ON A COLD ROAD

ON A COLD ROAD

Tales of Adventure in Canadian Rock

DAVE BIDINI

McCLELLAND & STEWART

Library and Archives Canada Cataloguing in Publication

Bidini, Dave
    On a cold road : tales of adventure in Canadian rock

ISBN 13: 978-0-7710-1456-7
ISBN 10: 0-7710-1456-2

1. Bidini, Dave. 2. Rheostatics (Musical group). 3. Rock music – Canada – History and criticism. 4. Rock musicians – Canada – Biography. 5. Guitarist – Canada – Biography. I. Title.

ML419.B585A3 1998   781.66'092   C98-931504-5

We acknowledge the financial support of the Government of Canada through the Book Publishing Industry Development Program and that of the Government of Ontario through the Ontario Media Development Corporation's Ontario Book Initiative. We further acknowledge the support of the Canada Council for the Arts and the Ontario Arts Council for our publishing program.

The author acknowledges the support of the Toronto Arts Council.

Text design by Sari Ginsberg
Illustrations by Martin Tielli
Typeset in Centaur by M&S, Toronto
Printed and bound in Canada

McClelland & Stewart Ltd.
75 Sherbourne Street
Toronto, Ontario
M5A 2P9

4 5 6 7 15 14 13 12 11

For my parents

✳   ✳   ✳

"Going down Highway 16 Johnny Crackle in the back seat of a 1962 Ford plays and sings sad songs riding ten years ago to a neon hamburger. Here I am, thought Johnny, and all I can worry about is the mustard and the relish."

— Matt Cohen, *Johnny Crackle Sings*

CONTENTS

VERSE

Rheostatics:

Dave Bidini: Rhythm guitar
Dave Clark: Drums (1980–1994)
Don Kerr: Drums (1994–2001)
Martin Tielli: Lead guitar
Michael Philip-Wojewoda: Drums (2001–present)
Tim Vesely: Bass

✳

Greatest Hits (1987)
Melville (1990)
Whale Music (1992)
Introducing Happiness (1994)
Music from the Motion Picture "Whale Music" (1994)
Music Inspired by the Group of Seven (1996)
The Blue Hysteria (1996)
Double Live (1997)
The Nightlines Sessions (1998)
The Story of Harmelodia (1999)
Night of the Shooting Stars (2001)
2067 (2004)

CHORUS

Dennis Abbott: 49th Parallel
Barry Allen: Singer, Wes Dakus and the Rebels, "Lovedrops"
Randy Bachman: The Guess Who, BTO, guitarist
Terry Black: Singer, "Sinner Man"
Tommy Chong: The Shades, Cheech and Chong
Bruce Cockburn: Three's a Crowd, guitarist
John Cody: West Coast drummer, Ray Condo
Geoff Davis: Lights and tech, Max Webster
Jerry Doucette: Guitarist, "Mama Let Him Play"
Rik Emmett: Triumph, guitarist
Richard Flohil: Promoter, agent
Gale Garnett: Actor, "We'll Sing in the Sunshine"
Amos Garrett: Session guitarist, "Midnight at the Oasis"
Peter Goddard: *Toronto Star* writer
Greg Godovitz: Fludd, Goddo, bassist
Gary Pig Gold: Expatriate Canadian musician
Rob Gunn: Road manager, Max Webster
Ronnie Hawkins: Singer, impresario
Bill Henderson: The Collectors, Chilliwack
Dave Henman: April Wine, guitarist
Richie Henman: April Wine, drummer

Jeanine Hollingshead: Mariposa Folk Festival organizer
Kelly Jay: Crowbar, singer
Jim Kale: Guess Who, bassist
Alan Kellogg: Ohio Express, guitarist
Ronnie King: Stampeders, bassist
Danny Marks: Edward Bear, guitarist, CBC's "Humline"
Dutch Mason: Maritime bluesman
Ra McGuire: Trooper, singer
Jim Millican: The Guess Who, road manager
Darby Mills: Headpins, singer
Kim Mitchell: Max Webster, guitarist, singer
Terry David Mulligan: Journalist, MuchWest
Alan Niester: *Globe and Mail* writer
Tom Northcott: West Coast singer-songwriter
Richard Patterson: The Esquires, Three's a Crowd, drummer
Jack Pedlar: Teenage Head, drummer
Bob Segarini: The Wackers, singer, broadcaster
Steve Smith: Jason, "The Red Green Show"
Frank Soda: Thor, Frank Soda and the Imps, guitarist
Skinny Tenn: Fludd, manager
Mike Tilka: Max Webster, bassist
Ken Tobias: Singer-songwriter, "Stay Awhile"
Shari Ulrich: Hometown Band, UHF
Donnie Walsh: Downchild, guitarist
Holly Woods: Toronto, singer
Denton Young: Zon, singer

PROLOGUE

"Zero degrees is where we start."
Max Webster, *"In Context of the Moon"*

I was nothing but a pimply little question mark on the day my sister and I first walked into Ken Jones Music in Etobicoke. Sunlight streamed through the windows, dappling the guitars that hung behind the counter and bathing the small music shop at the back of the Westway Plaza in warm light. The store was cluttered with drums stacked on top of each other, keyboards leaning three deep against the walls, dusty racks of unread sheet music, long outdated band want-ads taped to the cash register, and ashtrays scattered across old chairs and window ledges. At the back of the store, young boys sat in tiny rooms plucking guitars through amplifiers that buzzed like heat bugs, the sound of their hammer-ons and finger-rolls and string-benders snaking out to where I stood, sucking it all in like sugar through a Pixie-Stik.

After our first taste of this place, my sister and I signed up for guitar lessons, which I grew to hate. My disdain might have had something to do with the fact that Cathy had mastered the basic chords and strumming technique before I'd grown my first finger callus. She out-licked me on "Kum Ba Yah," "Michael, Row the Boat Ashore," and "House of the Rising Sun," which we debuted for our parents in our living room sitting on bridge-table chairs behind music stands. I'd like to tell you that I rose to her challenge and went on to become a blurry-fingered virtuoso of the fretboard whose technique set the world's pants on fire. But I did not.

Instead, I quit.

Cathy played her hand just right. My room was papered with an Aerosmith poster over my bed, 10cc above my night table, and Rush's *Farewell to Kings* staring at me each night as I hit my pillow. Every other inch of the walls was pasted with photos culled from *Hit Parader*, *Creem*, and *Circus* magazines, or purchased at Flash Jack's Head Shop, the scuzzy Yonge Street epicentre of high-school stonerdom, where they sold roach clips and hash pipes and lurid pictures of Linda Ronstadt. These pictures of my favourite bands were testament to my desire to be like them, but they were also witness to my failure to do anything about it. I'd wander into my sister's austere room – shockingly devoid of rock shrine-ography – and stare at her acoustic guitar, Mel Bay How-to-Play book, and music stand casually draped with belts, purses and other young-girl ephemera. In this display of cool-ness, Cathy seemed indifferent that she was better than me. My jealousy deepened. School ended. Summer passed. Winter descended. My sister played on.

But then a year later, mysteriously, she stopped. As soon as Cathy put away her guitar, I picked mine up again. I went back to

Ken Jones Music to sign up for more lessons, still a damp patty of clay waiting to be palmed, but this time confident enough to look into the future and see someone other than who I was: a nervous child dressed in brown, ankle-riding cords and a maroon sweater that scratched like steel wool. No, this time I could see myself as a figure straight from my walls – a sparkling giant outfitted in electrically lit platform shoes and a spangly jumpsuit, flaunting a great bramble of chest hair, and topped by a frizzy afro and bug sunglasses.

I approached the counter, where an unclean fellow sat with his feet up, plucking a mandolin.

"I was wondering about guitar lessons," I gulped.

"Do you play guitar, man?" asked the freak.

"No. Well, I did. But I'm not very good," I said.

"Excellent," he replied, strangely.

Stu looked like he'd just strode off a Three Dog Night album cover. He had that Jesus-as-folksinger look, thin-framed with a moustache and straggly beard. It was 1975. The first time I smelled pot, it was rising like steam off his flower-patched denim jacket. But while Stu was a prodigious stoner, he was a lot easier to understand than most of my teachers at school. He'd sit with me while I waited for my lesson with Ken and describe all the bands I'd never heard of whose music books he sold at the store – ZZ Top, the Eagles, Humble Pie, the James Gang. He told me about rigging a stage, setting up microphones, sound-checking, recording, tuning, and keeping your instrument in playable condition. He let me in on these mysteries as if he were spooling out paradigms from a lost language.

When a few friends and I finally got a band together, we set up

in the store so that Stu could teach us the basic tenets of song-
writing and arranging. We paid him with money given to us by
our parents, who had parted with their hard-earned dollars even
though they knew the money would be going to an indolent
hippie who wore love beads and smoked skunk-weed from a
water pipe. Stu took us through the looking glass, and we followed like Alice.

Our little combo was enthusiastic, if musically repugnant. We
were four fourteen-year-olds playing the Triumph version of
"Rocky Mountain Way" on out-of-tune instruments. Everybody
took a solo, even our drummer, Mario Molinaro, who played so
hard that he punched his sticks through his drumskins and
shredded the hi-hats into shrapnel. But no matter how hellacious
our din, Stu would listen patiently, bemused, and then show us
what a bridge was. We were thrilled. Every now and then, his own
group rehearsed in the store. We'd camp outside and listen to
them play Led Zeppelin and Rush songs with three-tiered syn-
thesizers, double-neck guitars, roto-tom drum terraces, disem-
bowellingly loud bass guitars, and vocal mikes cabled through a
Traynor P. A. To us it was like hearing the Stones at the Gardens.
We vowed that we'd be good enough to have gear that real and a
sound that big. Stu just tapped his head and said, "You will, you
will," then folded his hands in his lap.

Stu worked the front of the store, but the fellow whose name
was on the place did most of the work. Ken Jones was a round,
balding fellow who looked shockingly like Captain Kangaroo
without the mendacious eyebrows. Ken sold me my first guitar, a
white El Degas Stratocaster copy with a soft neck and a tone that
was as warm and forgiving as a tire crunching glass. Ken showed

me the basics out of the Mel Bay books, and soon I was putting two notes together, pretending to play "Rock and Roll Hoochie-Koo." That Ken had the patience to take me this far was remarkable considering that he spent most of his time locked away in a closet-sized room teaching sweaty teenagers with breath like milk gone bad how to cop Eric Clapton licks or strum church hymns. He eventually passed me on to a local long-haired rock troll who tried teaching me Frank Marino, Joe Walsh, and Domenic Troiano riffs while his girlfriend sat cross-legged smoking in the corner. This often led to lead-guitar duels with him in which I placed a distant second. I was put off playing solos for the rest of my life, but Ken and Stu had already turned me on to music and there was no going back.

A few years after I left the store for other musical experiences, the *Toronto Star* wrote an article about the Rheostatics' first gig at the Edge in February 1980. We were seventeen years old at the time and had to get a special liquor permit to play in the club. About fifty kids from high school came to see us play, and when we finished, the band we were opening for pleaded with us to get our friends to stay. But it was a school night. The *Star* found all of this interminably cute and dispatched a reporter to interview and photograph us on the bleachers of a high-school football field. I owe it to my mom for calling them and suggesting the idea in the first place. It was the first time I ever saw myself in print, and it was a shock. In the photo, I'm wearing blue trousers, a white striped blazer, and a T-shirt with an exclamation mark on it. Even though I'm sporting my most expensive haircut to date – thirty dollars at Super Cutz in Sherway Gardens – my head still looks like a luge helmet.

Canadian High
NEWS

DAVE BIDINI

BOTH SIDES NOW

Last year, 17-year-old Kipling Collegiate student Dave Bidini started writing about rock'n'roll as a hobby. It suited his interests and allowed him to "experience his future rather than wait for it to happen." One year later, that possible career continues to show promise, has given Dave a lot of excitement and developed into something more than expected.

"Writing about rock'n'roll was my way of sticking up for my kind of music and voicing a certain opinion that with any luck might be taken seriously," recalls Dave. "As the arti-

cles grew larger and more challenging, it became a part-time occupation rather than just an outside interest. Rock journalism suited my character and it just seemed to hang around me long enough to become fun."

But this is only half of Dave's musical tale. Seven months ago he got together with three buddies to form his own group, The Rheostatics, a name which they picked out of a physics textbook. Amazingly, Rheostatics have accomplished in months what it usually takes more seasoned bands sometimes years. For their first live performance, the boys managed to persuade the manager of The Edge (Toronto's premiere New Wave club which regularly features performers from the U.S. and U.K.) to give them a booking. He heard a tape of their music and on they went. Since then, they've played a return engagement and were featured at the El Mocambo (another Toronto hot spot) as part of CFNY-FM's Great Ontario Talent Hunt. In February the band produced and released its own single with "My Generation" backed "Satellite Dancing." "It's our greatest accomplishment to date. Things are happening so fast it's hard to believe," says Dave. The boys rehearse 30 hours a week, which puts a crimp in their social lives but they won't let it interfere with their school work. "School's still an intricate part of our lives; it's something to fall on. If this doesn't work out, we can always go to university."

Teen Generation, May 1981

Ken Jones posted the clipping in his shop. He drew an arrow pointing to me and wrote, "I taught him!" on it. He didn't do it because he had any intuition that we would dent the mug of Canadian rock, or grow up to dazzle industry captains or play sold-out concerts in hockey rinks or take champagne baths in rooms wallpapered with money. It was because of one gig.

One.
Three dollars. Tuesday night.
The Edge.

Sixteen years, handfuls of tours, walls of faces, miles of strings and cables, thickets of magnetic and electrical tape, lakes of beer, numberless clubhouse sandwiches, and six hundred gigs later, we were asked to do a national tour with the Tragically Hip in the winter of 1996 to support their *Trouble at the Henhouse* album. *The biggest tour by a Canadian band in the history of music in Canada.* It would put the Rheostatics in front of almost half a million people and finally give us a chance to play our music to the mass audience that till then had eluded us. Since our inaugural gig at the Edge in 1980, we'd gone through many changes in sound and had suffered the loss of our drummer of fourteen years, Dave Clark, who quit the band sixteen months before our tour. People like Stu and Ken and a million others had floated across those years, and as I set out to write down my experiences about being on the road, I found myself thinking not only about them, but also about the bands and musicians whose songs I'd heard on the radio as a kid, and whose bravura had founded the musical culture in which I now lived and explored.

I decided to track down these figures from my past. I wanted to understand, through them, the anatomy of making music in a country noted more for space and snow than for money or people. I was fully aware of the struggle it takes to sustain a musical career in Canada (I was painfully conscious that a small number of consumers supported Canadian bands — 19 per cent of total sales — and that our scant population meant that musicians shared the same audience in ten cities across the country), but I knew very little about the artists themselves. It became important to me to know what it was like for the early bands, the first to leave their home towns hauling P. A. systems and glitter balls, chasing down one-nighters in towns that barely existed. They'd established the east-west route that every Canadian group now travelled, and more than likely took for granted. Without their perseverance, neither we nor the Hip would have had reason to exist, let alone to light out for the coast, let alone to write this book.

It was in the old Reaction Studios on Stafford Street in Toronto — where we were recording our second album, *Melville*, in December 1989 — that I first became conscious of this musical tradition. In the foyer of the studio hung a painting which was signed *Ken Tobias*. The name sounded familiar, but I couldn't quite place it. Then I remembered that there had been a singer named Ken Tobias who had had hit records in the '70s, and whose songs, such as "Every Bit of Love," were on the K-Tel albums that I worshipped as a kid. I asked Ormand Jobin, who ran the studio, whether this was the same Ken Tobias who had been a pop star when I was a teenager. It was. I asked whether he was still alive. Ormand laughed, "Of course he is, man. He lives down there!" pointing to a door off to the side of the room. The door led to Ken's home in the basement of the studio. It stayed shut for most of the session, but I watched it closely, wondering if it would ever open.

One day, it did.

KEN TOBIAS: On my father's side we were Lebanese, and there was always somebody beating a chair and yelling "Dance the *Dubkee!*" which was a Lebanese dance. That's probably why I became a drummer first. There were a couple of jazz drummers in our family. One of them was in the navy, the other was an uncle who gave me a set of Olympic drums, with bongos that screwed on the side. That was influential. The first song I sang was in a Zellers store. They used to have stages in Zellers and they'd have fashion shows. I was four. I was modelling and singing. The manager of the store heard that I was a kid with talent, so they booked me. I did the "Maharasha Magador." It was one of those beat things where I had to hold my nose and go *aaaaaahaaawahaaaa* ... They gave me a bag of candy for doing it, and I dressed up in one of their suits. I have a picture of myself holding the hand of the store manager.

BOB SEGARINI: I started out on ukelele. I grew up in Stockton, California, home of Chris Isaak, Dave Brubeck, Janet Leigh, and a whole pile of crack dealers. When I was still in a crib, my grandfather, Bobo, gave me an old green Emerson table radio. I grew up listening to Glenn Miller and Kaye Starr, everything. By the time I was ten, I was hooked on music. In the eighth grade I wrote a song on the ukelele. My uncle, Elbert Bidwell, the inventor of the plectrum system of banjo playing, was the president of the Stockton local musicians' union. When I turned twelve, he gave me a Student Prince acoustic guitar from Sears and a union card. For the first couple of years I had the guitar, I took two strings off and played it like it was a ukelele. Then, when I was fourteen, I was in a talent contest – the Stockton Police Widows and Orphans Benefit at the Civic Auditorium – which was won by a band called the Jades. I came in third. Johnny Crawford was also on the bill, so was Dee Clark, and the group that did "Footstompin'." I brought my little book and got autographs. The Jades hired me to be their lead singer. I was a fourteen-year-old boy singing with guys who were eighteen to twenty-six. Eventually, I got thrown out of that band 'cause I grew my hair long.

DUTCH MASON: The first time I ever played live in my life was at school. I was on the guitar, with two other fellows playing drums and piano. We were terrible, just fuckin' terrible. And we knew it. The next week we played again and got another guitar player who worked out pretty good. We called ourselves Dutch Mason and the Wreckers.

GALE GARNETT: The big, famous song, "We'll Sing in the Sunshine," happened when I was fourteen. This was in California, Laurel Canyon. I'd been given a small amount of money to clean Hoyt Axton's house after a party. So while I was cleaning I made up this song for him to sing. This great feminist anthem that everybody went on about, I wrote for a guy to sing. I was fourteen years old; I wasn't thinking about feminist anthems. I gave it to Hoyt, and he recorded it on Horizon Records and nothing happened. Six months later, through the Clancy Brothers, I met Jerry Purcell. Tom Clancy, now dead, said, "Sing yer songs fer Jerry," so I did, and Jerry said, "These are great, RCA Victor's having a convention in Las Vegas, you should come."

But I didn't want to be a singer, I was an actor; I *am* an actor. I wanted my songs to be sung by other people. Singing with a voice as low as mine was a horrifying notion. But I went to this big hotel and into a large committee-type room and I sang a

Gale Garnett at sixteen

whole pile of songs for Ben Rosner, who was the head of A and R [artists and repertoire] for RCA Victor. I had long black hair, bangs, biggish tits, biggish ass, just like now. I was fourteen, but I looked older. In black clothing, I was able to pass for eighteen. I had a low voice, too, and I smoked. I could do the major sophistication thing, unless somebody asked me a real question.

So I sang for Ben and a whole bunch of other suits with shiny shoes and shot cuffs. They looked like the guys who worked for John Gotti, really. But I sang for them, and they said, "We want the songs, and we want her." I said "Noooo, I've got a four-note range!" but they really were insistent. I thought that it would be an adventure and so I recorded an album.

I was all kinds of illegal. I was under-age and I had no American documentation, and I was going to clubs where I could get in under age: Ash Grove, Troudabor. When you're a teenager, it's almost like being a drunk; you can fall from a great height and nothing breaks because you're so loose. And so resilient. You move through things that are dangerous because you don't know they're dangerous. You don't set up the victim signal that causes danger to move in on you. I moved through a lot of places where harm could come, and no harm came. Notorious bastards were very kind to me.

GREG GODOVITZ: My dad got me a three-quarter-scale Supro bass and a MagnaTone amp. The only reason I was allowed in my first band was because I had that amplifier; I didn't know how to play yet. At my first gig at Cedarbrae Community Centre, they had a cord plugged into the bass jack, but not into the amp. Instead, they ran the guitar, piano, and vocals through it. I had a Beatles haircut and a Beatles suit, and at thirteen, I was pretty darned cute. And I could sing. Brian Francis, the piano player who did the vocals, was terrible. The old man who put on the gig heard us doing "Twist and Shout," and in the middle of the song, he walked on stage, grabbed the microphone from Brian, and put it in front of me. Without missing a beat, I took over the lead and started singing. Afterwards, I was fired.

BRUCE COCKBURN: The first time I played guitar in front of people, I'd been playing for about six weeks. I was fourteen years old. I'd learned two licks, and both of them were rock-and-roll-based. Somebody had said, "Oh, you play guitar? You've gotta come down and play for our church dance!" They had an organ player who played schlock music, and they had me. I knew the organ player a little bit, so we played a couple of things together, then it was my turn to play. All I did was play my boogie-woogie, rock-and-roll licks, of which I knew two or three. I just played them over and over and over again. The kids tried to dance. It was humiliating; it was actually more humiliating than I knew, because I didn't feel as humiliated then as I do now, thinking back on it.

DAVID HENMAN: I had just learned to play the guitar. Some guy I knew who was a guitar player couldn't do a gig and so he asked if I'd do it. It was in Windsor, Nova Scotia, which at the time was a completely black community. I didn't know this, of course. I was waiting in my parents' house when this old beat-up convertible shows up with a black guy and a white girl in the front. I grabbed my guitar and ran out and got in the car. We played in a Legion hall; me and the drummer were the only white people in the entire place. Now, even to this day, Nova

Scotians are fairly prejudiced. But back then, it was truly ghet-toized. Fortunately, the black people weren't like the white people. They were really great and open-minded, and me and my friend were treated like kings, despite our race. The guitar still had the same strings on it as when I bought it, so they were rusty, and I'd never played for that long before. In the third song, my fingers started bleeding. I was playing songs I didn't know — they were just shouting out keys, Chuck Berry stuff. I got paid six dollars and forty-two cents.

DANNY MARKS: Nash the Slash — whose real name is Jeff Pluman — and I went to the same high school. His band and mine were both trying to get in on this afternoon concert. It was a big concert for me, maybe one of the first big ones. So I stayed away from school in the morning to get ready for the gig. We passed the audition, but the vice-principal, Mr. Snell, wouldn't let us play at the concert because I had stayed home that morning. He sent me home a lot of times, sometimes for having long side-burns, sometimes bluejeans, turtlenecks, whatever. He was such a mean bastard. Once, my mom bought me a beautiful turtle-neck to wear, so she had to go to Mr. Snell and say, "My son's a beatnik. Leave him alone."

RIK EMMETT: When my knee blew out I realized that I wasn't going to be an athlete, so music became everything. I got a gig, three nights a week, at the Robin Hood Inn in Pickering, Ontario. Sixty bucks a week for a kid in high school was pretty good. I had to wear a suit. The band was called the Amber Jacks, because the singer lived on Amber Jack Boulevard in Scarborough. There was a tubby, peroxide-blonde chick who played accordion, me on guitar,

Rik Emmett

and my friend Chet on drums. We used to go out into the parking lot, get pie-eyed and play. The singer was horrible. He was having an affair with a younger chick, but his wife, her name was Tammy, would come to the gigs on Saturday night, and they'd slow dance while he sang "Tammy" to her.

DENNIS ABBOTT: One time, the record player broke in my parents' house. There was this little plastic change purse and, because it was hollow, I could fit my ear into it. I was so desperate to listen to music that I put a pin through the purse, put my ear into the hollow and then put the pin to the record and turned it around and around. I was hoping that the sound would travel up the pin into the purse. I loved music that much.

I joined my first group in high school in Edmonton. We were called Four on the Floor and we were really, really bad. For our first gig, we set up all of our equipment on the stage of the auditorium in front of one microphone. It was one of those great big ones, the size of a volleyball. We were so naive that we thought that we'd do our song and it would go over the P.A. system. We had no idea that it wouldn't. We started playing "Fun, Fun, Fun" by the Beach Boys. Nothing went through the microphone except my voice, which was going into all of the classrooms with no music behind it. The auditorium filled up in seconds. They must have thought there was some kind of ritualistic killing going on in there. That was my first gig.

DARBY MILLS: My first time playing live was in Hundred Mile House, at a junior high school. I sang "Crazy on You" by Heart. I went out and bought a whole new outfit for it. I did one song, and I was shaking the whole time.

FRANK SODA: My first performance was a disaster. A humongous disaster. It was in our high school, and we were all still learning how to play. We were just trying to get our confidence up. They were having a talent night, and a friend of ours said, "Learn this song, and my sister will sing it." The song was "These Boots Are Made for Walking," by Nancy Sinatra. We learned it and we were ready to play it. But just before we went on, some mischievous, so-called friends of ours untuned our guitars. We started to play: the guitarist played a chord and he turned beet-red. He looked like he had a red light bulb on his head. I was playing bass, so you didn't really notice it from me, but the girl was singing to all this. It was a real disaster. I met the guitar player years later in Toronto and we had a laugh about it. He ended up being one of my big fans, and whenever I played Toronto, there he was, in the front row.

AMOS GARRETT: My first professional gig was at Carnegie Hall. I had a job as an accompanist for a guy named Mike Settle, who had written a hit record for Judy Collins called "Sing Hallelujah." This was in the winter of 1963, during the advent of the singer-songwriter era, which Martin Mull has called "the great folk music scare of the late '60s." Mike had gotten a gig as opening act on a tour of a comedy troupe led by Vaughn Meter, who had a huge hit comedy record of satirical pieces on the Kennedy family. The first gig of this tour was at Carnegie Hall.

When I walked into that place the first time, I was scared to death; I was twenty-two years old, and since my mother's family is from New York state, I had a lot of relatives coming to the show. I was in a tuxedo and patent-leather shoes. I was playing two guitars at the time: a Martin D-28, and a twelve-string Gibson flat-top. Their show was very choreographed, produced, and directed by big-time Broadway guys, and they didn't want me to have a second guitar on stage because they thought it distracted from "the look." I had to keep my other guitar on a stand behind the drop curtain. Drop curtains in those big opera houses and symphony halls are velvet and half an inch thick and they literally weigh several tons. They also have an overlap, which they call "the fly."

Now, in all of those halls, especially in New York City, there are union stage-hands, and you've got to watch out for these guys.

They are out to do as little as humanly possible to make their wage. Each of them has very specific things that they do or don't do. Just before the curtain was about to go up, I told the stage-hand that I needed someone to page the curtain, which means one or two guys on the inside of the overlap of this curtain – which draws horizontally – to pull the fly back. It's very hard; those two ten-ton curtains are pressed right up next to each other.

We do three songs and then it comes time to change guitars. Remember, this has all got to be very slick. I go back to the curtain; there's nobody there. I'm whispering through the curtain, "Page the curtain, page the curtain." Finally, I realize there's no one there, and so I start forcing myself through, cradling my six-string Martin like a baby because of the weight of the curtains. I'm wiggling through there in my tuxedo; the audience is starting to laugh. Mike Settle doesn't know what's going on because he's reading the introduction to the next song. Joe Lawrence, the bass player, is in hysterics, turned away from the audience.

Finally, I get through and I'm backstage. My guitar is gone; the stage-hands have set me up. I run around the back, find the twelve-string, and then I realize that I'm going to have to do this again later in the set, so I decide to take both guitars out and lay one of them on the floor. I squeeze in through the two curtains, now cradling two acoustic guitars. I'm pushing with all my might trying to get through. These curtains haven't been cleaned since Caruso sang there; there's almost an inch thick of solid dust and I'm in a black tuxedo. I come out on stage, and my hair's stand-ing on end, my glasses are dangling by one arm, my tuxedo is this pale, blotchy grey, there's dust flying off me, the twelve-string is totally whacked out of tune by the curtain. Mike goes into the fourth tune – which, incidentally, is the hit – and I look out. My relatives, especially my cousin Nick, who's in the front row with my Aunt Edith, is rolling around on the floor laughing and yelling "That's my cousin! Go get 'em, cuz!"

TOMMY CHONG: I was in the army cadets for a while. I met an Indian kid from Calgary – Dick Bird – and became the rhythm guitar player for him. We'd sit around the barracks and jam. He was addicted to guitar, then I became addicted. We'd stay over at each other's homes. We'd take the bus there with our amps and play Hank Williams songs. We'd sleep, then wake up, reach over and grab the guitar, and play all day until my fingers felt like they were falling off. When Elvis hit, Dick started doing an Elvis impersonation. He wore a white sports jacket, and he didn't look anything at all like Elvis. He had acne and curly hair and he was Indian. But he had this energy, and the girls would go crazy. In grade eleven I dropped out of school. Dick and I got a gig in Lethbridge, Alberta, with the Four somethings, a black group. They were gonna do a show, and we were gonna open for them. When we showed up, there was no one there. My mom and dad drove down from Calgary to see their son play; they were so proud of us, me and Dick standing up there with just two microphones going through one amp, no one in the crowd. Of course we got stiffed. Dick and I stayed the night, but they cancelled the second show, so we hitchhiked home. That's when I decided: Oh, man, this is the life. I love this life.

2

BRITISH COLUMBIA

"All the steps are necessary.
Even the ones that make you want to throw up."
Jim Kale, The Guess Who

When we first played Vancouver in 1987, we arrived at dawn. We sat four abreast in our ripe-smelling, rented Ram Charger, two thousand hard miles behind us, our faces blotched and worn, our bodies slump-shouldered, and bathed our bruised minstrel souls in the city's warm balm. Dazzling emerald light pirouetted off the unrippled water, painting the sky. It was dead quiet in the car for about two minutes, then someone started bawling. It didn't take much to loosen the taps. Dave emitted a foul gas and Martin, speaking for the first time all tour, called him a pig. It was our first journey away together, two and a half months on the road. My dad donated the family sedan — a brown 1979 champion Delta 88 four-door — then one day its timing chain snapped on a perilous mountain climb and we exchanged it for fifty dollars of bagged groceries in Revelstoke, B.C. We lost a lot of things that tour. Martin lost three shoes. He finished the tour with one ripped-up,

Rick McGinnis

Rheostatics, 1987

slime-caked Converse hanging off his foot, an orphaned sneaker destined to join the others along the shoulder of one of Canada's infinite highways.

We also lost Brett Clubbe, sort of. Brett was a young fan from Toronto who said he'd sell shirts and schlep gear for us if we took him across Canada. He was an agreeable fifth for the first, oh, thousand miles, but as the tour wore on, certain theories about how long a human being could last locked in the trunk of a car crept through our minds. Brett was known to sneak over to the local Hudson's Bay department store and load up on bacon and eggs in the coffee shop using his dad's credit card. Afterwards, he'd slap his belly and pick his teeth without once offering to relieve us of our brutal smokes-and-peanut-butter diet. That burned us a little, but his fate wasn't sealed until he made it his life's work to turn us on to the Grateful Dead.

I have no argument with the Dead. One of my favourite rock-and-roll yarns concerns the time Jerry Garcia played for mercy at the Fillmore while hallucinating that the audience was packed with mob hitmen, having accidentally licked the icing sugar off a chocolate cake laced with seven hundred hits of STP acid. The problem with Brett's Dead obsession was that his favourite piece was something called "Space Jam," which wasn't even a song. It was a torturous, forty-minute, tom-tom symphony — an ode to the drum fill. Uneasy listening. But it made no difference to Brett. He'd put his finger to his lips and slide the tape into its saddle, despite our groans. After a few minutes, his eyes would close and he'd be *lowing* rapturously in the back seat, his body swaying side to side.

He left us no choice.

We ditched the little hippie in Calgary.

Brett behind Crocks and Rolls, Thunder Bay, 1987

Brett followed us to Vancouver with Pig Farm, who found him stuck like spat-out gum to the floor of a band house in Calgary. Who knows what might have happened to him? He could have been picked up by the band Death Sentence, whose lead singer once climbed into their van with a meat cleaver wedged in his forehead. But as it turns out, I'd underestimated our young rainbow child; these days, Brett spends his time burying himself up to his neck in soil along the logging roads of the Pacific Northwest, an only marginally less dangerous vocation, it seems, than being a helper for an art-rock band from Etobicoke.

Once in Vancouver, Brett settled down, and so did the rest of us. The West Coast was redemptive, as advertised. Vancouver was an enclave of beautiful floating people, flower-lined streets, high-curved roads, mountain trails, and miles of long, sandy coastline. I had expected to find hordes of sandal-wearing tree-gropers with lettuce tied into their beards, but instead, these teenagers were exactly like us, perhaps happier. Evenings found us sitting on great slabs of driftwood, smoking tumescent joints, drinking wine, and watching the slow passing of oceancraft across the purple water. Vancouver was like a long kiss from a ponytailed girl. I left a piece of myself there.

Everybody does the first time.

TOMMY CHONG: We had a friend who owned Boystown, a community centre in Calgary. We rented the Legion halls, packed 'em in, made money. During the Stampede, we rented a flatbed and played on that. We split the money up and had a good time. It was 1958. Then one day, the mayor of Calgary contacted us – Don McKay was his name, I believe he wore a big white hat – and said that he wanted to see us in his office. I thought we were gonna get some award. But he asked us to leave town. It was during the Christmas season, and they were having trouble with kids from our dances, who would go off and fight, and ravish the local maidens. He blamed us for it. We said, "Good. Let's go to Vancouver."

SHARI ULRICH: I was going to college in the '60s, and I started to feel like California was not a good place to be, so I ran away from the United States. I was going to go to Canada and homestead, because, of course, there were no cities in Canada, just wilderness. That's how naive I was. I was pretty darned surprised when I hit Vancouver. I lived on a commune in Gibsons, and there was a guitar player with whom I started to play conga drum. We got a gig at a health-food restaurant for food. The place was the Nam restaurant, and we were paid in yoghurt.

BILL HENDERSON: The Collectors came back to Vancouver after having lived in California for a year. Down there, we played with all the California bands: Frank Zappa, the Doors, Iron Butterfly, the Dead, Jefferson Airplane. We influenced them, too. Our music was very original for rock music. A lot of our ideas were derived from classical music and jazz. Our first album, which we recorded in L.A., was voted by *Melody Maker* in England as one of the top ten albums of the decade, along with Jimi Hendrix and the Beatles. Bill Graham stood on the stage of the Fillmore and said, "This is a band that's taking rock-and-roll where it's going." We'd had some real critical success among our peers, not really from the sales point of view.

We came back to Vancouver having seen a lot of things. We came back with these huge transistor amps and created quite a stir. That's when we did the "What Love Suite," which was a bit of a watershed for music in our area. It was a twenty-minute piece, and it wasn't just a jam, it was a composed piece with structure to it, as well as places for jamming. Everyone was involved in creating the music. This particular piece was very powerful and it rarely failed on the West Coast. Among the heads, there was a real appetite for that kind of stuff.

TOMMY CHONG: We hit Vancouver just before the '60s. There were a lot of booze cans, a lot of black clubs owned by East Indian guys in Chinatown. Very ethnic. And there was a ton of junkies. I met my first junkie out there. I picked up this girl — I didn't know she was a junkie — and took her to a party. She kept dozing off, and I thought, "Oh, I guess she's tired." Then she'd spend an hour in the bathroom. One time she passed out in there, so I picked her up and put her on the bed, and she

The Collectors. Bill Henderson, centre

kept saying, "Just put the money on the table, man." But I still
didn't know.

We used to play a club called the New Delhi. The guy would
come out and shout, "Ladies and Gentlemen. Floor-show time,
everybody sit down, shut up, please!" Here I am playing blues for
a living! We'd do tricks and splits, the whole show. We had
record-company people come to see us; we were a good show
band. We were kind of what Ronnie Hawkins was to the East. A
few years into it, we opened the Elegant Parlour. It was an after-
hours club. It was there that I met Redd Foxx, Josh White, Jimmy
Witherspoon. The Supremes came down when I was playing
with Bobby Taylor, and they were the ones who saw us and told
Motown about us. Berry Gordy flew in and saw us and signed us
that night. We went to Motown and recorded "Does Your
Mama Know About Me?"

TERRY DAVID MULLIGAN: I remember going down to the Elegant Parlour to hear Smokey Robinson and the Miracles, the Temptations, the Supremes. They'd play the Cave supper club, then they'd go down and do a set at the Elegant Parlour. The Elegant Parlour was dangerous; all kinds of characters. It was my first time in a room full of black faces. It was a revelation. There were gangsters and shooters; white ties and black shirts. I remember seeing Four Niggers and a Chink – that was Tommy Chong. When they put that on the marquee, all hell broke loose in Vancouver. It was Tommy's sense of humour.

DARBY MILLS: Radio was nonexistent when I was growing up in Kamloops and Vernon in the '60s. I didn't know about music until I was in junior-high. I joined my first band in grade ten. We rehearsed in my parents' basement because they wanted to know where I was. I was ten years into serious figure skating at the time, and my parents didn't want me wandering the streets with some rock-and-roll band. We had the police at the door numerous times until finally my parents said, "Fine. We'll tell them to quit. We'll send those seven kids, who have been down here three times a week religiously, honing their craft, out into the streets." And the cops said, "Thank you very much, Mr. and Mrs. Mills; you go right ahead and let them play." The neighbours had to put up with it.

TERRY BLACK: When I was fourteen and a half, I started to go to a dance-party TV show, done out here in Burnaby. All my friends would go to it on the weekends. The host would ask everybody what they were gonna do with their lives. When he asked me, I said, "A singer." They got a lot of mail the next week because of that. This promoter thought it would be a good idea to make a record, so we cut a rough, rough demo on a basic tape recorder in a barn in Capilano and had it sent back east. My friends did background vocals in the kitchen and I sang in the barn. ARC Records pressed a couple hundred copies and sent them back west. I did the record on the TV show – I lip-synched it – and it got a great response, so the promoter sent a few records down to various record companies in California.

Dunhill Records was interested, so we went down and met Lou Adler. It was a hotbed of change down in California. The Beach Boys had just come out with "I Get Around," and Martha and the Vandellas had "Dancing in the Street." The Beatles had three or four top singles all being played at the same time. Everybody was cruising Sunset Boulevard at night, with the radios just blasting. It was a different time. Most times, it felt natural to me, but other times I'd be completely wiped out, like when I met Steve McQueen at a party, or Brian Wilson at Johnny Rivers's party. That kind of threw me a bit. I hung with Jan and Dean. They were surfin' and skateboardin' back then. When Lou Adler introduced me to his wife, he said, "I'd like you to meet Shelley," and Shelley Fabares came out the door. I flipped, because "Johnny Angel" was a killer tune. She was doing an Elvis movie. It was all happening there. In a way, it was tough bumping into all those movie stars.

P. F. Sloan and Steve Berry were starting to write for Adler, and they had a whole stack of songs that they wanted me to do. One of the first ones was "Unless You Care." Glen Campbell, Hal Blaine, and Joe Osbourne played on it. I had no idea who they were; they were just guys who played well, but they treated me with respect, especially after they found out that I could sing.

The record was made in a little studio, which isn't there any more, across from Wallach's Music City on Sunset. Lou gave me the music and said, "Learn this song. The session's in two days." I had no input into the arrangements, but it didn't matter; I'd never sung into a really good mike or had a really good headphone sound before. On the fourth take Steve came over the P.A. and said, "That's a take." I felt kind of shortchanged. I wanted to keep doing it because it felt so good. The record was a hit.

We cut an album called *Only Sixteen* and did Dick Clark's Caravan Tour down the coast. It all happened within three months. When I did American Bandstand, I met Duane Eddy and Brian Hyland backstage; it was great to stand beside Dick Clark and hear him talking about my new record and asking everyone, "What do ya give it?" and hearing them yell, "*We give it a ninety!*" Dick always made everybody look good. I did "Only Sixteen" and covered Rick Nelson's "Poor Little Fool." Lou wanted to break the record on KFWB and KRLA, and he thought a good show for me to do would be *Shindig*. I showed up at the studio and it looked great. Jay and the Americans were on the show, Billy Preston, Gene Clark. Glen Campbell was the emcee. We rehearsed in the afternoon and shot that night. The Shindogs were backing me up; Delaney Bramlett was part of them. I signed with Paramount Pictures and Twentieth Century Fox. I was doing screen tests and getting ready to be a big star. Then I was hit with the draft because I had a green card. I decided to go back home.

TOM NORTHCOTT: There was a guy in Los Angeles who made it a business of finding out who the up-and-coming artists were in North America and shopping them to record companies. His contact in Vancouver was Tom Peacock at CFUN. Peacock sent my stuff down to him, the guy took it to Warner Brothers, Lenny Waronker liked it, and sent word back up, through Tom Peacock, that I should get in touch. It didn't really register with me; I was just singing along, doing my thing, and I thought, "Oh, that's cool. Isn't that nice? Somebody knows my music!" But I didn't contact Warner Brothers. I do what I do, and if I can make a living at that, then I'm the luckiest man on the face of the earth. I've never sold myself, but if somebody's interested, I'll do it. I'm not a hard-driving artist. I succeeded in spite of myself.

Later on, I linked up with Jack Herschorn, who was just up from L.A., living in Vancouver. We started New Syndrome Records together. At the same time, I became friends with the Jefferson Airplane, and they got the Tom Northcott Trio a date at the Matrix in San Francisco. Tom Donahue, who was the father of FM radio, came down to the show with an airplane ticket and three hundred dollars cash and said, "If I give you this, would you please go down to L.A. and meet with Warner Brothers?" I said, "Sure, I'll go!"

BILL HENDERSON: In the late '60s, there was a whole scene that went from Vancouver to Tijuana. Some bands made forays east, but for the most part their existence was on the West Coast. There was a similar mindset culturally. But the Collectors didn't want to stay in the States. Being in California was rough on our families. By the time we'd done our second album, we decided we were gonna come back to Canada. Instead of working north–south, we'd work east, and then when we were big in Canada, we would just roll down into the States. This, of course, was a totally stupid idea. It wasn't stupid to save our families, but the

Tom Northcott with former Toronto mayor Bill Dennison

notion of making it in Canada so that you could make it in the States was really ass-backwards. It didn't work. The Toronto musicians didn't have any idea what was happening out west, and vice versa. In those days, it was much harder to communicate with your own country than it was with the States.

TOM NORTHCOTT: I got along with people in California, but I never felt part of the scene. There was an old-boys' network, and I was the boy from Canada. There were moments, though. I remember smoking a bunch of dope and going to the première

of Kubrick's *2001* with Eric Burdon. In the intermission, I was
taking a piss standing between Eric Burdon and Steve McQueen.
I thought to myself, "I've arrived!" I was in San Francisco, it was
the summer of love, my record, "Sunny Goodge Street," was
released, and within twenty-four hours, it was the number-one
requested song on the number-one radio station in San
Francisco. It remained there for days, which stretched into weeks.
The same day that it hit number one, I heard the Beatles' *Sgt.*
Pepper album for the first time. I was convinced, in that one
moment, in one magic day in San Francisco, that I had become as
big as the Beatles. It was heavy stuff. It was very big stuff.

Pacific Coliseum, the Pacific National Exhibition.

The rink is beautiful in its own way, the redwood-panelled
rafters fan the round ceiling like the bottomside of a sand dollar.
The first time we played here, we opened for the Barenaked
Ladies, the biggest show of our lives to date. That night, the performance got off on the wrong foot, literally. We started with a
difficult song, "When Winter Comes," a ten-minute triptych
which begins with Martin finger-tapping his guitar alone at the
foot of the stage. It looked and sounded huge from the wings, his
sharp body soaked in foggy blues, his rubbery sound filling the
cavernous sports bowl while young kids spilled in excitedly and
found their seats. But from there, things went terribly awry.
Spindly-armed, tub-bellied, wild-haired Dave – not the world's
smoothest runner – jaunted across the blackness towards his
white Milestone drum kit and stepped on a foot pedal, which

completely shut down Martin's guitarworks. Hearts panicking in the wings, bassist Tim Vesely and I climbed on stage. Humming silence filled the arena. Not exactly *Live at Leeds*. We stood there frozen. I felt like voiding my bowels. Martin fell to his knees and pounded his gear like a caveman taking a rock to a coconut. Finally, his sound kicked in, but so did forty minutes of misery.

At rehearsal, we see the stage for the first time. It's star-shaped, with three ramps spearing the centre, right, and left. It's the size of a baseball diamond, deep in the back and long at the sides, where guitar and monitor tents are staked, cleaved by a long ramp running up behind the drum kit. Massive black scrim is hung in a huge semicircle around the stage's perimeter, giving way to a painting as vast as a cruise ship's flank, swabbed with greys, dull reds, forest greens, and crestfallen blues, all coagulating as if rising in a dark coastal mist. The painting dwarfs the tiny amplifiers and guitars that are set up along the backline. Above the drum kit, a laser-light rack is being programmed by an elfin man with a pencil in his mouth who waggles swords of cold green light that shoot out at the clapped-up seats. He draws diamonds and O's around the arena, and I feel their points flare out from over my shoulders, giving me the feeling of a rare and spectacular power.

Walking from edge to edge of the giant platform, I see that the Tragically Hip like to set up within sweating distance of each other. This is good news. At the Barenaked Ladies show, we spaced ourselves as far apart as possible. We did this after having endured many years of playing together in rooms the size of my sock drawer, of having our asses pinned to the back wall of clubs. That night, each of us had our own yawning laneway, but we were so far apart we couldn't hear what the others were playing.

This resulted in a mangled sound, which dumbfounded us as well as the thousands of zit-speckled teenagers, who, like us, had no idea what was supposed to be happening.

Today we set up a few feet from each other. We are so close that I could easily wave my Gibson over my head like a drunk windmilling a cat, and konk Tim or Martin hard enough that they'd start drooling and singing in Tagalog.

Of course, they could do the same to me.

I make note of this.

It's quite a sight. Not so long ago, I was a kid waiting outside a concert hall, trying to imagine what things looked like from this very spot, this maw of rock-and-roll fantasy. The closest I came to knowing was the time my friend Kenny Huff crawled on-stage at a Clash concert. Kenny was our high school's first punk. He was once asked by the principal to change out of his Sex Pistols T-shirt, and in the storied tradition of suburban rebellion, did so. I've often wondered what Mick Jones thought when he saw Kenny lunge at him that night at Exhibition Stadium. Twelve thousand punks looked on as several large security gorillas bounded from the wings to get him. Kenny did a little pogo-hop around Joe Strummer, waving his arms over his head like a dancing skeleton, eluding one tackle, then at the last second dived desperately at Mick before being intercepted by a biker who launched him face first towards the Astroturf.

In the parking lot after the show, we found him, sweating, bruised, eyes glazed over.

"Kenny! What was it like?" I wanted to know.

"It was wild, man!" he exulted, sweat pouring off him.

"What did you see?"

"Rows of lights, bodies, way, way up!" he laughed.

"What did the sky look like?"

"The sky? That was a fucking twenty-foot drop!"

Tim Mech, our cherubic guitar tech, calls out my name, and I snap into the present. We gather at the tip of the stage. Clemens Rikken, the Belgian photographer hired by the band to photograph the tour, shoots the crew, bands, and management standing together. I smile in my woolly red tuque, and as the shutter clicks, a voice tells me to beware. First, it says, you are poised to sound a chord in the collective teenage unconscious, then the next thing you know you're complaining about the quality of champagne in the dressing room.

The next day, there's champagne in the dressing room. It's part of the most Lucullan rider we've ever had. Across white linen tablecloths, great bowls of hummus and guacamole and cream cheese have been laid out beside baskets of pita and nut bread, pepper-speckled tortilla chips that fan out across my palm, wheels of fine brie and exotic cheeses, fennel spears and smoked salmon, trays of icy soda pop and sparkling water and beer, a bottle of expensive Australian wine, a forty-ouncer of vodka, and a fruit basket stuffed with pomegranates, kiwis, grapefruits, and fresh flowers plucked from the sunny banks of the Pacific. The room itself – well-lit with long couches and pillowed chairs – almost makes me forget the rat-cellar dressing rooms that we've inhabited throughout the better part of our career. Band rooms are often the most derelict parts of venues. Many of them are mouldy fire-traps covered with petroglyphic scribblings (usually of R. Crumbian cocks, tits, and asses) of transient bands desperate to leave their imprint in black Magic Marker. Even in fabled clubs like the Bottom Line in Manhattan, the dressing rooms are an afterthought. Twice we've been billeted in the men's washroom (both times in Kingston, Ontario) and once, at the Townhouse in Sudbury, we were so disturbed by the drawings on the walls of the club's living quarters (thank you, Headstones) that we booked ourselves into a hotel.

The champagne is a gift from the Hip and their manager, Jake Gold, a man whose reputation precedes him like a cur on a leash. Jake was once a very round fellow, but not so on this tour. "Christ, you're looking good, Jake," I hear them say while moving quickly past him in the hallway, giving Jake pause to reach inside his blazer and stroke his slimming tub. Jake is feared by those who have crossed him. He's already worked over our manager, Paul Davies, who is the bookish opposite of Jake. But I like Jake, and while it's true that the music biz breeds a particularly repugnant kind of slimeball – draped in fine fabrics with coke spoons corkscrewed up their noses – I also believe that Jake is not half the monster his enemies make him out to be. His idea of power and achievement is relatively prosaic compared to the wildings of other managers: a little muscle around the deli tray, a spliff as fat as your thumb, the odd blow job.

We talk with him about last night's "surprise" gig at the Gate, which we played with Toronto's Mrs. Torrance. Here's what happened: At four o'clock, an overzealous CFOX announcer released word that the Hip would perform an impromptu gig at the Gate. By six o'clock, five hundred goons were swarming the club on Granville Street. Policemen on horseback were called in. Friends on guest lists were badgered away, and those who wormed inside the club waited out the Hip's arrival on stage by pounding back ales and fifty-cent shooters. Mrs. Torrance played an opening set and were ignored. A half-hour later, we plugged in, sounded a few chords, and were footballed with boos. In the dressing room afterwards, the club owners brought down trays of fresh crayfish and oysters; we wondered whether they were meant for the Hip. The next day, *Vancouver Sun* reporter Katherine Monk published this column:

To tepid applause and deriding cheers of "Hip! Hip!" (no hooray), the Rheostatics finished what could have been a sweet, touching and tight set at the Gate Thursday night.

Unfortunately, no one was there to see Toronto's off-beat contenders. The sold-out house was sitting pretty for a "surprise appearance" of the Tragically Hip.

After four radio plugs from CFOX, hundreds of would-be Hipsters lined Granville mall hoping for a once in a lifetime encounter with Canada's "biggest" band.

Sadly, not one Tragic figure emerged to save the Rheostatics from the angry — or at least completely disinterested — mob who filtered out of the venue exhaling giant sighs of disappointment like some bald, leaky radial flapping down theatre row.

A struggling Dave Bidini at one point introduced a female guest vocalist (Tamara Williamson) as "our good friend Gord Downie" — and as the room turned its collective head toward the stage, the partyers in the room started booing.

Disturbing as it was, the evening was a perfect Rheostatics moment. After slogging the huge stone uphill for the past six years, the band has garnered much critical affection but has yet to break into the mainstream consciousness. Not even their *Whale Music* album – or soundtrack film score (complete with single, "Claire") – managed to make a dent in the public imagination.

This tour with the Hip should have been the ideal vehicle, but gauging from Thursday's reception – the 'Statics might have been better staying at home.

DENTON YOUNG: We played the Forum at Ontario Place to fourteen thousand people. We'd played the high schools all year and every kid that we'd played for came that night. It was really a good show; nothing went wrong. The only guy that gave us a review was from the *Globe and Mail*, and he was an idiot. I came home on such a high, and then I read the paper the next day. The reviewer said that we should have stayed in the garage, and that the very mention of the name Zon evoked bugs curdling in the drain. It was scathing. Then I read one line that said, "This four-piece band . . . ," and that's when I realized that he'd reviewed the opening act. He had come to the show, watched the opening act, thought it was Zon, and then went back and wrote the worst review we've ever had.

BILL HENDERSON: New York was where we got our first bad review. It was in the *Village Voice* and it said: "The best thing the Collectors can do is break up and leave music." That was devastating. That was nasty.

PETER GODDARD: I was the first person hired full-time to write about music in Canada. That was with the *Toronto Star*. When I first started, I caught all kinds of flak. I came back from a James Brown concert, and I was going over some photos when an editor came by and said, "Just swung down from the tree, eh?" The guy who suggested the job to me said, "Okay, here's the deal. You write five times a week and you cut your hair." I had to work for two years before they let me write anything about rock-and-roll. As a result, I think the bands were put through a wringer with me. They really hated me, because I would say stuff that other people wouldn't. It would surprise me that they hadn't seen these things themselves. Joni Mitchell and I used to get into terrible fights. I used to criticize her for being airy-fairy. I called Rush a bad Led Zeppelin cover band. I came to respect them, but that's exactly what they were.

RA MCGUIRE: Writers like Keith Sharp would look for your weakest moment and try to get the ugliest thing coming out of your mouth. Once this CBC guy, right before the interview, asked if I wanted to talk about [keyboard player] Frank Ludwig quitting the band. I said, "Actually, if you're giving me the option, no." We get halfway through the interview, the recorder's running, and he says, "Before this interview started, you said that you didn't want to talk about Frank Ludwig leaving the band . . ." I looked at him and said, "You fucking asshole." He was scrambling to turn off the machine. There was this other asshole from Vancouver named Alexander Varty. I reviewed his band because my friend, Tom Harrison, was in it, and since Tom was a music writer, he figured that it would be a hoot if I did some record reviews. They were awful, but I tried the best I could. Not long after, Varty interviewed me himself, and when he printed it in the paper, he put in these clever retorts after my answers which he

hadn't said during the course of our conversation, all this snarky
shit. He'd led me on to say stuff that he could make fun of later.

We play the arena anyway. I'm scared shitless. At first, my voice
sounds Herculean, but it balloons out to the farthest reaches of
the rink before I can get any idea of its true dimensions. I sing
too loud, I sing too quiet. Sidestage, the Hip watch our show,
doubling the pressure. We wear matching burgundy sharkskin
jackets that change colours under the lights, so at least we look
good. We play eight songs, stiffly, to perfunctory applause, then
leave the stage bewildered. It's all we can do to keep from tucking
our heads under our collars and skulking back to our empty
dressing room. Our debut is inauspicious. We have floundered
through our first show.

You always dream of playing stadiums, but you never dream
you're the opening band. Backstage, Tim looks like he's been
bonked by a cricket bat. Martin sits on a chair and smokes. Don
laughs and cracks a beer. I trace my way back to the stage and
peek through the curtains at the crowd. There are apple-cheeked
kids in baseball caps, slugs in moth-eaten tour T-shirts, packs of
excited girls, a parent chewing a nail, Billy Corgan standard issue
#25478, your entire high-school's grade-twelve class, a laughing
office pool, lots of kids on awkward dates, and acres of mall
denim. As I suspected, none of them look like they've been
affected whatsoever by our distinct brand of Canadian Shield art
rock. Seconds after our last chord, they're busy working on gluey
orange nachos, eyes wandering around the rink, readying themselves for *their* band: the Hip. A half-hour later, the group takes

the stage and the crowd explodes. It's still exploding two hours later, and one thing becomes perfectly clear: tomorrow, I bite the head off a pigeon.

Show Two.

A stoned yeti in a Team Canada jersey and Canadian flag headdress stands at the tip of the stage and hollers "ROCK-AND-ROLL!" throughout our forty-five-minute set. We play well and the pigeon is spared.

Leaving Vancouver, we think this bird will fly.

ALBERTA

"The crowd roared, four thousand jack-in-the-boxes suddenly sprung, all of them laughing at me. Orr raised his hands in salute and turned, just as I hit him."
Roy MacGregor, *The Last Season*

A word about Edmonton:

Northlands Coliseum — where we played two sold-out shows before heading south — sits on a snowy desert. From the road it looks like an enormous bathtub plug. It's flanked by cloudscraping wheat silos on one side and a liquor store with blackened windows on the other, surrounded by a white expanse that floods in all directions, making one feel ridiculously northern. When we arrived at the Coliseum from our hotel, it was already filling up with kids whose excited voices sounded like sparrows teeming high in the trees. Before the gig, I met a teenager who told me that he had driven twelve hours from the farm for the show. He is typical, it seems, of Albertan youth. Earlier in the day at a college-radio interview, Martin and I ran into two kids who'd sleuthed us down and were looking for autographs for their CDs. I was reminded of the times when my pals and I used to dog after bands, too. Often, we weren't as interested in talking to the musicians themselves as we were in proving that they could not hide from us. The new-wave era was our heyday. We once found out where Devo were staying in Toronto and presented them with a bag of potatoes and a box of Cap'n Crunch. Singer Mark Mothersbaugh invited us up to their rooms, but I wish I'd never gone. Drapes drawn, television blaring, four po-faced men in jeans and T-shirts sat around a lone, teenage groupie, smoking a joint. I felt like asking: "Hey, guys, where the fuck's the plastic hair?" but it was no use. I haven't listened to much Devo since.

So we try to do better than that. Martin and I invited the kids to talk with us on radio, but they were button-lipped and nervous. It was hard to tell if we fulfilled their notion of what rock stars are supposed to be like, but I've learned that every encounter with a hero comes with some degree of demystification anyway, and there's nothing you can do to prevent it. A friend once told me he was visiting New York City on his holidays when he spotted his idol, jazz saxophonist Pharaoh Saunders, wandering around Times Square wearing a purple velvet suit. Starstruck, he dropped everything he'd planned for the afternoon and tailed him, waiting for the perfect opportunity to ask him for an autograph. But he didn't get the chance. Pharaoh wandered into a peep show, and didn't re-emerge.

Alberta kids. Strong-jawed, wispy-haired. In the afternoon, a handful of them showed up at our HMV in-store performance at the West Edmonton Mall, even though the store had neglected to advertise our appearance. It wasn't the first time. In-store performances are the most stressful, self-defeating kind of promotion. You're rarely allowed to perform on instruments you're used to, as limited space and set-up time make it impossible to deploy your travelling rig. This often results in terribly self-conscious performances. Familiar music redesigned for acoustic performance was once a novel, even musically beguiling, exercise, but these days every musician – even the ones with pierced willies and spiderweb tattoos – must pretend that they've been latent little Stevie Forberts all along. And the fact that the Unplugged phenomenon helped warm the careers of geezers such as Eric Clapton and Rod Stewart hasn't lent it credibility. Perhaps the industry and public has to accept that once a song is crafted and laboured over and sweated out and committed to tape, it is definitive, distanced safely from bongos, djembes, nylon-string guitars, and the threat of Billy Joel dropping by to sing harmony.

Tim and Martin abhor in-store performances, and in the afternoon, I discovered why. At the end of our twenty-minute set, we'd sold more copies of the *Friends* soundtrack album than of our own. Aloof shoppers stepped around our equipment to get to CDs, and the crappy, in-store P.A. made us sound like we were being broadcast over ham radio. On top of that, the store clerks refused to play our record after we'd finished. If there was an upside to this exercise in humility, it was that it made us yearn for the loudness and bombast of the stadium, or at least the opportunity to hide behind it. So, stressed-out and pissed-off, we attacked the evening show with a little extra tooth.

At exactly 7:45 p.m., the lights fell. Our show opened with "Earth/Monstrous Hummingbirds," a seven-minute, theatrical song about the history of civilization. We began the set by crawling up on stage out of the audience; it was the first time this tour that we'd opened our show with any kind of razzle-dazzle, as opposed to just strutting out there and playing. But we'd done our homework. Peter Gabriel used to play arenas where he'd jump off the stage and start running around the perimeter, wind-milling his arms, and his fans would follow him, in a crazy train of running swimmers. Similarly, Iggy Pop amazed the crowd at the Cincinnati Pop Explosion by standing on their outstretched hands while he caked his body with peanut butter, and in Toronto, Tex-Mex legend Joe King Carasco once ran out of the Colonial Tavern, crossed Yonge Street with his hundred-foot cable, and continued his guitar solo in the Eaton Centre.

These were the events that we had in mind as a purple light shot down on Martin, who skittered like a mechanical spider across his star-point to his amp. Under cover of darkness, Don and Tim sneaked out from behind the stage and began playing a rhythmic pattern that sounded like it could ripple cement. A green light hit me, and I pretended I was, er, *hatched* out of an imaginary egg. I took small, deliberate steps towards my guitar, acting like I'd never seen it before, then reached for its neck, only to recoil in terror. Get it? *It was the friggin' dawn of music!* Opposite me, Martin pantomimed eating a banana. Gary Stokes on the sound board soaked the song in beautiful reverb and sent it roiling over the crowd. Behind the band's propulsive rhythmic fist, I pressed my eyes shut and sang, *"The Earth was born . . ."*

Three verses later, I opened them.

Edmonton was yawning.

DENTON YOUNG: In Zon, I started to come up with gimmicks. You know those 150-watt spotlights that you set up in front of your house at Christmastime? I used to put one inside a socket (or a pigtail, as we'd call them), tape it up really strong, flick it on and swing it around stage. It was a fantastic effect. One night, I hit myself in the head so hard that it blew the bulb. I nearly knocked myself out.

RIK EMMETT: I got blown up once, by a flashpot, in Port Hawkesbury, Nova Scotia. I was blinded from the magnesium powder in my eyes. I was playing near the front of the stage, and the flash went *boom* at the wrong time. My hair was burned. I lost my eyebrows and all the hair inside my nose. I had second-degree burns across my nose and cheek. They walked me back to the dressing room and, thankfully, there was a registered nurse in the crowd. She helped me wash my eyes out and was very reassuring.

In Triumph, Gil Moore used to do a shtick where he'd have magician's flash-powder that he'd curl up into a little funnel. He'd fill it with magnesium powder and then he'd have a burning cigarette on the edge of his tom-tom drum. He'd be doing his rap, pounding his kick drum with his hand raised — "ARE YOU READY TO ROCK?" — and at the end of his shtick, he'd touch the flash-paper to the cigarette and then throw it. It looked amazing. It was like this ball of fire was flying out of his hand. But, one night, at the Piccadilly Tube, he was a little bit drunk, and he didn't quite get it out of his hand in time and he burned his hand really badly. In order to do the rest of the gigs that week, he had cream spread all over his hand inside a rubber glove, and a bucket of ice water at his side. He'd play until his hand started to hurt, and then he'd stick it into the bucket and play with one hand and his feet until the hand got numb again.

RONNIE KING: I once saw Crowbar play at Massey Hall. They came out of a cake with a topless chick.

Denton Young

KELLY JAY: I used to ride motorcycles when I was a kid, and if you wore Canadian insignias in the States, you got free drinks. I wore the flag on my clothes for a while, but I started covering myself in maple leaves the week after Woodstock, after I saw Hendrix with his American-flag vest. A month later, we did the Strawberry Fields festival, which was a rock-and-roll festival in Oshawa — eighty thousand kids, the largest of its kind up here — and I wanted to do something special. I was glad people took to it, 'cause that's what I wanted to happen.

Captain Canada was born when we did Massey Hall a while later. I had a beautiful tuxedo that I was going to wear at the gig, but it didn't get delivered to the show. I walked up Yonge Street to Lou Miles to get it, but on the way there I saw these red tights and red sweatshirt in the window and I had the guy put CAPTAIN CANADA up the leg. I was so sick of hearing that Canadians were benign; it pissed me right off. I couldn't see how we were any different from Americans when it came to playing, so why would our attitudes be different? We didn't have anything to be shy about. I remembered there was Captain Canuck, but Canuck to me was like calling a guy "nigger." So I became Captain Canada instead.

RICHARD FLOHIL: McKenna–Mendelson Mainline would play sitting down in a row. At the end of the stage would be this giant alarm clock. Joe Mendelson would come out and turn it to forty minutes. When the bell went off, the band would get up and walk off stage, even if they were in the middle of a song.

SKINNY TENN: Mainline had these posters that said MAINLINE PLAYS FOR MONEY. They were no bullshit; their attitude was, if you're a good audience, you'll get an encore. Skip Prokop of Lighthouse had the slogan LIGHTHOUSE PLAYS FOR PEACE, so Joe Mendelson turned it around. Fludd took it one step further: FLUDD PLAYS FOR THE CHICKS.

JOHN CODY: When I saw the Collectors — who later became Chilliwack — opening for Tiny Tim and Country Joe and the Fish, they brought a couch with them on stage so that they could sit down while their drummer took a solo.

DAVE HENMAN: Matt Minglewood, Sam Moon, and the Universal Power from Sydney, Cape Breton, were an amazing band. The guitar player was Diego Gun. He once did this thing in a high-school auditorium where he went running off the stage with a sixty-foot guitar cable, then ran *backwards* at the stage and did a backflip and landed at his spot right in front of the microphone while playing the guitar.

FRANK SODA: We took the train across the country from Terrace, B.C., to Toronto to join Thor, a muscle-rock guy. Thor didn't really know music, and he'd say things like, "I got an idea. I want you to write a song called 'Ya Gotta Eat!'" He wrote "You Gotta Keep the Dogs Away," which became the title of his record.

Thor's show, I think, incited violence. The worst incident I remember was in St. Catharines, Ontario. He used to put these concrete bricks on his chest and he'd get guys from the audience to come up and take a sledgehammer and break them. One night, the guy from the audience was really drunk and he decided to hit Thor where it hurt. Before you know it, one guy jumped him, and another guy jumped that guy, and it became a

riot. They had to close off the whole block. Somebody went
through the window.

Thor did other things in his show; he used to pick me up with
one hand and carry me into the audience while I played guitar.
We lasted for two years. After a while, we were writing songs
that Thor just couldn't do. We had no choice but to leave to do
our own thing. When we told him, I think he punched a hole in
the wall.

RONNIE KING: Mel Shaw came to us one day with an idea. He had
found some Murine — the stuff you use to soothe your eyes. He
used it to write FUCK on his forehead, which you couldn't see
unless you put a black light on it. It was vivid. There was also a
kind of paint that reacts to black lighting, and we did the whole
stage up in it. We did our Stratocasters — we put tape around
them and spraypainted the bodies — we did the sombrero hats,
drumsticks, shoes, everything. We had three or four black lights
at the base of the stage in front of us and people would stand
back and think, "What the hell is making these guys glow like
that?" We renamed the band the Paint Brushes. We were so
popular that when we went out of town to play, we'd have other
bands sub for us. There was one band called the Rebounds,
which consisted of Rich Dodson and Kim Berly, who later
became part of the Stampeders. One weekend, the Rebounds
renamed themselves the Turpentines. When the Paint Brushes
broke up, we joined forces with the Turpentines, and that's how
you got the Stampeders.

FRANK SODA: I had this song called "TV People" about people
getting brainwashed watching too much television. I imagined a

guy's head turning into a TV. I thought, wouldn't it be funny if we could get a TV and put it on someone's head and just blow it up? So I got this old TV from a used-electronics shop, gutted it out, put it about twenty feet away and we blew it up with these pots. We realized that it didn't move too much if you loaded the powder right. It made a lot of noise, but it didn't appear that dangerous. So we padded the inside, and I tried it on my head. I added more and more powder and it worked great. Later on, if the roadies were a bit drunk, they'd put too much powder and I'd burn my hair. But it sounded and looked great in arenas, like cannons exploding out of my head. The first time Goddo saw me do it, he came running to the stage, saying, "Are you okay?" because he thought that I was hurt. It looked and sounded unbelievable.

RICHARD FLOHIL: Peter Goddard and me and my wife went to see Bobby Bland at Joe Louis Arena. We were the only white people in the place. Opening for Bobby Bland was this incredible band who played really weird music. The sound sucked; they had a crappy, sixty-watt sound system, which was terrible inside a big hockey rink. The band was in the middle of the ice, and the lead singer wound up staggering into the audience wearing nothing but a silver-lamé jockstrap. The cops went crazy and the house lights went up. Cords were pulled out of amps because they were afraid there was going to be a riot. I turned to the guy beside me and asked, "Who the hell is that band?" He said, "That's the Parliament-Funkadelic." Not knowing, I said, "Oh, where are they from?" and he said, "Toronto, Canada." They were managed at that time by a man named Ron Scribner, who also managed Alice Cooper when he was in Zoom.

Dee Lippingwell Photography

Frank Soda

SKINNY TENN: Kenny Shields and the Witnesses toured western Canada with Cream. Those guys were so fuckin' heavy. We were petrified. It was the biggest band and the biggest gig we ever played, places like the Edmonton Coliseum, three thousand people. At the time, Cream were on the verge of breaking up; it was always very volatile. We'd never seen a group from England before. These guys were so strung-out, man. They were like animals. I see this Gentleman Eric Clapton thing now and I just laugh. Ginger Baker, he'd come out of the dressing room, with all these rings on and wild hair and clothes like we'd never seen a man wear before. Then the band would go up there and jam. They gave the poor kids in Alberta a really half-assed show. They'd do "White Room," but it would last twenty-seven minutes. They'd do the intro, a verse, then jam. They played "Sunshine of Your Love" for an hour. Two songs. No encore, either. I'm sure they were all thinking to themselves, "What the fuck are we doing in Edmonton?"

Highway 2, monstrous snow.

Dog Pound, Balzac, Ma-Me-O Beach. Savage cold, impossible wind. *Apocalypse winter.* Reliable Gary Stokes, who boasts of having driven this wonky north-south arrow to Calgary thousands of times before, gnaws his lip and clutches the van's steering wheel like he's working the horns of a bull. We pass clusters of ditched cars and trucks, many of them buried under huge churches of snow, their side mirrors sticking out like little frostbitten hands. We hunch to look out under the frostline on the front window and see other cars shimmying wildly across

lanes as if rebelling against years of moving in a straight line. A
policeman stands outside an emergency cruiser, holding out his
glove, and we slide towards him like a curling stone. Wisely, he
windmills us through and we inch closer, slow as erosion, south-
bound to Calgary.

Gary Stokes is our road manager, soundman, and principal
driver. I'm beginning to wonder about him. Gary claims he's
from Grande Prairie, a big farming town in northern Alberta.
But Gary's baseball cap is way too clean for someone who comes
from anywhere near there. I have proof of this. My friends from
Brandon, Manitoba – Tyler, Rod, and Pat, who play in the hip-
hop group Farm Fresh – once held a contest in nearby Virden for
the first person who spotted anyone not wearing a soiled baseball
cap. There were no winners; it simply could not be done. Gary's
hat looks like it's just been picked out from a glass showcase at a
Husky truck-stop. I'm menaced by its absence of dirt, but
because our fate is in his hands, I ignore this niggling detail.

Below Gary's hat trails a black ponytail, and this I cannot over-
look. The ponytail suggests breeziness and insouciance, piano-
key ties and people who listen to Dire Straits. Gary is not, to my
knowledge, among these dweebs, yet his shiny mane implicates
him. I decide that I must harvest this hair, perhaps with Martin's
X-acto knife. I also ask myself whether I should trust my life to
a man with a ponytail. The blizzard boots the sides of the van
like a pack of rampaging thugs. Wind knuckles the roof and
snow spits through the windows.

The question is answered for me.

Gary Stokes is a man of many bands. He is Sarah McLachlan's
soundman, with whom he navigates the globe. A month before
driving us to Calgary, he was mixing live sound for Hayden at

Neil Young's Bridge Concert in California, clinking glasses with David Bowie and Pearl Jam. The Cowboy Junkies played there, too, and reportedly ended up staying at Neil's ranch for a week. I ask Gary if this is true.

"Yes, it is," he says. "I'm sure I could have gone if I wanted. I'm sure Hayden was invited."

But no. I had to come up here and drive you morons across the tundra. Gary doesn't say this, but I'm thinking it. Wouldn't he rather be playing pinochle with Ziggy Stardust? One would think. But instead, Gary has returned to mix sound and squire around the Quirk Kings of Canadian Pop, turning down an audience with the very Legends of Rock and Roll just to be with us. I decide that's one helluva gesture. Sure, you could hoist lagers with Pete Townshend, but you could do other things, too, like play hockey with the Tragically Hip. Our man Stokes understands this, and that's why, six hours later, he pulls the van into Calgary, where we suck long, deep breaths of the terrible blue cold, tramping over the new crust and scrambling for a drink.

I first played hockey with the Tragically Hip at Bill Bolton Arena in Toronto. Jim Cuddy, Michael and Peter Timmins of the Cowboy Junkies, and a few of the Skydiggers played, too. I went into rock-star lock the first time I saw the boys standing there in the arena's foyer.

"Hello, there," they said, their tuques socked over their heads, sticks arced across their shoulders.

"Uh, hello," I replied, staring down at my boots.

At the time, the Hip were Canada's fastest-rising rock band. I was pretty jealous. We'd done a small tour of Canada that year, and their song "Little Bones" had hounded us every step of the way. Once, in Red Deer, Alberta, at Mortimer's in the Capri Hotel, the disc jockey sank into his dark cubicle and listened to Hip records on his headphones while we played our set. When we finished, he blasted "Little Bones" at us before we'd said goodnight. The song goaded us. There were only four people in the audience that night, including two guys who'd just come back from putting out the oil fires in Kuwait. We knew that Red Deer would be a bad gig as soon as we entered the city limits, where a giant Shell sign with the S burnt out blinked at us from a sixty-foot pole.

Welcome to HELL.

After playing our dismal first set to no one, our then-road manager, Richard Burgman, came backstage and gave us a little pep talk. Richard is Australian, from Wagga Wagga, New South Wales, and has a face like a knife. He was born with a long black scowl that suggests he wants to kick your head in. His favourite tour story is about Pierce the Pieman, the escaped Australian convict who once cannibalized his travelling companion and fashioned a tobacco pouch from his scrotum. Whenever he told this tale, he'd finish by asking, "Now, lads, put in that position, could you ever see yourself resortin' to this kind of . . . savagery?" He chewed off that last word like a strip of peppered jerky. With a thin snake of grey smoke curling over his lip, he looked you right in the eye when he spoke, and Christ, he could scare the balls right off of you.

Richard also had the charming habit of addressing people as "scum." He'd often start a sentence with, "All right, scum," or "Now, listen, scum," and sometimes he even used the word as a term of endearment, usually in the morning to get us out of bed. After a while, I stopped taking it personally, though Martin and Tim never got used to it, nor did they warm to "maggots" or "filth," two other witticisms favoured by our *éminence grise*.

That night, Richard gathered us behind the little stage at Morty's, called us scum, then read us his riot act. It was quite moving. Spitting out brown flecks of tobacco from his hand-rolled cigarette, he said, "I know there are only four people out there tonight, lads, but prove something to me. Prove to me that you care. I want you to go out there and play *the greatest show of your lives . . .*"

We went out and got hammered. I nearly fell into the drum kit. It was years before I finally realized what Richard was trying to tell us. He was saying, "Get your shit together so that you can make something out of your careers. Treat this lousy gig like it's the most important thing in your lives. Prove to me that you don't have to take shit from anyone, especially the Tragically Fuckin' Hip."

Looking back, we probably owed him the effort.

We haven't been back to Red Deer.

In Saskatoon on that same trip, Tim and Martin were ambushed by a drunk in a blues club. He told them that, in order to be successful, they had to be more like the Hip. This was the last thing they wanted to hear in the middle of a mid-winter prairie tour. After finishing their beers, they left him and wandered back to the band house, half-canned in the ass-rattling Saskatoon cold. A car at a stoplight blared "Little Bones" at them from the road. Tim and Martin looked at each other and lowered their heads. When I heard that story for the first time, I felt like crying.

Cathy Bidini

Richard Burgman

So this was how we'd crossed paths with the Tragically Hip.
From a distance, they'd tormented us. They'd evolved as weird
inventions of our paranoid subconscious before we ever saw
them as real people. Watching them hack around with the puck
and flutter shots at the net on that cold spring morning at Bill
Bolton Arena, their transformation from ethereal rock lions to
feckless scrubs was so unsettling that I didn't go back to that
game for years.

I'd been spooked.

I am snapped and locked snugly into a white, spaghetti-webbed
mask. I am suddenly very fat. I can barely walk from the weight
of the pads, which are wrapped around my legs like two sloths
hugging a stump. Inside my helmet, my breathing sounds
amplified. I look out at the bright oval rink of the Max Bell
Centre as the Zamboni does one last long lick down the middle
of the ice. Then the gate swings open and the first few skaters hit
the frozen water, their skate blades *shwicking*. Pucks are shot
against the boards *boam!* and hiccup through skates carving eights,
oblongs, rhomboids, and other geometric jigsaws in higgledy
patterns across the beautiful translucent ice.

I skate to my net.

A few days ago, when the Hip crew asked if I thought that I
was good enough to play shinny with them, I gave them a choice
– I could vanquish them from either end of the rink. I go both
ways, having become a recent inductee in the union of goaltenders. I became a part-time puckstopper after Dougie – the
fellow who stands between the pipes in our Sunday-night scrub

games – asked if I'd consider taking his prehistoric gear off his hands while he upgraded. I accepted because I knew that his pads, gloves, and bulky underthings had had courage beaten into them, and that I'd have had to scour used-equipment shops to find such rubber-tested tools of ignorance. (Upon examining the equipment up close and under a strong light at home, however, I noticed that the waffle-board had two fingers and a thumb missing and the chest-protector provided about as much ribbing as a French tickler).

I am aware that goaltenders are supposed to have wild mood swings and general antisocial behaviour, and for better or worse, I'm well on my way. I only recently learned to embrace the basic principle of tending goal: to actually enjoy being hit with a hard frozen rubber thing travelling at high speed. I do like it. I also like the solace of being the only person in the empty half of the ice once the action moves up-rink, and I like the warm-up: while the skaters are swooshing around me whacking at pucks and dogging after each other, I'm leaning placidly against my cross-bar, shrouded in calm and implied poise. Christ, I could be sleeping. What I'm really doing, however, is watching Canada's number-one rock star carve up his crease at the far end of the rink. Gord knows his onions; he once backstopped his bantam team to the all-Ontario championship, and because he's the god-son of Boston Bruin GM Harry Sinden, I assume that he's picked up a few ideas about how to play the game along the way. Taking warm-up shots, he shadows his corners ably and is deft with both hands. He exudes a fundamental understanding of the position, something that guys like Dougie and I can learn only from sitting in front of the television on Saturday nights.

So, being only Canada's 249th-biggest rock star, I try to

Dave with Gord Downie, Max Bell Centre, Calgary

Clemens Rikken

remember what Felix Potvin did the last time I saw him warm up
on television. I drop to my knees and arc my back, my cushion-
padded legs pinned under me. While I'm down there, I make a
few notes. The arena's ice-level odour, for instance, reveals itself
to be a northern cocktail of diesel, lumpy coffee, du Maurier cigarettes, French fries, mildew, old mountains of grey arena slush,
and grape bubblegum, five balls to a sleeve. I also notice a sign
posted on the wall behind me. Apparently, last week the Shaolin
Monks — a touring martial-arts outfit who were on last year's
Lollapalooza — performed here, and two days before that the
Superstars of New Country were booked in for a sold-out
evening of some of the worst crap you'll hear this side of
Bolton's Best. Clearly, we are in the ideal place for tonight's
follies, and as I climb to my skates, suddenly, without semaphore,
the first shot arrives.

It is soft and generous.

The rest of the Hip are here, save drummer Johnny Fay, who
is probably somewhere sharing a foam bath with two ladies. The
band's married stiffs — guitarist Bobby Baker, bassist Gord
Sinclair, and guitarist Paul Langlois — are all skaters of com-
mendable skill. Like Tim Vesely — who is dressed like a jewel
thief in black jeans, turtleneck, and tuque — they move in short,
choppy strides, with tongue-wagging élan. I wish I could say the
same for poor Don and Martin who, when they finally manage to
get moving, simply hold their arms out like two frightened
tightrope walkers, and try not to take anyone out.

Mike Cormier, the Hip's shaggy-haired, got-no-sleep, pushing-
forty, two-packs-a-day drum technician, is the game's revelation.
He cannot be stopped. His evening goes something like this:
skate like the wind, score, race to the bench, puke, skate some

more, score, vomit, rest, hack up some blood, score twice, retch on some green stuff, make faces like your head is going to explode, then score again. Mike's aplomb puts him in a beer league all his own, outclassing the other hard-scrabble arena moles, tavern-hardened production rats, sensitive-to-the-touch songwriters, and corpuscle-busting management types who should probably be back at the hotel on this off-night sitting in the tranquillity of a soundless tub, but instead are out here tapping their near-dry font of youth for a bit of wahoo on a snowy, quiet prairie night, unencumbered by corporeal realities and the better sense of adulthood.

I could puke, too, but it wouldn't help. The first few minutes are nerve-wracking, but I settle down after my first save, which comes when Langlois tries to beat me on the short side. My pads absorb his shot, and the puck bounces to a defenceman, who slings it away. At the other end of the rink, Gord shoots out a leg and stabs the puck with his foot, then sprawls across the crease to get position on the rebound, which is hiccuping near the side of the net. I should mention that, while Gord is a commanding performer in concert, on the ice he is a flopper. The word doesn't evoke images of heroic and graceful athleticism, but most floppers get the job done, albeit with their necks and stomachs pasted to the ice. So Gord, having flopped, holds the puck for a few seconds, then slides it to his defenceman, who rushes down the ice and tests me with a wristshot. It's as if Downie has whispered to him, "Bidini's glove hand. Looks weak." I swipe at the puck with my mitt like a butterfly collector waving his basket; the disk floats into the top corner of the net. Ricky Wellington, the Hip's bodyguard who cannot skate, is pointing at me and laughing from the bench. At the other end of the rink, Gord is

Clemens Rikken

Paul Langlois, Max Bell Centre, Calgary

spanking the ice with his stick while the scorer is being hugged by his teammates. I spit and call Jesus a terrible name. Sweeping the puck from the back of the net, I feel my confidence fall limp, and then things go from bad to worse.

Gretzky is cruising over the blueline.

Glen Gretzky, actually. It turns out that Wayne's cousin is an employee of the provincial junior-A champion Calgary Canucks, and, along with a few friends, he's distinguishing our scrub teams with a rare quality – skill – ensuring that Gord and I will, unfortunately, be challenged by skaters who actually know how to do a thing or two with the puck. Not surprisingly, Glen moves a little like Wayne – back hunched parallel to the ice, stick fully extended in front of him, tongue fluttering in pursuit of the puck – so it's easy to dream that instead of standing in a small rink in suburban Calgary, I'm crouched low with my knees angled together in a sold-out, rafter-packed hockey stadium, staring ruefully out at history's greatest scorer, who is moving towards me like a viper.

Gretzky descends on a two-on-one. Our defenceman (who, as my luck would have it, is related to no one) is caught flatfooted and scrambles to skate backwards as quickly as Glen is moving forward; he cannot. Glen's winger – another of the swift-skating Canucks employees – swings wide to his right and forces me to read not one but two plays – the pass or the shot – neither of which I am particularly good at. I must stay even with the shooter while somehow maintaining shape on the other side of the net, creating the illusion of moving both ways across the goal at the same time, a tactic that seems to require two brains, even though most goaltenders lack one good one.

Glen holds the disk until the absolute last second before

tipping his hand. The defenceman slides his body flat across the ice towards Gretzky, who slips the puck under him. The winger takes the pass and I fall sideways away from the rubber, throwing my legs out. My pads, stacked together, move across the crease like a small chesterfield. Ice gnashes into my mask and I end up face down, looking out the back of the net. There is no crowd to tell me what has happened. There is no tsunami cheer, no Bic lighters being flicked, no Les Pauls getting air-slashed, no kids howlingly ill on cheap sherry, no young girls screaming through the quiet parts, no chairs, paper cups, or cigarette butts being flung, no Gord up there working out a hard case of the vocal yips, no careering, pin-lit guitar solos, no end-of-gig clean-up, no idling buses spewing black fumes in the bowels of the arena, no metal door being swung shut by silver-haired security guards. Nothing, in fact, except the small sound of skateblades *snikking* up the ice.

It appears that I have stopped Gretzky.

At the Saddledome, the crowd is zonked, crazy. In Toronto, fans applaud; in Vancouver, they cheer; but in Calgary, they howl hair-raising, guttural paroxysms of zeal. Wandering the concourse, I see a very bad girl in a leather jacket being hogtied by security and heaved length-wise out of the stadium. A few minutes later, I watch a fellow so drunk that he is crawling on his hands and knees to get to the washroom; inside, a kid barfs into a urinal, then high-fives his friend. There are scrums of sour-faced young men raising cups of beer, totally ignoring the music, detached from the ambience of the performance. Then again, perhaps they *are* its ambience. After ten days, it's still hard to tell which best represents the Big Rock milieu: the hairy-armed lout, the angelic teenage girl with the green glow ring around her neck, the bookish, nail-biting kid mouthing Gord Downie's poetry, the row of suburban girls with their arms wound around each other, or the small native kid who looked up at me during our show like I was Zeus casting down bolts of lightning from a mountain peak.

The kid was eight, maybe ten. He was sitting in the Henhouse with his parents on either side. The Henhouse is the area reserved for fans who have donated to the local food bank, submitted their names, and had theirs drawn, and got their seats upgraded to the front of the rink. Jake Gold got the idea from Hootie and the Blowfish, which proves that some good comes from MOR after all. The Henhouse is supposed to stop the seat-hoarding practices of industry types and scalpers who often people the finest chairs in the house. It's comforting knowing that those audience members who sit closest to us, the ones we see first, are enjoying one of the finest concert experiences of their lives even before our first chord is struck. Their enthusiasm is palpable and infectious. They cannot hurt us.

By our third song, the kid couldn't look away. He was agog. He even stood up to watch Don Kerr smite his shiny red tom-toms. Mid-song, I flashed him the Family of Rock finger salute, and he glanced down at his hands.

I felt mountainesque.

The first musician to acknowledge me in the audience was Nigel Bennett of the Members, a punk-influenced white reggae band from London, England. They opened for Joe Jackson at the Seneca Fieldhouse in Toronto in 1979, and I was at the front.

Nigel had wildly afroed brown hair and crooked teeth and he chewed bubble gum furiously while he played. His band's performance was unlike any I'd seen; I'd watched ELO, Triumph, Zon, and a handful of other bands perform live before, but I'd never been that close to the stage before, nor to an actual rock-and-roll musician. So as a crowd kid, I gave it all I had, and after one song, I cheered so stupidly hard that Nigel came over and looked down at me, and, well, he *laughed*.

It made my year.

Before leaving the stage, I threw the kid a T-shirt. I'd hoped that during one of these shows, I'd look out and see myself in the crowd, and there I was, with my parents, no less. It was quite a day. *We brought some boxes of Kraft Dinner from home and handed them to the woman at the front gate who tossed them in a giant bin and then we were sitting up in the reds before the show when the deejay from the Bear came on and he went up to the mike and called out our names and they echoed around the rink and so we went down and I met the deejay and we were upgraded to first-row seats and I got a T-shirt and a guitar pick thrown to me by the openers and we had hot dogs and nachos and popcorn and Cokes and later the Hip came on and they were amazing and now I think I wanna be a rock-and-roll star, so Mom, Dad . . .*

Can I?

After our set, we went to our dressing room, where Richard Lewis, the director of the film *Whale Music*, was sitting drinking a beer.

"So?" I asked him.

"So what, buddy?" he said.

"So what about that?" I asked, meaning the show.

"Oh. You looked so *small* up there."

GREG GODOVITZ: The first concert I ever went to was the Drifters, the Coasters, and the Platters at Maple Leaf Gardens. I was eleven years old. I went on my own. I was pretty independent as a kid. My dad had a smoke shop at Dundas and Yonge — Ted's Smoke Shop — and I used to deliver the coffees. My godfather, Jimmy Leone, had Leone's Beauty Salon right around there. There were lots of places I'd deliver to. There was an element of danger to the area, but it was pretty safe and it had a certain excitement. I remember going up to the Ford Hotel at Bay and Dundas, which was a real hot spot for jumping. It was the highest building downtown outside of the Royal York, but since it was too expensive to stay there, you'd rent a room at the Ford and you'd jump. I remember walking up with this big tray of coffees and sandwiches for the customers at Leone's and seeing a crowd gathered on the sidewalk. I went over and there was this guy just smunched on the ground. I was about nine or ten, so I was shocked, but what really struck me was that there was this band standing there — the first band I'd ever seen — and they looked very surreal. They wore iridescent green mohair suits and had greasy dyed-green pompadours. They were called Johnny Green and the Green Men. I just stood there staring at them. I thought they were stranger than the body oozing blood.

FRANK SODA: In the late '60s when the psychedelic thing was happening, I heard a band from Denmark that forever changed my life. They were called the Young Flowers and they had just finished touring with Cream when they came to Kitimat, British Columbia, to our high school to play. The guy had a wall of amps on one side and a wall of amps on the other. Nobody had seen this. It was the days when everyone was just drugging and smoking. They cranked and they were amazing. The guitarist was doing Indian-style things and thirty-minute solos. He'd be tripping, but he'd just go. They travelled in that whole northern area; I think one of the guys had a relative up there, so that's how they ended up coming. I think they stayed a year, just hanging around. They reminded me of Gypsies. Later, they were judges for this battle of the bands, which my band ended up winning. We were called the Roots of Innocence. But when I saw that guy with his Les Paul and big stack of Marshalls, it changed everything for me.

KEN TOBIAS: The first bands I saw played at places like Lily Lake, which was a small lake in the middle of Fredericton, where everybody used to swim. They had a boathouse – a big building – where they sold their concessions and stuff, and there was a dance hall. You'd walk out on the verandah overlooking the lake. Lily Lake, to me, was like Hollywood. If you played there you *happened*. Dutchie Mason played there and he dyed his hair a different colour every night; Dutchie Mason and the Esquires. He stuck a cigarette between his teeth and played keyboards, horn, guitar, and the boys would play everything that was happening in r&b. We'd sneak in, grab a beer, sit in the corner, get drunk, throw up. We'd see all the old black people – not the young black people – gathered together, all dancing. It was adult, it was a little bit seedy, but very alluring, very free. If you couldn't get in, you'd just stand by the door. Eventually, I played there. And there were those same black people, dancing in the corner.

DONNIE WALSH: When I was a kid, my dad owned a hotel in North Bay. It was a place where they had Saturday-night dances;

sometimes they had a live band, but usually just a jukebox. The whole room was a dance floor. The room beside it was where everybody sat down. There was enough room for maybe two hundred people to dance. They'd pile these quarters in; you'd get three plays for a quarter. Because of the God laws, at eleven-thirty you had to turn the jukebox off; at twelve o'clock everybody had to be out of the room. The next morning we'd plug the jukebox in and because everybody had been putting their money in all night, it would run all day, from nine in the morning till after dinner, playing every tune that was on there: "String of Pearls" by Glenn Miller, "Hound Dog" by Elvis, Chuck Berry, Fats Domino, Pat Boone, lots of cowboy music, too. That's where I heard my music.

RA MCGUIRE: Believe it or not, the most impressive kid's concert I ever went to was Vanilla Fudge opening for Jimi Hendrix, who just sucked. He was really bad. He just stood there and was rude. He played one song, and then he said, "Now, I'll play ya some bubblegum shit," and proceeded to play a half-assed, half-length version of "Purple Haze" before fucking off. Vanilla Fudge, on the other hand, were just so strong and emotional. I remember the bass player the best. Every time he whacked his bass, it was though someone had pushed him backwards. He was getting thrown all over the stage by the power of his playing. I loved that his performance was keyed to the actual music, more than just waving his arms or dancing. He seemed to connect with his instrument in a very visceral way.

HOLLY WOODS: Jimi Hendrix was the first concert I ever went to. It was at the Dortan Arena in Raleigh, North Carolina. We had our state fair there. Cows and concerts. I was in grade nine and I went with my boyfriend, whose name was Larry Nine. I had on a little green wool skirt and turtleneck and high heels. Everybody around me had tie-dyed shirts and when Hendrix walked out, I went, "*Whaoooo!*" He was incredible. From that day on, I dressed differently, I talked differently. It changed my life.

TERRY BLACK: It hit home that I wanted to be a singer when I was thirteen and James Brown came to the PNE. It was my first concert. I skipped school and went to the show with some friends. When I was standing backstage, a woman who was taking care of Stevie Wonder asked if I could stand with him for a minute while she went to the dressing room to get his brush. I started talking to Stevie and he knew right away that we were almost the same age. He was feeling my face. Meanwhile James Brown was on doing his thing. Stevie started to practise "Fingertips" on the harmonica and he asked me about the new dances. I showed him a few of them, moving his arms and telling him what they were about. Then the woman came back and said it was time for him to go on. He was great. He did the arm thing.

RICHARD FLOHIL: I came to Canada in 1957, and on my second day in the country, with no job, maybe two hundred dollars in my pocket, I walked down Yonge Street and passed a bar called the Colonial Tavern. I saw a sign outside that said, "All this week: Earl Hines." I was blown away. Upstairs there was a guy polishing tables, and I asked him if it was *the* Earl Hines, the guy who'd played in Louis Armstrong's Hot Seven in the '20s. He said it was. I asked him how much it cost to get in. He said, "Well, it's free, but you have to drink two beers." The next night, I found out there was a big show at the Gardens with Fats Domino, Paul Anka, Cliff Richard, and John Lee Hooker – Dick Clark's Parade of Stars. A week after that, I went to the Town Tavern and discovered hockey on a black-and-white television set while a rotund black man named Oscar Peterson racked the joint. This was my first week in Canada. I knew right there that I was in the promised land.

4

SASKATCHEWAN

"I gotta keep on keepin' on."
BTO, *"Rock Is My Life & This Is My Song"*

 Das Bus.

Yesterday, we picked up our tour bus. Before I ever set foot on it, I imagined lying across a velvet bench in my bathrobe, sipping a beer, my guitar across my stomach, watching wrestling on television, perhaps with a maiden or two standing over me, feeding me grapes and fanning me with palm fronds. I never once imagined I'd be curled up like a scampi in a cold, dark cell, rocking back and forth on a hard bunk trapped between two doors sealing in the foul emissions of six men living on pizza and black coffee. Now I know why rock musicians used to stay up all night chasing ladies and shooting dope: to avoid having to sleep near each other. Maybe those dinosaurs had it right after all. No one ever envisions, say, Nikki Sixx blearily making tea at the kitchenette and having it spill scorchingly down his trousers. Sadly, this happens to us quite often; our eight-bunk sleeper is more than a tad bouncy, and even the simplest task is often the stupidest adventure. Navigating from the back of the bus to the front, for instance, is like being trapped on a funhouse ride, and more than a few times I've been thunked on the side of the head by hurtling suitcases and CDs shot at me like ninja stars. Even playing the guitar and singing meditatively in the back lounge invariably results in a hapless battle between one's own artistic meanderings and the bus's grunting engine. (There's another rock-and-roll myth shot to hell. All those stories about the Stones and Little Feat and other bands jamming and writing albums on their tour buses? Forget them. They were parked.) The bouncing is hard to figure considering that we are currently navigating the flattest strip of Highway 1, where the scenery rarely shifts and the road just keeps on going.

The best thing about Das Bus is its massive front windshield and side windows, which turn Canada into a dreamy, cinematic epic. The bleak winterscape outside looks as if it's being shot by Eisenstein (or Egoyan), and we spend a lot of time staring dolefully at this film. Otherwise we occupy ourselves by reading, sewing, and writing. Unfortunately (or not; it depends on how you feel about space and existential beauty), today's movie is *Saskatchewan*, and while it's rife with tone and possesses all the stretchy languidity of a film by Lars von Trier (whose yarn *Breaking the Waves* is an oft-chewed bone of contention between me and Don, who claims to have actually enjoyed it), it's a little thin on plot and could probably use a few actors, like, say, maybe, one.

There are no people here.

But while Saskatchewan may appear vast and empty with only "miles of wheat and indifference" (Mordecai Richler) to recommend, I've always found this expansive province to be an excellent place for thinking. On our first tour, in '87, I discovered this while on the return leg of our journey. My girlfriend, Janet, was sitting in the back seat of the Ram Charger reading a magazine she'd bought at Chuck's Snappy Foodway, a remarkably well-stocked convenience store just outside Moose Jaw, where you can find current issues of *Modern Drummer*, *The New Yorker*, *Goldmine*, and, if you happen to be a fugitive running from the law, *Prison Life Monthly*. After leaving Chuck's that afternoon, I took the wheel and drove (actually, the term "drove" is misleading when applied to travelling across the prairies; a better verb might be "pointed," which is all one has to do when moving in a straight line with about ten thousand feet between vehicles). I remember looking in the rear-view mirror at her smoking with her sunglasses pulled down across her small face, her lovely black hair dappled by the light of the flaming sun, a golden sea of wheat-straw stretching under the cloudless azure sky. The rest of the band were smoking and jabbering away, and I thought that I had never before experienced a more memorable scene. There I was with my young, beautiful girlfriend and three best friends, and something about this conjunction of love, camaraderie, and the Canadian landscape defined my life. The openness of the land, the sultry summer air, my left arm slung down the side of the door – for the first time I felt like I was where I should be.

Free.

The moment sustained itself and I lolled it around for a while like a jawbreaker thinning on my tongue. I said nothing, but my mind spilled a river of soundless thought. I put one hand on top of the steering wheel, lit a smoke with the other, and wrestled with ideas of existence and experience and other concepts upper-most in the consciousness of a twenty-three-year-old in the sudden throes of epiphany. I was able to drift untethered into these canyons of philosophical thought, I think, because of the sheer boundlessness of the land. This couldn't have happened in the city because the setting that had engaged me in the first place remained unchanged well until sundown, so I was able to play out my ideas like a magician's infinite helix. For me, Saskatchewan is the place where everything suddenly collided — if only once — and where I was truly born for the second time. Those who simply put their head down and power through this unsung province are denying themselves its subtle powers.

DENNIS ABBOTT: The 49th Parallel had an old 1949 Brewster courier bus, and it had a glass roof, a sightseeing roof. We cleaned it out and we a put a long horseshoe-shaped booth in the back and up the sides. We had double bunks, two sets, on each side. We stuffed the equipment underneath and sometimes towed a trailer or also took a little van that our equipment guys drove. I had a top bunk so I could just lie there all night and see the stars and feel the highway, just looking up. One night, we blew a tire. Whoever was driving didn't catch on right away and by the time he did, it was red-hot. We thought we'd just pull over and wait at the side until morning. But the brake lining had caught on fire and some of the flames started licking up on the inside of the bus. We all bailed and starting yanking all the equipment out from the loading bays underneath. We finally yanked everything out onto the highway. And the bloody bus burnt. That was the end of it.

There's the sign: Melville. Das Bus speeds past it, ignoring all
distractions so we can reach Saskatoon's Sask Place by showtime.
It could be worse, I suppose. We could be slouching towards
Regina, that dreary white-collar suicide capital of Canada. Over
the years, we've had many Reginian moments, most of them
absurd and tragi-comic. In our past couple of tours, we've been
cursed with two off-days there, both Sundays. The first one was
wasted at the cinema watching *Speed*, so the next time I was determined to find an activity for the group. In the morning I scoured
the newspaper until I came upon the magic words GIANT RECORD
SALE. Feeling hopeful (not to mention achingly bored out of our
skulls), we climbed into the van and drove towards the suburbs.
An hour later, we arrived at the address in the paper. There,
sitting on two lawnchairs inside the cleanest garage I've ever seen,
was an elderly couple guarding four crates of Christian albums
propped up on a bridge table. Within this pious mess, Mike
O'Neil of the Inbreds miraculously found Donny Most's first
solo record, so the day wasn't a complete waste. We spent the rest
of the night in the band house trying to fix a broken VCR and
looking for a bootleg Who videotape that Mike had bought in
Winnipeg. We never repaired the machine, nor did we find the
tape, but at least we found out what passes for a GIANT RECORD
SALE in Regina.

Another sign: Melville, Yorkton. We became associated with
Melville through our second album, which shares a name with
the town. While it's true that we titled the record after pedal-
steel guitarist and band guru Lewis Melville, the CD also featured
a song called "Saskatchewan" and was adorned by Martin's cover
painting of a colossal fish on a yellow prairie. So when we
embarked on tour in the fall of 1991, we decided to experience

Melvillean culture first-hand, having accidentally appropriated it in our wheatless Etobicoke homes.

We were booked for one night at Slo-Helen's restaurant and tavern in the Waverly Hotel. The Waverly was run (and still is, I believe) by Brian and Helen Hicke, and it was their son-in-law, Steve Tunison, who convinced them to hire the band sight-unseen. The first thing I did after settling into the Waverly was put two dollars down on a fifty-to-one horse — Gordie's Mistake in the seventh — on Helen's off-track betting game. I watched the race live via satellite from Winnipeg's Assiniboia Downs as my pony lurched impossibly across the finish line, earning me ninety-two dollars before I'd sat down to my coffee. I was ecstatic. Afterwards, we set off for Melville Arena, where the Saskatchewan Junior Hockey League's Millionaires were playing. It was here that I left my substantial winnings in the hands of the concessionaire, who provided me with a bounty of Millionaires beer steins, buttons, stickers, T-shirts, and other priceless SJHL paraphernalia. I'd simply escorted my ninety-two from one side of Melville to the other.

As it turned out, playing the friendly wooden tavern at the Waverly was a revealing musical experience, and not just because Jim Walters, the impish mayor of Melville, presented us with a Millionaires jersey on stage. Rather, having accepted congratulations from the thirty or so patrons in the bar after our set, I found myself staring at a wall covered with photos of bands who'd performed at Slo-Helen's over the years. Two acts stood out: a local new-wave combo called FX, whose members looked like apple-cheeked kids from a W. O. Mitchell story except for the shocking-pink and blue hair; and the bizarre McRory, a musclebound keyboardist with drum pads fastened to his upper

Rheostatics in Melville, Saskatchewan

body, giving him the look of Lawrence Gowan on steroids. Their photos were stapled among hundreds of other faceless groups, many of them with generic names, and while I'd sworn as a young rock pug that I'd never end up being a forgotten musician on a beer-soaked plank, looking at these groups, I suddenly felt drawn to their heritage and forgotten leagues.

I realized that these artists *existed*. Even though few of them would ever be heard outside Saskatchewan, this hadn't stopped them from writing songs, doing a photo session, pressing a record, requesting their own songs on the radio, renting a van, booking a tour, and kissing their girlfriends goodbye, a routine that was no different from, say, the Tragically Hip's. I finally saw these groups for what they were, not for what they weren't, and the more I thought about it, the less it mattered whether our own careers were Juno-bound. Standing there in the Waverly, it seemed enough to be part of the common musical legacy of bands making music in brutal winters across our hard country. While I'd always wanted to be considered in the tradition of artists like the Band, Neil Young, Joni Mitchell, and Rush, that was only part of it; I realized that I was already born into one. Looking at those faces on Helen's sticky tavern wall, another fathom of Canadian music had been revealed, one that I'd always missed seeing, perhaps for fear of finding myself in it. So before leaving Melville, we signed an eight-by-ten and Helen went over and put it up.

We joined the ranks.

We existed.

RA MCGUIRE: There was a place in the middle of Saskatchewan, near Melville, called Barn 22. The guy who did the shows lived in the downstairs of the barn, and upstairs, there was a floor and windows without glass. It was only open in the summer. Kids came and parked their cars in fields that went on for miles. It was a rock show. You could probably hear the music ten miles away. Some of the greatest rock moments of my life were in that place. Everyone was just pissed and sweating, and afterwards, the kids just went to sleep in their cars. It was a place where everybody could just go and be. It was perfect.

GREG GODOVITZ: When we were on tour we drove through this town, I think it was called Churchbridge, somewhere on the prairies. I said, "Stop. Let's play *here* tonight!" We were in the middle of nowhere. These people probably never had a show through there ever. So we went down to the local high school and we set up our full concert show in their gym, with free admission.

Goddo

We came out dressed in the school's marching-band outfits, which they gave to us and which I wore the rest of the tour. The jackets were orange with brass buttons and epaulettes, and the pants were black with an orange stripe down them. To this day, I get people coming up to me and saying, "I was at that gig. We remember what you did for us that night."

BARRY ALLEN: We played outside of Saskatoon in a hall in the middle of the prairie. There was nobody around. Finally, some guy showed up who had the keys to the place and he opened it up. We said, "Are you sure we're playing here?" It was weird. But then at ten o'clock, sure enough, the place was packed. People came from miles around, out of nowhere, for the big dance.

RICHARD FLOHIL: The Stampeders were the masters of playing towns that nobody could find on a map. They would go into town and buy a full-page ad in the paper for a dollar-twenty. They'd go in with lights and exploding effects and smokebombs and play these places like Morden, Manitoba, population zip, and everybody for forty miles around would drive in for the show. They'd pack the local arena. They were the first band to avoid just doing the big cities.

I remember going on the road for a few days with Stompin' Tom. Tom would drive his car, which had CB contact with the other van. They'd go into towns like Leamington, Delhi, and Petrolia, and they'd have an advance guy — like in the circus — who'd go in three weeks before, book the high-school gym, buy a big ad for nothing, stick up posters everywhere, give the school the coat concession for the use of the space, make sure anybody could come to the show and that kids under nine were free, and he'd sell out everywhere. Tom was the first person on the road I ever saw sell merch. He sold tons of it. Songbooks, records, caps. He'd sell seven hundred seats at three dollars each and the show would cost maybe a hundred bucks to promote. He was making a fortune, and working every night.

RONNIE KING: Around 1970, the Stampeders had a hit with "Carry Me." We were becoming a big band, but still Donald K. Donald, who was our promoter, would conjure up the most bizarre towns for us to play in. We were emerging rock stars playing in Digby, Nova Scotia, at the local elementary school.

DONNIE WALSH: Downchild have done thirty cross-Canada tours. Flin Flon, The Pas. Even the Twin Cities: Onaping and Lavac, just north of Thunder Bay. They call them the Twin Cities because one had a laundromat, the other a Chinese restaurant. In those days, you played every night. We played all kinds of rooms. We played an arena in Wikwemikong, a reserve on Manitoulin Island. It was a regular-sized hockey arena, small-time. The band was in the middle of the arena, there were about four hundred people there, all standing at the other end. It didn't have any lights, so I had to go to the local hardware store, where I bought eight lawn lights. I stuck them on top of the column speakers. You still couldn't see a damned thing in the whole place.

DUTCH MASON: We'd go to Labrador and play for two weeks. There was a good bar in Wabush. Lots of mining people, mill-workers, too. There were no roads in there, but all these guys were driving around in Corvettes; they had them shipped in on the train. They could only drive a little way in them, but they had to spend their money on something. And they made good money, too.

JOHN CODY: With the top-forty bands, I'd go way up into the lumber towns, into the Yukon. We'd play every town, no matter how small. I got to know Canada way more than I ever wanted to. We'd do one-nighters in towns that didn't really exist. I did a New Year's Eve at an Indian reserve where, when we finished playing, they said, "Okay, you can leave, or we'll kill you." We had no choice. We had no recourse. You'd get messed around all the time, and the agents wouldn't stand up for you.

KELLY JAY: We once played the Red Pheasant Indian Reserve in North Battleford, Saskatchewan. We stayed there for a week with Don Francks and a guy named Al Niester, who was a writer for *Rolling Stone*, and Lester Bangs, who wrote for *Creem*. We decided we were just gonna party for a week: ride horses, motorcycles. We had a baseball game on Saturday afternoon and a concert on Saturday night.

ALAN NIESTER: The record company and the band tipped off *Creem* that this concert was going down on the reserve. I jumped on with them in Regina and jumped off in either Winnipeg or Thunder Bay. It was a great thing for a rock-addicted twenty-year-old to do. I'd heard that groupies would follow you everywhere, but Crowbar weren't the prettiest band, so there was a dearth of that. There were bean-bag chairs and beds all over the place, and the bus was divided into two factions: those who

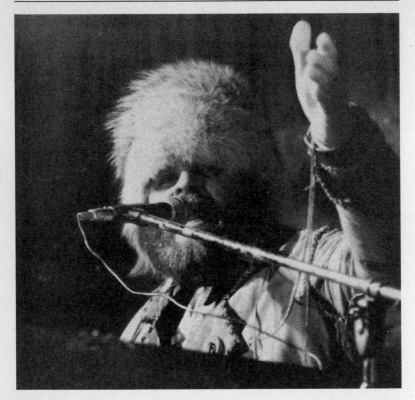

Kelly Jay

smoked dope and those who drank beer. Those of us who liked
to drink beer had to piss out the window because there wasn't a
washroom. Whatever Kelly says, Lester Bangs wasn't with us at
the reserve. Kelly probably met him when the tour stopped in
Windsor. Lester was spending a lot of time in Canada just
hanging out at the beer halls.

It's too bad he wasn't with us up there at Red Pheasant because
it was an amazing time. The band was visiting Don Francks and
his wife, Lili. It could have been 1870. There were kids riding

around bareback on horses and the band stayed in a sod hut that, literally, had buds germinating out of the walls. It smelled like you were sleeping in dirt because, in fact, you were. The concert itself was performed on a flatbed truck. They hooked it up to a portable, gas-driven generator and they did the show with their whole shtick. Kelly would carry around both guitar players – one of them over his shoulder, the other under his arm – and he'd hop across the stage. He did the whole show in front of about 150 people, basically everyone from the reserve, including the elders. It was very bizarre.

RA MCGUIRE: We did an amazing two-date thing on the Queen Charlotte Islands. It coincided with the arrival of *Loo Taas*, Haida for "wave eater," which was the canoe that Bill Reid carved. This was the day of the first Haida crossing from Vancouver to Haida Gwaii [the Queen Charlottes] in a hundred years. There were media on-site from all over the world, plus all the ancestral chiefs, with all the pomp and circumstance. We were hired to play the community centre after the potlatch and we did two shows. We did one for the kids – maybe fifty of them – and one for the grown-ups. That gig was both remote and awesome.

We also played an amazing gig up near James Bay, a place called Gessasabi. It was a dry reserve, and they checked your car for alcohol when you went in. We spent three days there, and we travelled around with the Cree warriors. The reserve was near all those Hydro-Québec developments, and they were involved in political action. We were taken out in canoes to the island that the tribe had been relocated from; we were shown the homes that they had lived in. Those are amazing experiences that no tourist

could buy for a million bucks. We were Trooper and these guys
wanted to take us into their lives.

On this seven-hour marathon from Calgary to Saskatoon, we
stake out our territory, the four square feet that will be ours until
we reach Toronto. The back coach is Martin's domain. It's a
horseshoe-shaped room with two windows masked by pullaway
brown curtains and a television and cassette player. The TV,
which receives one blurry channel, is boxed by a mirrored frame
of groovy, yellow pinlights, and all you have to know in order to
conjure up the seamiest of CanRock fantasies is that both Hugh
Dillon and Gordie Johnson travelled in it last year. I believe that
Martin originally claimed this desirable territory for two
reasons. First, it's a place where he can lock himself in and
attempt to break his record for most smokes smoked on tour,
and second, he can seek easy refuge from the Dow Chemical farts
that make sleeping in the bunks almost unbearable. Martin's
original idea was to build a bed in the back using two fold-out
slats of wood, but as it turns out, he has already slept fully
clothed through two nights collapsed on the bench. I'm not
anticipating this routine will change. On our first all-bus tour –
Another Roadside Attraction – in 1996, Martin's back coach
looked like the rubble of a collapsed flat. One morning I awoke
to a peculiar smell wafting through the door which I later discovered to be emanating from a rotten banana peel stuffed into a
sock. Notepads and sketch paper, empty cigarette packs, dead
butts poking like teeth through the ashtrays, and ruinous clothes
heaps made the area unusable for the greater part of the trip, a

journey that consisted of a mind-numbing four-day nonstop drive from Chicago to Seattle (with the two-member Inbreds as our guests), which is where I believe the tawdry Tielli reached his squalid nadir.

On this trip, however, it turns out that both he and Tim — equally prodigious smokers — must journey to the front of the bus to light up, so Martin's domain appears a little more stately. Still, while many travellers carry with them tightly secured hard-shell suitcases to protect their belongings, Martin tours with an old brown saddlebag lacking a working zipper, so his earthly possessions (which regularly include fully stocked paint kits, coffee-table art books, stacks of journals and sketch pads, seashells and insect casings, prehistoric rocks, the beginning of a bottlecap collection, and, on our only U.S. tour, an oversized novelty harmonica) are already spilling out before the first piston strikes. Not surprisingly, he's also this band's King of Lost Things, and over the years, not counting hundreds of dollars in bills and coins, I'd say that he's lost at least one complete suit of clothes (including vest and suspenders), a barrel of shoes, five sketch pads, and countless writing journals, some of which have been returned, but many that have been lost to the beavers.

That said, Martin provides our moving gulag with a remarkable easygoingness. This is odd, in a way, because he's also the most intense person I know. But whenever the minutes drag or the days seep into one another, or whenever you want to talk or cannot sleep or need a drink or a smoke or are desperate to play a song despite the nasty metallic grind of the engine, Martin is upright and wide-eyed and ready to go. The man does not sleep. This may partly explain his astonishing cache of songs, poems, lyrical fractures, stories, jokes, and lists which he compiles in his notebooks. Yesterday, for instance, he whispered to me while I was half-asleep in my bunk, "What were the obscene names we gave the Group of Seven?" and after I told him, I looked back to see him writing it down in his journal under a dim lamp, giggling to himself and tugging on a warm beer.

In many regards, Don is Martin's opposite. For example, while Don is in the front of the bus carefully sewing a button on his shirt, I'm pretty sure that Martin is somewhere in the back tearing open an elbow. But while sloth and insomnia are Martin's nature, assiduity is Don's. This, it seems, can be attributed to his diet, which requires more work daily than you or I put into ours in a year. Part of Don's code is that he only consumes food that comes in clear plastic bags with tiny writing and incomprehensible names. Actually, that's a bit of a lie: it's true that I know what a carrot is, it's just that Don's is smeared with grainy black goo. Don is always chewing something odd — rice cakes, almond paste, miso, seaweed — yet he weighs half as much as I do and has little problem moving through the narrow passageway between the bunks. The reason for his particular diet, I'm told, is complicated, though Don once confided in me that it was because he ate too many Pop Rocks as a kid. I still don't know if this is true, or whether he said it to stop me from asking so many stupid questions, like, "Hey, Don, what's that funny green stuff on yer yam?"

When he isn't eating, however, Don's not just sprawled around tugging at his gitch and reading hot-rod mags; no, this is a man committed to his joints; that is, his body's. Don will habitually enter a room and immediately start designing a space where he can stretch his body out as if he's trying to spell the Cyrillic alphabet. I've watched him many times pretzel his legs over his shoulders, arms under his feet, elbows behind his neck, as if

auditioning for a macrobiotic circus act. Many a time I've awak-
ened to look over at the empty bed next to mine and wonder,
where's Don? only to be surprised by a leg or a hand shooting up
from the floor below. Every day, from his first, yawning second,
Don is busy pulling, yanking, kicking, and stretching his limbs
into impossible angles. And when he's not doing *that*, he's playing the cello.

At each rink, we float away to our own islands. I scale the arena
seats and start writing; Martin takes a guitar and finds a quiet
place to strum; Tim searches out a telephone to call his wife, Lisa;
and Donny escorts his cello to where he and it can spend time
together. There are eight bunks on our tour bus and one of them,
naturally, is for the cello. This instrument – handsome, dark
brown, old, and marred with the striations of time – resembles
its owner in that it, too, is tall, thin, and relatively quiet. The two
of them have developed a symbiotic relationship; at airports,
while the rest of us are busy dragging suitcases and hauling
jacket-bags through customs (or, in Martin's case, recovering a
trail of razor blades and pencils which have fallen from his sack),
Donny is often consumed with trying to swing a seat on the
plane for his cello. And most of the time, he's successful,
proving that very few people actually have anything against the
cello (it's not as if you're trying to check in a set of vibes). I
believe that the only time Don was ever met with any scorn or
ridicule from an authority figure was on the Another Roadside
Attraction tour in Calgary when a security guard, after listening
to him play a neo-French-Canadian folk song for about ten
minutes, told him that he was fighting a losing battle. It upset
Don, but we had to laugh. Other than that, playing the cello in
public places has been a great way for Don to meet people (as in,

"Hey, what the hell's that guy doing over there?"), and while we're used to our drummer carrying on this way with his treasured instrument, I think that some members of the Hip find it odd, which makes me like the cello even more.

Tim Vesely loves his instruments too, maybe even more than Don. I'd like to go on record to say that I have never once wiped the oily, black grunge off my electric guitar. Tim's Fender Telecaster, conversely, looks like you could serve crumpets to the Queen off it. It is shiny and clean and sparkling, despite the *grnnngg* of Tim's rhythm hand, and I believe that the only time he ever stickered one of his instruments was when he stamped a Sonic Unyon sticker under the bridge of his Takamine acoustic. It's not that Tim is particularly fastidious about his belongings. We once played a gig near a swamp in Sackville, N.B., where the bassist for Ginger blew up Tim's bass amp. While many other musicians would have thrown a shit fit, Tim was simply nonplussed. It's his nature to be disarmingly calm in alarming situations, which is why, after seven gigs on this tour, he can strap on his bass, walk out to the middle of the stage, stand in front of thousands of anxious people, and perform, well, disarmingly.

Incredibly, I first encountered Tim at Walt Disney World in Florida. I think I was thirteen, but time warps, and I'm not certain about the year or the particulars of the occasion. Hell, I'm not even sure this really happened. But if my memory serves me well, I was at a free concert outside Cinderella's Castle given by Bo Donaldson and the Heywoods, who had a minor saccharine hit in the '70s with a song called "Billy, Don't Be a Hero." I remember being there in the crowd with my parents and sister and looking out across the sea of bodies and setting eyes on a nameless face that I knew from back home in Etobicoke. I was

Tim Vesely

Timothy Bonham

trying to place this person when the face, horribly, looked at me. Being a frightened, self-conscious little nerd, I jerked my head away, nearly injuring my spinal column, and left it at that. But for years afterward, the face and I passed each other in the hallways of our school, sharing our terrible, unspeakable secret with no one, least of all each other. Little did we know that we'd go on to spend half of our lives together.

Eventually we became friends, and one evening we found ourselves sitting in the same row at a Yes concert at Maple Leaf Gardens. I don't remember much about the performance other than the bass solo, and I remember it not because it was wonderfully emotive or technically dazzling, but because it was the loudest sound I'd ever heard in my life. I could feel the low end of Chris Squire's strings rattle through my chest cavity like a pneumatic drill, and, frankly, I couldn't see much point in *that*. But it made a strong impression on Tim (who held down first bass in the school's orchestra). After the performance, he declared while walking down Yonge Street that he had decided during the concert to buy an electric bass. And just like in those stupid rock-and-roll-group movies, that was my cue to announce, "Well, geez, I play guitar! Let's form a band!" A few weeks later, we were standing together around a friend's parents' Bon-Tempi organ, butchering songs by Triumph, Cheap Trick, and Eric Clapton. We never performed any Yes, neither then nor now, which is strange considering that the Rheostatics were born the day that Vesely went electric.

MIKE TILKA: I first met Kim [Mitchell] at the University of Windsor. He was playing guitar in a country band. He was just a skinny little kid, and he'd been on the road since he was thirteen.

I'd been jamming with a keyboard friend of Kim's who suggested that I meet him. He had told Kim the same thing, and so Kim wrote me from a Greek Island where he was playing: "I understand you want to be a musician and move to Toronto. I want to be a musician, too." After he came home to Sarnia, he took the train to Windsor, and we jammed two or three times. We were really bad; we had no vibe — but we both had the same drive. We got a house together in Toronto; all of this with a guy I didn't even know. I left my girlfriend, I left my job, all of my friends. I knew two people in all of the city. The first gig we did was at some resort in Bracebridge. We played to two people.

KEN TOBIAS: I met this guy by the name of Bill Sweeney up at a place called Nashwaak Bridge. Bill was a true motorcycle rock guy. He had short hair, jeans, a leather jacket, and sideburns, a real Elvis type. I was so impressed with him. I was drawn to the attitude. He was a tough guy, he didn't hang around with anybody, but for some reason, he took me under his wing. One day he said, "You sing a lot there, kid. Do you play guitar?" I said no, and he said, "Well, I gotta get you a guitar." The next thing you know, he showed up where our family was staying in Fredericton. He was on his motorcycle and he had a guitar slung over his shoulder. It had no strings on it. "Here," he said. "You have to put strings on it and get it together."

RANDY BACHMAN: We had this song in the Guess Who called "White Collar Worker," which was more or less "Paperback Writer" by the Beatles, except with twelve or fifteen chords in it and an opening line that went: "We get up every morning from the alarm clock's warning, take the eight-fifteen into the city."

When I formed BTO, I played around with it some more, and
then one night in Winnipeg, C. F. [Turner] came to me after our
third set and said that he was too hoarse to sing. I'd only sung
harmonies in the Guess Who, and was no lead singer, but I sang
anyway, because you don't have to be a great singer to get away
with sounding like Neil or Santana. I figured that I'd play a long
guitar solo in the middle to stretch out the set and get it over
with. But pretty soon, the audience — who were pretty drunk at
this point — started yelling for some rock-and-roll, so I just
started in with those three chords — C, B-flat, F — and told the
guys to come in loud and clear on the chorus. When we went to
record it, I gave the words to Fred, but he said, "No way, pal. It's
your song, you sing it. You can sing, anyone can sing. Look at
Dylan." So I sang "Takin' Care of Business."

RICHIE HENMAN: My brother David, my cousin Jimmy, and I
formed April Wine after deciding to make a go of it in music.
We needed one more guy to complete the group, and Myles's
[Goodwyn] name was on the tip of everybody's tongue. We
knew that he was living and writing songs up in Cape Breton
with a band called East Gate Sanctuary. We called him, and he
agreed right away. He was down two days later. I picked him up
at the train station with all his possessions: one guitar, a Fender
amp, and two green garbage bags full of clothes. He and Jimmy
moved into a little unheated cottage right on the lake in Waverly
that had belonged to our grandparents, which was only a couple
of miles from my parents' house. It was easy to pick them up
every day and bring them to practice. From that moment on,
that's all we did. My dad took out a loan on a window van and
we headed for Montreal, April 1, 1970.

Richie and Dave Henman, 1964

DAVID HENMAN: In the Maritimes in 1969, April Wine started to get into writing our own songs. Before that, I was in a band called Prism — not the West Coast one, another one — and I wrote a couple of rock operas; I was into Zappa and Beefheart, Edgar Varese, stream-of-consciousness, bizarre stuff. But at the time, in the Maritimes, if we tried to play an original song, people would yell, *"Play something we know!"* We thought it was ridiculous, but what could we do? As it turned out, my cousin Jimmy and I were sitting in the Old Mill Tavern in Dartmouth, N.S., drinking beer, going, "Man, this really sucks. What're we gonna do?" I said, "Let's put a band together." Jimmy said, "I know this guy

Myles Goodwyn," and we got together in my parents' basement with him and my brother Richie on December 1, 1969. We weren't sure what we were gonna do. All we knew was that we wanted it to be new and different. Myles started playing this song he'd written that had this sort of Led Zeppelin riff, and we went nuts. Within four months, we had a bunch of great songs. Our agent in Montreal said he knew promoter Donald K. Donald, and wrote him a letter on our behalf. We got a response saying, "If you're ever in town, stop by and see us sometime." We interpreted it as, they want us out there! We piled into a GMC van with a hundred dollars between us and headed for Montreal. When we got to Montreal, we called Donald's office and they said he was at this club called Laugh In and we were told to meet him there the next day. Eleven in the morning, we walk in and the place is empty except for a podium set up with tables and microphones on the stage. We told the bartender we were there to see Donald, and he said, "Oh. Would you like a drink?" We thought that was cool. Pretty soon people started coming in and the tables starting filling up and we were thinking, "Wow. They really *were* expecting us! What a reception!" We were completely naive. It was for some Woodstock-type festival. Later, Donald came in, so I stood up and announced, "Hi, Donald! I'm David Henman! We're April Wine!" He looked me over and said, "Oh, uh, call my office on Tuesday."

RICHIE HENMAN: The response we got from Donald was a "Don't call us, we'll call you later," but none of us really saw the words on the page. We zeroed in on what we wanted to see. Somewhere in there, it said, "Send more demos," but to us that meant, they're crazy about us! We were lucky that they were such nice people that when we met them, they said, "Well, seeing as you're here, we'll help you get settled in and find you a place to play."

Sask Place, upper level, sound-check.

What about the Tragically Hip? Truthfully, our days unfold with very little opportunity to sit down with the boys and ask questions like, "Now, Paul, tell me, were you unloved as a child?" We arrive at the show, unpack our stuff, attack the spread in our dressing room, wait for sound-check, sound-check, eat, get dressed, manage a quick game of Ping-Pong, play the show, eat some more, drink a beer, watch a bit of the Hip, then sleep. The moments that we spend with the Hip are often wedged into whenever our mealtimes overlap or after both bands have played, and, so far, the only fellow to hang with us post-show has been Gord Downie, and that's only after he's finished signing autographs and meeting fans and hanging out with friends.

Still, it's a treat to observe Canada's biggest band at such close range. After having lived in this bubble for a few weeks now, I'm convinced that one of the reasons why the Hip are THE HIP is because they more or less look like you and me. I mean, if Gord Downie pierced his face and wore a unitard or Bobby Baker draped himself in chain mail, I'm not sure they would be as well loved. But since they look like the band who covered R.E.M.'s "So. Central Rain" at your high-school talent show and whose rhythm guitarist could be bagging your groceries down at the

Safeway, it's easy to find yourself in their style and sound; they're familiar. Of course, there are folks out there who would argue that this is not altogether a good thing, who would suggest that by parlaying their parochial image into superstardom, the Hip are merely enforcing Canadians' fear of exotica, giving us what we know rather than what we need, perpetuating the CanRock trademark of stolid rock played in plaid jackets.

But I've grown to like it. Their jams are fluid and suspenseful, the hits exciting, and Gord's narratives are his own. In rehearsal, Gord is very low-key. There's no mad-dog-nipping-at-my-pant-leg dance or attacked-by-bees hand ballet or jacket-caught-in-the-door-of-a-moving-subway pantomime; in fact, you'd hardly notice him up there the way he just puts his head down and scrubs the guitar with the crook of his hand. But that's the beauty of Gord as a rock-and-roll front man; for half of the show, he's a skittish marionette, but for the other half, he comes across as a guy with a sock on his head.

Watching them during sound-check, I'm reminded of a chevron of geese, with Gord at the arrowhead and the band flanking him, angled precisely. I remember being on stage with the group in Markham, Ontario, and being startled by how rousing Gord Sinclair's bass patterns were (not to mention by how tight his T-shirt was). But like most bassists, Gord is often overlooked; he rarely comes across in a theatrical sense, because it's hard enough for bassists to bend their fingers around their double-width strings let alone reinvent the scissor-kick or the hammer-on. Sinclair may appear like window dressing across the Hip's front line, but once the music is studied and disassembled, you discover he lends it many of its defining melodies (listen to "Grace, Too"). On a great new pop song which they've been working out on tour, he is the tune's melodic anchor, dabbing the song with little flurries of notes while handling his instrument with the strength and single-mindedness of a man climbing a rope.

DANNY MARKS: Bass is a dangerous instrument. You know, those low notes'll get ya. You can get very sombre with those notes, and it's a very under-appreciated instrument. Bassists often have to remind the band, "Listen, I don't get the glamour; I don't have a fabulous instrument like the drums, with all the shining cymbals, or the guitar, all loud and fast." The bass player thinks to himself, "I am the most unloved guy in the band, but if I stopped playing, you'd all be in trouble."

DUTCH MASON: When Little Jimmy Dickens came to the arena in Kemptville, he had an electric bass. First one I'd ever seen. My father bought me one, but we couldn't get an amp to run it, so he took these old 78 jukeboxes from the restaurant and tore them apart and got this electrician in to add an extra tube and jacks to these boxes that we'd put the speakers in. They sounded good. Whenever anyone in town got a bass, they'd come around and ask us to make them an amp. All they had to do was get us a couple of jukeboxes; they were worth nothin' back then, but now they go for thousands.

RONNIE KING: Around 1969, there were three of us left in the Stampeders. We stayed a trio. Two of us played guitar — me and Rich — so one of us had to play bass. Sure as hell wasn't gonna

Ronnie King

be me. You couldn't get chicks playing the bass. We argued long
and hard over this one. Finally I said, "All right, I'll switch to
bass, but I want to still play a few tunes on the guitar." Eventually,
though, I proved them wrong: You still could get chicks if you
played bass.

To Gord Sinclair's left is lead guitarist Bobby Baker, whose playing gives the Hip's songs their painterly colours. If I were fourteen years old, I'd covet his shiny pants, long polished hair, and single glowering eye; I'd have his poster on my wall and would practise moving like him in front of the mirror, my air guitar close against my hip, head lowered, ass angled just so. But whether I'd actually become him would depend largely on my ability to learn the signature riff from "New Orleans Is Sinking," which, at least for me, would be no automatic job. Chances are, I'd probably end up like his guitar counterpart, Paul Langlois, instead. That may read like a slight, but it's not. While Baker solos windingly through the songs, Langlois's playing is resolute; he marks his chords like a strongman hammering nails into hardwood. A lot of kids look up at him and think, "You know, man, I think I could do that," and that's how most musicians start playing. And since thousands of youngsters will have bought guitars and formed bands as a result of this tour, the quiet guy with the prodigious hair will have played a large part in shaping the future of rock in Canada.

As for Johnny Fay, I must admit straight off that I've never seen a drummer whose playing I didn't like. All told, if I could do it again, I'd sit behind the kit. While I take exception to their vanity gloves, track pants, headbands, their obsession with bottled water, their penchant for getting naked (not to mention that little stick-twirling thing they do), I still think that drummers are the acrobats of rock, and that playing with one's hands and feet is unimpeachably cool. Johnny plays with an unflagging confidence and even touch, with propulsion rather than flair. His arrangements are spare yet poignant, and while I could always hear more fills in most of the Hip's songs, there's obviously a reason for his Teutonic approach. Since many of their songs veer off into exploratory jams, I suppose it makes sense that someone steer.

While the Hip check their monitors, test the P.A., and tighten up the odd melody or orphaned rhythm, all around the concourse of the arena the rock show is being born. Alabaster-skinned prairie girls working for minimum wage are arranging stickers, buttons, T-shirts, hockey jerseys, hemp hats, keychains, belt buckles, tour posters, and other saleable Hip-ernalia on tables in the mezzanine. They pause occasionally to render crudely drawn price guides and apply the odd fine stroke of lipstick. At the same time, concession workers are filling condiment trays from great squirting bags of mustard and relish. They're wiping down countertops and cleaning soda lines and spearing weiners onto spike-wheels and loading popcorn chutes and brewing bad coffee and making sure their nametags read straight. Security staff are patrolling the hallways in polished shoes and fresh crewcuts, testing walkie-talkies and trying on earplugs. Gainfully employed high-schoolers are bagging garbage bins and flipping fresh blue pucks into gleaming urinals, bored ticket-takers are sipping Cokes and trying to sink a rumpled paper ball into a trash can, and ticket-sellers are Windexing their glass kiosks and sliding tickets into little paper sleeves. Outside, on the top steps of the building, fifteen to twenty kids are looking in through the front entrance of the rink, trying to draw from fragments of muffled sound the shape of a song or two which, when played later tonight in concert, will trigger wild cheers of *hip hip hip hip hip hip hip hip hip hip hip hip*, which will get me wondering what it would be like if those letters spelled a three-syllabled Tuscan name instead.

Bidinibidinibidinibidini . . .
It would go straight to my head.

A few hours later, we take to our pre-gig preparations. Drummers are always the busiest. They seem to be partial to stretching. Dave Clark became devoted to arm and hand warm-ups, and later moved on to eyebrow-raising, Om-like incantations. Don used to kick his legs out repeatedly like a Rockette, though he seems to have stopped doing that on this tour (perhaps he hurt himself; maybe he should try stretching). Tim and Martin, who have been snookered by provincial smoking laws, take the opposite physical approach, compensating for forty smokeless minutes on stage by doubling their pre-gig tobacco intake. It's a reminder of the old days. Back when I smoked, there'd be three of us hauling on Winnies and Player's and Marlies and Exports. Our old tour manager, Jay Scott, recalls driving nonstop from Toronto to Thunder Bay, spending the night in a motel, then going out to the van in the morning to warm up the engine, only to be sent retching by the acrid stench of burned nicotine. But since I don't smoke any more, my pre-show activity is more practical, less cancerous. My job is to scribble out the set lists and feed them to Tim Mech, who in turn passes one to Gary Stokes and another to the Hip's lighting technician, who's moonlighting with us. I'm also responsible for consulting with Gary about what kind of walk-on music to use. We've prepared some beauty clips for the tour: "Good Times" by Chic, bits of Stompin' Tom, "Popcorn" by Hot Butter, snippets from *The Wizard of Oz*, and the play-by-play of Paul Henderson's winning goal in 1972, in both French and English. These clips are designed to set a musical tone for the evening as well as disguise our entrance on the stage. They also help settle our nerves. Except for opening night, the butterflies have eluded me, though I must say that Tim and Martin seem nervous and ill-at-ease before most gigs. I don't believe that Martin has ever been relaxed on stage anyway, which may account for his shockingly wired performances. Mind you, the atmosphere in the dressing room doesn't exactly ease the nerves. Once the place empties of friends and crew, you start to notice the hum of the fan and the buzz of the ceiling lights, which make you feel more like you're about to get your tonsils out than make sweaty rock for eager sponges. I sometimes try to diffuse this tension by singing or going *uuummmm*, but inevitably, I end up feeling like I'm auditioning for *Cats*. It's just not me. Besides, rock-and-roll isn't supposed to be the kind of activity that you have to warm up to do. It's at times like this that I wish I were in a punk band, and that someone would simply push me off the couch, and holler *"Get the fuck on stage!"* into my ear. Away I'd go. I make a note to try this out tomorrow.

Tim Mech retrieves us and we take our walk. Our blazers glint and flicker as we make our way under the bleachers towards the stage. Tim flashes his Mag-Lite in our path to make sure that we don't trip over any cables or plummet through any fissures. We arrive at a ladder that takes us up to the platform, where the Hip are sometimes hanging around. Gord Downie, it seems, is always there. He takes in every second of every show, flattering us nightly. As the rink falls dark, the crowd's exultation hits us like a splash. But since we haven't yet appeared on stage, they're more or less applauding the fellow who just turned the lights off. Sometimes this hurrah is just a ruse to get us to go out there at all. The show begins when the walk-on music starts. With the stage lights low, I make my way on stage, pick up my guitar, and sound a note, maybe pluck a chord. More dubious cheers. The walk-on music fades as I step up to the microphone. Sometimes I say hello and sometimes Martin beats me to the punch. I notice a face in the Henhouse, maybe two. I see the rink like I haven't seen it all day and the thought crosses my mind that I'll never see it this way again. So I take a good look. Somebody counts in the first song. It's either there or it isn't.

MANITOBA

"I mooed on the lonely roads of Canada."
Mack Sennett, *The King of Comedy*

The Peg.

Considering what we've been through in this city, playing Winnipeg Arena means as much to us as playing Maple Leaf Gardens. Although our first serious out-of-town gigs were in Kitchener and Thunder Bay, Winnipeg was the first city to roll out the welcome wagon. Playing the Royal Albert Hotel in 1987 was our baptism into rock-and-roll and the road. Until then, I'd only ever slept in my house with my parents in Etobicoke (not counting the odd holiday and a few months away in Ireland), but four days out of town on our first tour, I was flopping down in a room with a yellow pillow and sheets stuck to the bed, and thieves and junkies living next door. To a twenty-three-year-old suburban kid just out of Air Guitar College, it was thrilling. In the Albert, I wrote a thousand songs. The band jammed endlessly. Then one morning, ambulance attendants wheeled out an old fellow who'd died in the room next door. A pall fell over the Albert. Spooked, we packed up our guitars.

We got the fuck out.

The Albert's figurehead was a fellow named Tex, a six-foot-tall yokel in a white cowboy hat who sprayed a mysterious confection of eggs and fish to clear patrons out of the bar after last call: farts in a can. I never heard Tex speak. Whenever he was confronted by a bad drunk, he'd spray that stuff in that direction and before you knew it the guy had his hat and coat on and was out the door. You could smell Tex's scent in your sleep. After a while the Albert felt less like the setting of a great Stompin' Tom song and more like the place where dreams go to curl up and die. One of my darkest days ever was the time I celebrated my birthday at the Albert. I was turning twenty-four and, worse, I was out of cigarettes. It sucked. That morning, I roamed the streets and dreamed of getting home. Our tour had started beautifully, but ended up hounded by trouble. Our records hadn't arrived for us to sell on tour; we missed gigs; and if not for the kindness and mercy of the Toronto group 13 Engines, who were touring the country concurrently and agreed to squire us home, I might still be standing in a wind-battered phone booth trying to explain to my dad what had happened to the family car. Uprooted, heart kicked in, I hacked around the streets and wrote miserable thoughts down in my book on a bench in the park:

Dear loser,
Having a terrible birthday.

Then, to my astonishment, I discovered ten dollars in the pocket of my jeans. It was money I'd kept from a T-shirt sale at a gig the previous evening. None of us had any money back then, so it was quite a discovery. We'd survived on a steady diet of beef jerky, donuts, and Old Dutch potato chips, and fashioned free smokes from tobacco and a rolling machine appropriated from the Engines. That ten-dollar bill was a godsend and I kept it for myself. It was *my* friggin' birthday.

I should have gone straight to the Wagon Wheel or the Downtowner and ordered a clubhouse and fries and coleslaw along with copious refills of coffee, but, instead, I bought a pack of smokes – Player's Light, twenty-five – which in those days cost something like $7.50 in Manitoba. I sat in the park and smoked miserably, cursing everything. I was broke, hungry, and sore. I missed my home. I missed my bed. I missed the person I was before I climbed into the car at the bottom of Martin's parents' driveway in Etobicoke. When I'd finally had enough, I skulked back to the Albert, head down, fists shoved deep in my pockets, the waning light of the blazing prairie sun flickering across store windows and bus shelters, turning the streets Hallowe'en orange. I found the guys gathered in my room. "Happy birthday, Dave," they said, and tossed me a deck of Turkish cigarettes, which they'd bought with money scrabbled together from their pittance. Shamefaced, I picked up the smokes and turned them over in my hand. For the rest of the night we sat in our room in the Albert smoking, the thick, purplish tobacco plumes floating like ghost tails out the window, Tim and Martin strumming guitars softly in the corner, the fire escape rattling with the wind, and just outside our door, the sound of tubercular, bathrobed miscreants coughing as they walked the plank.

Lonely, together.

The Peg.

KEN TOBIAS: We formed a band called the Crystal Staircase in Montreal. We had the suit jackets, the look, everything. We made low money, but we were dressed up to kill. We went all the way up to Baie-Comeau, singing this beautiful, original stuff with these layered vocal parts, chords. I hated this gig. I'm on stage, I've got my suit jacket on, and then they tell me that because we're not doing so good in the club, they're gonna bring a stripper in. She was going to twirl her pasties. She was a nice person. They wanted us to play for her. Of course, with my ego, I said, "I'm going to New York, I'm going to be big, I don't wanna do this!" and the management was saying, "No, no. You gotta do this." I was the angry young man saying, "All right, I'll do this." I pulled all the microphones back, I opened my jacket up, I got my harmonica out and we do "Kansas City." She's twirling her things, and I've got my eyes closed because I don't want to see it. *This is not where I want to be.* I've got the harmonica pressed against the microphone to get that nice distorted sound. I've got the thing in my mouth, right near my teeth. Well, unbeknownst to me the woman is coming towards me and she's got her crotch to us. Then she thrust out her crotch and slammed my microphone. The harmonica hit me in the teeth and I fell right into the drums. I knock the friggin' hi-hats over. I was so embarrassed and angry that I turned red and *I decked her.* I skimmed her jaw, enough to put her into the first row. Of course, the guys in the first row loved that. But I hated hitting her. I felt so bad. I apologized, then turned around and said, "*I'm done with this fuckin' tavern hole here. I'm tired of this fuckin' shit. I'm leaving. I'm quitting the band!"* I walked off stage. It was terrible. It was debasing.

JOHN CODY: Between 1972 and 1975, I played in all the strip bars in Vancouver. The third-rate joints. We accompanied the strippers, we played behind them. The best place was called Fort Boogie. On the outside, they had giant cartoons of Donald Duck whipping naked women and a thought bubble that said, *"Dance, girls! Dance!"* The band was called Smilin' Jack Smith. Smith was a hippie from the United States avoiding the draft. The gig was six days a week, noon till eight at night for one hundred dollars per person a week. The dancers were either junkies or extremely unattractive. I saw a fair number of road-burgers and heavy drug deals. At one point, both of our strippers were men. You couldn't tell, though.

DENTON YOUNG: My first band was a three-piece called Tamarack, and I played drums. We had a girl singer, and I sang background vocals only. We played places like the Red Pine Lodge in Swastika, Sturgeon Falls, Dangerous Dan's in Sudbury; miners coming in to drink on the weekend, a brawl every night. We played the Penthouse Motor Inn on Military Trail in Scarborough, and the whole place erupted at the end of the night. Somebody would take somebody else's jug of beer and then they'd just go at it, big, big guys. There were topless girls dancing on these big round tables, which was really risqué back in 1970.

DENNIS ABBOTT: In Oklahoma we played a place called the Oriental Club. A guy called Scotty ran it, who they said was

John Cody, far left

mob-connected. He shot the place up once and he wouldn't let black guys in. It was full of Vietnam vets, who were all speed freaks, and real cheesy-looking women. We played behind strippers. One of them had an act where she stripped down to her white, Nancy Sinatra go-go boots and ran across the stage in a backwards crabwalk. We'd whistle up to them between sets because we were just boys and we thought that what they were doing was actually pretty cool.

RONNIE KING: In 1966, we left Calgary for Ontario. Our first gig was in North Bay, which we were told was a resort town. We said, "Resort town? Man, we're gonna get chicks feeding us grapes at the pool!" The club was called the Blue Spruce, about eight miles out of North Bay, and it was the biggest, most scrappy place I'd ever seen, with two or three fights a night. And as far as a pool went, there was a slough out back full of bloodsuckers. Unless you had dibs on the car for the day, you'd be stuck out there. The next gig was in Sault Ste. Marie, a real heavy dockside place with sailors fighting and beating on each other. After a while, two or three guys in the band went nuts.

JOHN CODY: In the summer of '75, I did five weeks at the Royal Hotel in Prince Rupert, B.C. We thought we were getting into rock stardom. But it was an extremely tough place. One night our guitarist was knocked unconscious after someone threw a bottle at his head while we were on stage. While we were trying to stop the bleeding and get him to the hospital, the audience was chanting, "One more song! One more song!" They didn't want to let us out. It was a crazy area where the police wouldn't come in. The reason we stayed so long was because the owner of the hotel wouldn't pay us. Every week we'd go up to his room to get paid, and his light would go out when we knocked on the door. He ended up burning down three of his hotels, and on the third one he got caught. He killed himself by smashing his head into a wall.

JACK PEDLAR: When I was in a group called the Magnetic Sound in Hamilton we had pretty cool band shirts. They had black backgrounds with bright polka dots: banana yellow, pink, and teal. I was thirteen years old, the youngest in the group. I was playing up in Tillsonburg once when, all of a sudden, I was grabbed from behind and put into an armlock with a knife to my throat. I felt this hot voice in my eardrum and I could smell whisky. The voice was saying, "Gimme yer shirt . . ." He liked my shirt and he was gonna cut my throat to get it. But the last thing I was gonna do was take off my shirt. His girlfriend saw what was happening; she came over and punched the guy in the face. They got into a brawl and I kept my shirt.

DAVE HENMAN: I once spit into a biker's jug of beer. For the song "Street Punk," I'd start it off with this dramatic punk intro whereby I'd fill my mouth with beer, stagger up to the front of the stage, and just spew it out. After the set, I got word that there was this biker who was very unhappy and who wanted a new jug. I went to the bar, got a jug, walked over, sat down and said, "Geez, man, I'm really sorry." He didn't kill me.

STEVE SMITH: There was a club in the west end of Toronto called the Mad Mechanic. This was a rough club, lots of bikers. The roughest guys were the bouncers. You'd be playing your set and they'd have guys in headlocks, ramming them into the walls. Our roadie, who'd also mixed the sound, would be hiding under the table. You'd go out to the parking lot after the show and there'd be a dent in your car from somebody's head.

JACK PEDLAR: There was a bar in Hamilton called the Home Side, which we renamed the Homicide. The worst I saw was the night guys came in with ski-masks and baseball bats. They'd cut the telephone wires. The room was packed, and they backed everyone into corners. They whaled on the whole bar staff, then left. This was all within thirty seconds. We were doing "I Shall Be Released." Bang.

GREG GODOVITZ: We were playing up in Timmins. We had a day off. It was the big sports day, when all the locals got rid of their wives and went to drink at the motel where we were staying. By this time I was wearing velvet pants with mirrors down the side and ballet slippers. So I go mincing down the hall and these two guys come out of their room and they go, "Holy fuck, what is this?" They grab me and pin me up against the wall, and, thank god, just at that moment Ed, our singer, comes walking out and the guys go, "Aw. Check out Goldilocks." One punch and they were both out cold. Another time, we went down East and we had the first platform shoes they'd ever seen. Our hair had glitter in it, dyed green, and they had no concept of what it was all about; you were either from some other universe or you were a faggot. You were gay and they were gonna kill you.

RIK EMMETT: I was recruited to play in the Justin Page Band. They did songs about being gay, sung by a heterosexual man, a very glam-rock thing. Justin wore garter belts and fishnet stockings and he was a cross-dresser. He'd go everywhere with two Afghan dogs. He had his hair dyed so the back was white and the front was dark, and he had a moustache; come to think of it, he looked like an Afghan himself. It was a trip. We played standard rock clubs.

We'd go down to the East Coast and I'd walk on stage wearing Davy Crockett boots and a woman's black gymnastics leotard with a white padded hand clipped to my crotch, black eye make-up, black lipstick, playing a white Strat. I noticed folks in the crowd going, "What the fuck?" and I realized what showbiz meant. That was a big thing, to be able to take my musicianship and subvert it to an entertainment venture.

DUTCH MASON: We played for bikers, miners, everybody. We played in a gay bar in 1966 in Halifax, off and on for a year. We had no problem at all. They hired us to get rid of the gay people, but we attracted more. We started attracting women who'd come in to see the gay guys. It was a big joke. They're all good people anyway. We never had no problem. Finally, the owner said, "I give up!"

Marillion.

Martin and I are stuck inside the 92 ROCKmobile with a disc jockey who is broadcasting live across Manitoba and who says we remind him of Marillion. We're idling in front of the old arena, surrounded by kids without jackets shivering in the skin-peeling prairie cold, whose luminous eyes are peering in through the tinted windows. A teenage girl asks, "Hey, man, is that the Hip in there?"

"Uh, no, it's the openers," says the radio tech, who is doubling as van security, and who has forgotten our band's name.

"The Rheostatics?" asks one of them.

"Uh, yeah," he says, turning around to look at us.

"Cool," she says.

I bet she's never heard of Marillion. We get compared to Max Webster, Neil Young, Talking Heads, XTC, David Bowie, and Rush all the time, but never Marillion. If you don't know (and if you don't, good for you), Marillion was one of those third-generation British progressive-rock bands who took it upon themselves during the thrilling days of new wave to revive fourteen-minute synthesizer solos and songs about forest nymphs. Their lead singer was a self-aggrandizing fellow named Fish, who considered himself something of a romantic, a jazz-rock Fabio. Apparently, there is someone in our group who reminds him of Fish. While it's true that Martin once strapped himself to a giant crucifix and walked around his neigh-bourhood, and Don recently completed an epic poem based on the life of a young princess with a flower-sniffing fetish, I still have no idea what this announcer sees in us.

"So what's this, fellas, your third album?" he asks.

"Actually, it's our seventh . . ."

Sometimes, there's just no point in doing interviews. I actually like the process, having conducted hundreds of them myself. The first interview I ever did was with a Winnipeg band called Harlequin for a high-school newspaper called, embarrassingly, *The Sunshine News.* When I went to the band's hotel room, I was so nervous that, when I looked at them, their heads started swelling and shrinking as if I were seeing them through a funhouse mirror. That wasn't nearly as bad as when I interviewed Joey and Johnny Ramone a few months later at the TraveLodge on the 401. It took me hours to ask my first question, which made no sense by the time I spooled it out. I'd wanted it to be the best question they'd ever heard, but it was probably the worst. When I arrived home after the interview, I listened to the tape, only to discover, in horror, that I'd pressed PLAY instead of RECORD. Half sobbing, I called my editor, Sheila Wawanash of *Shades* magazine, who told me to write down everything I remembered. I was fifteen. I didn't remember much.

In a way, I've associated every interview I've ever done with those two experiences. That's why when this jockey asks, "Now tell me, fellas, what's it *really* like touring with the Tragically Hip?" I feel my stomach sink. Every jockey since our first show in Vancouver has asked us this question, and there's nothing worse than hearing the same one over and over again, especially if you didn't feel like answering it the first time. Gord Downie has said that the Hip's most-asked question is, "So why aren't you guys big in the States?" I wonder whether a trade could be brokered. Answering why we haven't broken in the States would be easy. "Um, because we rarely play there," we'd say. Similarly, if the Hip were asked, "What's it like touring with the Rheos?" the boys could say, "Fine!" and just leave it at that. But these fellows who work for radio stations named after wild animals ("THE MARMOSET! GRRRRAUWWW!") often ask questions to which they think they know the answer. Not only does this makes them feel smart, but it also makes their job easier. So the reason they want to know about opening for the Hip is that, in the past, opening bands have been molested by their audiences, and from us, he expects horror stories.

We have none. The first gig we played with the Hip was on Canada Day, 1994, at Molson Park in Barrie, Ontario. It was a great bill: Change of Heart, the Odds, Spirit of the West, Eric's

Trip, Treble Charger. We performed in the gloriously sunny middle of the day. At one point I threw a Nerf football from the stage and watched it sail about two hundred feet in the air and fall into the lap of a stoner reclining on the grass. It was the day after Wendel Clark was traded to Quebec and I remember shouting, "Goodbye, Wendel," and getting all choked up, forgetting the words to a song.

Our show was a ton of fun, but since the Hip's most abusive fans were still in the parking lot getting hammered, we were able to perform without being pelted with garbage. Later in the day, however, Jane Siberry narrowly missed being clopped in the head by a twenty-sixer, and Daniel Lanois, who went on second-last, was bombed with more than three hundred water bottles; someone actually counted them. After the gig, Lanois's bass player – a linebacker-sized fellow from New Orleans who wore military fatigues on stage – told Dave Clark, "If I had had a gun out there, I woulda killed me somebody." Gord's first words at the beginning of his set were, "This song is for assholes who throw shit at musicians," and it was clear how humiliated and angry he was. Over the years, the Hip have been cursed with some dubious fans.

"So tell us a little bit about the band's history," continues the deejay, reading notes scribbled on the back of our bio. More kids have swarmed the van, cupping their hands around their eyes, staring through the dark windows. Doing interviews on mainstream stations is when rock-and-roll is most like selling shoes. You're really just a commercial between commercials, so I try and keep my answers short and snappy. I've never had much use for those how-to-make-it-in-the-music-biz texts, but I'd imagine that that one's in there. *Remember to be concise and colourful; there are other stations for the listener to switch to.* But in thirty seconds or less, it's hard to draw a thumbnail sketch of sixteen years, even though I could probably do it right now, provided I spoke quickly. Let's see. Formed in 1980. Made a 45. X Records. Toured the country in 1987. *Greatest Hits.* Intrepid Records. *Melville. Whale Music.* Signed to Sire Records. *Introducing Happiness.* Dropped from Sire. *Whale Music* soundtrack. Genie Award. Clark quits, Kerr joins. *Group of Seven. The Blue Hysteria.* Hip tour, then another. There. Easy. Instead, this is my answer: "Well, we've been around for a long, long, long, long, long, long, long, long time."

He appears confused. He tries again.

"So what about Winnipeg?"

"Oh, Winnipeg's great. We have a lot of good friends here, people we met on our first tour."

"When was that?" he asks.

"In 1987. We played the Royal Albert Hotel, which is where Joey died," says Martin, obliquely referring to a song that the deejay has never heard.

"Well, what can we expect from tonight's show?" he asks.

"Lots of songs about Winnipeg!" I say.

He thinks we're kidding, but we're not. He might even suspect that we're making fun of his city, but we're not doing that, either. *Never make fun of the city you're playing in.* We have two songs — "King of the Past," and "Royal Albert Hotel" — about being in Winnipeg on our first tour. *In order to make your song appealing, have it take place in a familiar setting, like New York or Los Angeles.*

"Great. Well, thanks a lot for coming down and talking with us, fellas, and have a great show tonight," he says, ending the interview.

"Thanks," says Martin.

"Okay, folks: Rheostatics!"

"Thanks, Winnipeg," I say, waving to the kids outside the van.

"Great! Now here's a song by the Cranberries!"

SKINNY TENN: I got on the radio because I wanted to have *all* the records. Even in high school, I used to write to *Billboard* and tell them that I was a deejay and they'd send me records. I got my first job as a disc jockey at CKLM in Saskatoon. *"Ninety-Nine Point Two Pounds of the Slimmer Thinner Skinny Spinner!"* I would talk real fast and sound real cool. I identified way more with the guys I saw play at high-school hops than with the guys who were running the radio station. Back then, there were groups who were called station bands, which was great because there was basically no music scene to speak of in Saskatchewan. Since we were 1250 on the dial, one station band was called the 125 Witnesses. I was hired to emcee a concert and they were the group; I got fifty bucks and they got fifty, proving once again that the business guy always gets more. I turned them on to cool records, which they would immediately cover in their sets. Because no one had heard the songs before, people thought they were their own. That's how I became their manager.

BARRY ALLEN: Whatever town you were in, you'd get in touch with the radio station. When you did a gig, the first thing you did was hire a deejay to emcee for you. Right away, you became friends with these guys. They were busy promoting the scene and the bands, and they couldn't wait for your record to come out. They'd move all across the country, and if you heard that your record was getting played in, say, Moncton, you knew that it was because one of these deejays had got a job out there. Nowadays, stations are so insular and the formats are so tight. Radio stations want to be part of the community, but they're not really; they're so busy playing the big stuff that they can't be bothered to play the little band that's starting up, the one that lives in their community.

RICKY PATTERSON: When we got into the town we were playing, we'd make a phone call and, nine times out of ten, we'd get the deejay who was on the air. Then we'd say, "Hey, we're the Esquires. We're playing in town tonight, can we bring you a copy of our record?" and they'd say, "C'mon down." We'd walk in and there'd be no guards, no special buttons to push; we'd go right in, sit with the deejay, they'd spin the record and talk about the gig. Today, that's impossible. You may not fit the station's format. It would mean going on the air without being screened.

HOLLY WOODS: My brother was a deejay when I was growing up. He brought home the first Beatles album on reel-to-reel. He'd bring home all the 45s. He was only fifteen, going on sixteen, at the time, and he was the all-night man. He would fall asleep on the air. My father would stay up and listen late at night to make sure he was okay. Whenever he heard some dead air, he'd get on the phone and ring till he woke him up.

MIKE TILKA: There was a big teen deejay out of Detroit called Tommy James. Our trio did a local TV show for him. We played a jazzy arrangement of "Age of Aquarius," which was probably pretty awful. Piano, bass, and drums. Our idol was Les McCann.

Todd Rundgren was on the show, too, with his first band, the
Nazz. They kicked their amps off the stage and did all this out-
rageous stuff and had blue hair. Todd had a presence then; he was
an ass, but he was amazing. He was so loud and good. I'd never
heard loud and good before, only loud and bad.

Another guest on the show was the number-one black deejay
in Detroit, a middle-aged guy, deep voice, the god of black
radio in Detroit. About a month after we did the TV show, the
keyboard player and me were at the Masonic Temple in Detroit
seeing Lou Donaldson and other funky jazz acts. Outside of a
few hookers, we were the only white people in the place. By the
second break, I had to go to the bathroom. The hallways were
packed, and I was being jostled a bit. It was just a little weird for
this eighteen-year-old white guy to be in this hallway with these
adults all dressed to the nines, out for the evening. I looked
like a bus boy or something. All of a sudden, the deejay saw me
and he said, "Hey, Mike! How's it goin'?" It was like the parting
of the Red Sea, because everybody knew who he was and he
acknowledged me.

RONNIE KING: We had a big hit Stateside in 1971 with "Sweet
City Woman"; the record company – Bell Records – could barely
catch up with it. Chicago and L.A. were on it right away. We still
had to do a few southern Ontario gigs – we'd already committed
– even though our record was taking off around the world. We
were driving home one night from one of these high-school gigs,
out on the lonely highway, and tuned into WABC in New York,
which only played the top twenty. We heard their jingle, and the
announcer came on, saying, "Hey, brand-new band from Canada
right here!" We stopped the car, ran around like idiots, and

jumped on the hood, yelling *"Ahhh!! We're top twenty in New York! Holy shit!"*

TERRY DAVID MULLIGAN: I started out in radio in Red Deer, Alberta, then went to Calgary and then Regina. My air name was Terry Dee and my shtick was to invite people to come on the air, then insult them. I couldn't really announce, so I had to come up with something. I screamed and I yelled. I did what I did. Years later, in 1968, when I was working for CKLG-AM in Vancouver, I got good. It was boss radio. Then one day management came to me with the idea of taking rock music to the FM band. That wasn't done at the time. Rock-and-roll just didn't exist on FM; it was all Mantovani. So they sent me to San Francisco to KSAM and Big Daddy Tom Donahue. I spent a week with him and a guy named Abe Voko Kesh, who was the manager of Blue Cheer. I sat in with Tom and watched him work. He'd come in with 150 albums, throwing tracks all over the place; he'd take people on journeys where one track led to another which led to another. I brought the concept back to Vancouver. It was the best. I remember Alan Anaka, the sales manager, coming out of his office holding flattened-out letters from people who had been listening. There must have been one hundred letters. He said, "I've never seen anything like this in all my years of radio."

BOB SEGARINI: In 1966, Tom Donahue. Big Daddy Tom was a big man who started Autumn Records, recorded the Beau Brummels, Sly and the Family Stone, Hi Five, all that. Tom found a Chinese radio station in a church basement that stopped broadcasting at 5:00 p.m. He proposed that he would pay the bill if he could go from 5:00 p.m. to 5:00 a.m. That was KMPX. *That* was the first underground FM-radio station, not WLS. KMPX was where the San Francisco scene happened. *"That was a guy named Captain Beefheart out of Los Angeles . . . cool stuff. Right here. We're gonna play a whole side B. If you need any smoking paraphernalia, the Purple Haze at 155 is the place for you."* That's where it started, and that's when local bands started pressing acetates and bringing them down, their rehearsal tapes. That's where I first heard the Mystery Trend, the Airplane, the Opposite Sex, which became the Warlocks, which became the Grateful Dead. That was *radio*. They played whatever came through the door. If people liked it, they'd play it again. Radio should always be that, but now the majors control radio stations. It's bad. It's wrong. It's done.

Winnipeg Arena. A warm and beautiful place, yellow, red, blue, and gold floorboards stamped with one-hundred-year-old boot-dirt, exposed steam pipes crawling along the walls, THE PEMBY DRAFT HOUSE: YOUR NO. 1 DRAFT CHOICE, grey aisles crumbling in the upper decks, BROUGHT TO YOU BY SILVERWOOD DAIRIES. Rows of scuffed wooden chairs arc upwards into the smoky ceiling light that dances around an enormous painting of Queen Elizabeth. I wonder how many prone goalies or felled boxers or Ozzy Osbournes or human cannonballs have stared up at Her Majesty and wondered if they'd been knocked into some weird dream. How many of them looked for guidance at the old banners — WINNIPEG VICTORIAS, STANLEY CUP CHAMPIONS 1901, 1896 — only to be left wildly guessing as if batted about by the hands of a great clock.

Winnipeg Arena is all about the past. Here, you're sent reeling back, not forward. October 15, 1972, is the date inscribed under a plaque in the arena's concourse commemorating the first ever WHA game. Al Hamilton took the face-off for the Alberta Oilers. Muttonchop sideburns. Fu Manchu moustache. Spherical afro. The Golden Jet was there. So was Anders Hedberg and Ulf Nilsson. Black-and-white photographs of Winnipeg's WHA teams line the walls, and if you follow them around the rink, eventually you find yourself at the entrance in front of a wall patterned with gilded bas-relief portraits: the Manitoba Sports' Wall of Fame. On it are the faces of Steamer Maxwell, Bullet Joe Simpson, Joe Hall, Turk Broda, Andy Bathgate, Scott Young, Trent Frayne, and Jim Coleman, the last three being sportswriters whom I used to emulate as a kid. That's what I wanted to grow up to be.

Charlie Gardiner's there, too. Jocular, acrobatic, beatific, Charlie Gardiner was born in Scotland, moved to Winnipeg as a kid, and was drafted by the Chicago Blackhawks, where he backstopped them to the Stanley Cup in 1933, the team's first-ever championship. But two months later, Charlie was dead in a Winnipeg hospital, the result of an illness incurred while playing net for the Hawks. In his time, he was the most beloved player in the league and the greatest goalkeeper of his era. He hosted a weekly radio show in Winnipeg and was famous for joking with players and singing to the crowd. After winning the Cup, he was pushed around the Loop in Chicago in a wheelbarrow chased by five hundred adoring fans, youngsters who were probably no different from the ones who are pulling into the hoary, snow-covered parking lot outside the arena in their parents' cars, their engines coughing steam, stereos reefed, fingers drumming expertly on the dashboard, passing under a sign in front of the rink that says: HIP TONIGHT. NEXT MANITOBA MOOSE GAME FRIDAY.

Kids are lined up on the steps. The locks on the doors slide back and the first teenager spins into the foyer, his fists raised in a V above his body. To him, it matters little that Charlie Gardiner was once Winnipeg's most famous athlete. This kid's dream has little to do with the past; in a few minutes, he'll hurry through the arena to find his seat, wait out the opening band, and then, for two and a half hours, scream along to his favourite Hip songs. He's spent countless winter nights envisioning himself doing just this. The security guard rifles through his jacket, then shows him the passageway. The kid bolts through the turnstile and runs past the fellow in the red tuque and long coat who is moving his hand over the bust of the chimeric goal-keeper who, sixty-four years ago, died within a short walk of where he is standing. I'm running my fingers over Charlie's gilded mouth and nose, sliding my hand across his crimped hair as if wiping frost from a windshield. Hundreds of other kids have now filled the foyer, laughing, screaming, and calling out to each other. I turn away and leave them. One by one, we are swallowed into the dark rink.

Youngsters. The Local Rabbits and Farm Fresh are with us back-stage. It's always good when friends show up, not only because you enjoy their company, but because they put a little distance between you and your band-mates, god bless them. The Rabbits are a surprise: they're touring the country at the same time as us, and their day off has coincided with our Winnipeg show. The first time we met them (Pete, Ben, Jason, and Johnny T. Starr, who hail from Pointe Claire, Quebec), they couldn't have been much older than sixteen or seventeen. They showed up during an interview at Concordia radio where we autographed their CDs. One of them mentioned that they were in a band and that they'd done a version of "Record Body Count" in their basement, so we challenged them to come down to our gig that night at Club Soda and play the song. The Rabbits are loud, boisterous fellows who tend to speak excitedly at once, but this time, they fell silent and turned red. I asked them again, and they stared at each other. I asked them a third time and they said that they would. When we left the station, we looked back and they were jumping around and hugging each other. They performed the song, and the crowd went nuts. We've been friends ever since.

Over the years, many young bands have contacted us, seeking words of encouragement. A few positive thoughts can go a long way towards boosting a young person's confidence. I know this first-hand. After our first gig at the Edge, I sat in the dressing room with the flute player for Popular Spies, the headliners, and asked him if he had any advice for a fledgling band.

"Yeah," he said, pulling on a cigarette, his fedora angled across his face. "Never break up."

He probably meant to be flip, but, as you can see, I took his advice literally. So the weight of one's words upon young musicians cannot be overestimated. I'd be remiss, however, if I didn't present an example of what not to do. The incident occurred after a gig at the Rivoli, where we were selling tapes to help finance our ill-fated tour of Ireland. I was impressed by the B.C. group 54-40 at the time — they'd had hit records like "I Go

Blind" and "Baby Ran" and were fast rising among the ranks of new Canadian bands. So when I spotted them in the club, I appealed to them to buy a tape. The reaction of their guitarist, a lanky, ponytailed fellow named Phil Comparelli, was less than encouraging.

"Man, don't quit your day job," he said.

To this day, I harbour deep resentment towards him.

Johnny T. Starr suggests smoking a joint. I don't usually smoke on the road because my voice is already on the verge of sounding like an air horn. I'm the type of musician who shouldn't be singing in the first place; I have a tone that makes certain people wish there were rules governing these sorts of things. But tonight, we twist a rope then burn it down to its bitter end. Afterwards, we help ourselves to great trays of beer and cola and tortilla chips and salsa and pie. For musicians who don't sell millions of records or live in ancient Irish castles, free pie pretty much represents the apex of commercial achievement. Stacked high, they travel past our dressing room on great trolleys propelled by men and women in white cloaks — raspberry, blueberry, rhubarb, and apple. It's a stoner's delight.

Through the old brick walls of the rink, we can hear the crowd's applause rising and falling like a weather balloon and eventually the Hip's "At the Hundredth Meridian" pulls us down the hallway, out to a landing beside the stage. By this time, we're zooming. Right there in front of us, in his white turtleneck, Gord is leaning over the mike stand. The band is coaxing the song towards a respite as if carefully guiding a great ship through a narrow channel. A few yowlers in the audience are crying out, but for the most part the crowd is silent. The dope gently guides me through the music. The bass is droning a low note *thum thum*

Gord Downie

thum and a cymbal is swelling *shwaaa* and Gord is standing there howling, *"She's gone sellers,"* and the stage behind him is bathed in gold. He pulls his hand out of his pocket and begins to waggle it beside his head. His eyes are closed and his body is rigid except for the hand. He forces it forward like a man reaching into a hole while Paul Langlois strums a lazy, dirty chord *planggg planggg* and the bass adds *bwing* to the end of *thum thum thum*. *"She's gone sellers!"* It's as if Gord has just learned English and hasn't yet quite figured out how to put the right words together. His nervous-sounding voice keens up the register, his face widening, jaw falling open, and I'm reminded of Jacques Brel, whose words I can't understand either, but don't have to. Gord's performance is astonishing. The crowd, most of them standing, press their hands together and gaze at the stage. It is the best thing I have ever heard by the Tragically Hip.

KELLY JAY: We got to play the Fillmore East in New York with Ronnie Hawkins. We opened up for Joe Cocker, Maggie Bell and Stone the Crows. It was amazing. We met Bill Graham, who sent us down flowers and T-shirts, and Leon Russell, who sent us a huge, two-ounce bag of pot that was laced with THC. By the time we went on, we felt like we'd taken animal tranquillizers. I couldn't even remember how to breathe.

TOMMY CHONG: At the Elegant Parlour, there was no liquor served, but people brought their own. Cops would come in and try to raid the joint, but the people were very discreet. Pretty soon the pot scene hit and no one was drinking. They'd be laughing and having a great time; it confused the hell outta the cops. Cops were busting people left and right, though. Sergeant Stedenko from *Up in Smoke* was a real cop around that time in Vancouver. He tried to bust me many times. He would sneak around outside the club, waiting for someone to spark a joint. He once followed me home. He threw my dad up against the wall, rousted my family. He wanted to get me so bad. But he became famous from our recording, so they had to transfer him to Turkey. Really, Turkey. He retired just recently, and his fellow narcs gave me a poster with his name on it.

DAVID HENMAN: When April Wine moved to Montreal in the summer of '70, they put us up in St-Sauveur in one of those places that skiers rent in the winter, which were empty in the summer. The whole area was like a hippie commune. People were wandering around stoned, half-naked. The local chemist would come to your door on Saturday night. He was a little guy with long hair and he'd say, "Open up," and drop something in your mouth. Then away you'd go.

BOB SEGARINI: In California, we used to be able to get really pure organic mescaline and psilocybin. We used to drink electric root beer. I'd take a number-five horse capsule of real mescaline and put it in a glass of root beer, drink it, and spend the next nine hours looking for god in a three-way G.E. bulb. I spent the entire year of 1968 on acid.

MIKE TILKA: Everybody's got a Goddo story. One night they were playing with us in an arena in Timmins, maybe North Bay. It was the end of summer, a little cold. Greg [Godovitz] came into our dressing room after he'd played, took one look at the deli tray, and said, "Wow. You guys got all this shit, we didn't get nothing." We said, "Help yourself. We can only eat so much cut meat." He headed for the bottles and started pouring himself stiff drinks. We were getting ready to go on and we thought, "Ah, who cares? We'll just leave Greg in here." When we got to the encore of our set, Greg, who'd been drinking this whole time, ran out on stage. He'd taken a cut salami and stuffed it into his pants. He started doing these obscene gestures, just blasted out of his mind, and we were all laughing. Then he pulled the zipper down and started flicking slices of salami all around, at which point we looked at the crew and said, "Get him outta here!" The next day, he didn't remember doing it.

FRANK SODA: I've seen Goddo literally run out into the audience and punch someone. He'd put his guitar down and away he'd go.

RA MCGUIRE: Goddo came into our dressing room with a fire extinguisher and proceeded to get that white shit all over everything, thinking that it was really hilarious. Later that night he ended up with a French-Canadian girl in the lobby of the hotel; he was wearing a silk dressing gown and a bandanna around his head with what looked like a switchblade stuck in the band. There was a banquet going on and they were sitting on the floor against the wall and I was just sort of hanging, curious about what was going to transpire. The hotel called the cops to eject Greg from the lobby. A cop came and stood over him, at which point he reached up and pulled out his switchblade. He hit the little button on the handle and a comb popped out. Greg said, "Do you have any idea who I think I am?"

GREG GODOVITZ: Hamilton was always the wildest place for us to play. In our heyday, we had three guys that followed us around. One night, they were all there together. There was a guy named Mac, who used to get up on stage in a jam-packed hall and grab those little stubby beer bottles and smack them on his head until they broke. His head would be all bleeding. He'd get on the mike and grunt, "This is for the Goddo Man!" There was another guy called the Lizard Man. I had this song called "Let the Lizard Loose," which is about getting your cock out. I'd be playing guitar and this guy would come up and he'd whip out his dick and I would finger the neck while he thrashed the strings with his dick. *How much has that gotta hurt?* Okay maybe not the A or the D, but the B and the E's gotta really hurt. And I'm actually playing thinking, "Oh, geez. This guy's got his dick all over my guitar." The third guy used to come up and he'd look at Gino and me and he would show us his ass. He'd just pull his pants down teasingly, and he had the faggiest look. Well, this one night, the Lizard Man's on guitar, Mac's on stage, and I see Mac grab this guy, who by now has his pants around his knees. Mac throws him over his shoulder and grabs a fuckin' beer bottle and shoves it right up his ass. The whole fuckin' thing. And this was a Molson stubby. This wasn't no delicate Heineken, man.

BOB SEGARINI: When the Family Tree album came out, we were living at Sandy Koufax's Tropicana Motel on Santa Monica Boulevard in L.A. Everybody knows this hotel. In the hotel that week was Them; they drank seventy thousand cases of Scotch and never changed their clothes. They wore the same clothes that they had on the cover of their album, I swear. We threw a celebration party, and I bought an ounce of cocaine for 450 dollars. I put it in a pie tin. I rolled up five one-hundred-dollar bills, taped them shut, and stuck 'em in there. At the end of the night, half of the coke was gone, but the one-hundred-dollar bills were still there, even though it was an open-door party. That's the difference between then and now, right there.

JERRY DOUCETTE: When I was in the Reefers, we'd take a syringe, fill it full of vodka, and shoot it into about twenty or thirty oranges. We'd be walking up the stairs to some hotel room in Kitchener – the Walper Hotel, I remember – and we'd have this big bag of oranges over our shoulders. Because we were kids, no one thought anything of it.

KEN TOBIAS: Everybody took turns taking care of Freddie McKenna, the guitar player on "Singalong Jubilee." He was obese, huge, and he was blind, and he also drank a lot. You know, he was an authentic country guy. He had over seven hundred songs in his repertoire. *Sing Out* magazine, which was huge in America for years, came up to see him just to document the guy. He could drink, boy. I had to take him down to the tavern once, and I said to Fred, "I'm going to the bathroom." He said, "So order me something. Order me fifteen or eighteen drafts." They brought over the tray, laid it down, and I'm not away more than three minutes. When I came back, he was downing the last one. He had this technique where he'd grab the glass, put it up to his lips, and turn it as he drank. Very effective.

DENTON YOUNG: After a while, you see the damage the drugs and alcohol can do. I won't deny that I probably indulged more than I should have while I was in Zon. When there was trouble in the band, when we weren't seeing eye to eye, everybody would turn to their personal vice. It's tough being on the road. When your whole livelihood depends on four other guys you're not getting along with, and you're not making money, you feel like you're pretty alone out there. Then you start killing yourself with booze.

BOB SEGARINI: I had a severe drug problem for ten years. I've been clean for two years from free-basing cocaine. I used to do it once a year, just like we'd do rocket fuel once a year, which is when you mix heroin and cocaine in a joint. Once a year, like Christmas. You used ether and all this stuff; it was very dangerous. But it wasn't in the music industry that I got heavily into cocaine; it was radio. In those days, we ran on cocaine. It was in abundance everywhere. I learned how to free-base myself, which is the biggest mistake any boy or girl can make. I spent the next ten years just killing myself. When my mother got ill, I went to California, and I ended up spending fifty thousand dollars building a screening room in the garage with a ten-foot motion-picture screen and THX surround sound, everything you could imagine. I spent two years sucking on a crack pipe watching laser discs. It was like *Leaving Las Vegas*. I lost my home, my wife. It was the classic scene.

Wherever they play, the Hip like to find a room to jam in before hitting the stage. I know where this room is, so I take the Rabbits there. If there's one thing that youngsters love, it's someone else's gear, especially when they're still playing their first guitars. We plug in, tune, fall out of tune, then spiral around for a while on a little guitar riff, believing, as many stoners will, that we are creating some of the greatest music ever made. Pete Elkas, the Rabbits' stage-left guitarist, is playing a dwarf-sized drum set that was made for Johnny Fay by Ayotte of Vancouver, an amazing instrument that you could fit inside a suitcase. The rest of the Rabbits are playing through practice amps, going *twang, skronk, berrang.* Meanwhile, back in the hockey rink, the Hip are slamming full-throttle through their most famous song, the one about the dead hockey player. The first fifty rows of the crowd have balled their hands into fists and are waving them like maces around their heads. Backstage, we're really starting to cook. Pete yells, "Ben! Solo!" across the room. Ben goes *plonk, plink, whangggg, skreee.* Outside, Paul Langlois's last mighty guitar slash ricochets around the rink; Ben goes *skrrang,* his tongue curving around the side of his mouth. "Rock on, Ben!" "*Gordie! Gordie! Gordie!*" The Hip walk down the ramp off the back of the stage, white towels wrapped around their necks. Back in the jam room, a string pops from its saddle, *proingggg*.

The song is over.

So is the gig.

Wearing a bathrobe, Johnny Fay wanders into the room and sees Pete playing his drums. Pete pauses in midair like a toy monkey drummer whose batteries have just died. Johnny Fay's look suggests that he fears his precious kit is being clobbered beyond repair. Perhaps it is. A few minutes later, Dave Powell, the Hip's road manager, tells the Rabbits to stop playing. I walk over to the Hip's dressing room to apologize for letting things get out of hand, but on my way there, I'm shouted after by three greasy-haired teenage girls, who are calling to me from behind a security curtain.

"Hey, hey, opening-band guy!"

"Hey! You! You're *soooo* cute!"

"C'm'ere! Please! Talk to us!"

"Do you know the Hip?"

"Please! You're *sooo* gorgeous!"

Now, I'm no fool. On good days with the sun hitting me just right, I may indeed resemble a young Telly Savalas. But I am hardly what one would consider cute or gorgeous, and even though a fair number of women and the odd fellow have mooned over Martin, Tim, and Donny (in that order), we are not a band of smooth-skinned poster boys. Come to think of it, neither are the Hip.

"Did you like the show?" I ask them.

"Oh, it was amazing!"

"Do you think we could meet them?"

"Who?"

"THE HIP!"

"They're our favourite band!"

"You were good, too!"

"Well, you see that door right over there?" I say, pointing to the Hip's dressing room. "That's where they are right now."

"Really? Omigod . . ."

"Could you please get them to meet us? Please?"

"Oh, I don't know . . ."

"C'mon. We'll do anything!"

"They're probably just sitting around relaxing or something. Maybe if you wait outside by their bus, you could meet them . . ."

"C'mon. Could you just get us a guitar pick?"

"Yeah!"

"Yeah! *Pleeeeeeeze?*"

"Okay. Hold on," I say.

I walk backstage and find a guitar pick in my suit pocket.

"Here. Here's one of their picks," I say.

"Oh. Oh, man. Amazing."

"Thanks. Thanks."

"Whose is it?"

"Oh, it's Bobby's," I add.

"Wow."

"Bobby's? Really?"

"Yes, Bobby's."

DUTCH MASON: We had girls hanging around us all the time. We played this place one time, it was up in the Rodin goldmines or some fucking thing, and we were playing this high school. The girls were just screaming and we didn't know what was fucking going on. We were just playing Elvis tunes, no big deal. After we finished, I was out back, and about fifteen or twenty girls were standing there and they said, "Just shake for us." I went, "What?" They said, "C'mon. Just shake." So I gave 'em a few moves like Elvis, and they all screamed, and I said, "Fuck. I gotta get outta here."

JERRY DOUCETTE: All the high schools in Hamilton would get together and have a sports day at an outdoor stadium. There were six thousand kids there. We had just a small P.A. – a Bogan sixty-watt amplifier with column speakers. I had an old Hofner guitar with white alligator-skin covering. It was fabulous. This was back when the Beatles were doing their thing, back when the chicks were going crazy. That day, after our set, we got mobbed. I couldn't believe it. We were chased, and just like in the movies, I had to run away or risk being caught.

BOB SEGARINI: In the old days, groupies were called road angels. Back then, I was on the road twelve weeks solid. Once, I was in Michigan, and I'd had it. I was living a horrible existence. Somebody had to write down what city I was in and put it on my monitor. One time, I opened the window of my hotel room and I didn't know where I was. I went to look in the phone book, but there wasn't any, so I asked for the local paper, but they sent me the *New York Times*. Now I was really confused. As it turned out, I was in Providence, Rhode Island. But how pathetic that was, calling the front desk and asking, "Could you tell me where I am?" The road is horrible. But then, here comes this little girl, who took me by the hand and put me in a Volkswagen with my luggage, took me to her house, lit candles, and bathed me and made me a homemade meal and, most important *she did my laundry.* She saved my life. People look down on a lot of groupies, but let me tell you, if it weren't for the people who are adamant fans of what you do, this industry would have been dead years ago.

DENTON YOUNG: Nobody ever did my laundry for me, but just having chicks coming on to you was pretty interesting. But then you'd find out that she had come on to the drummer in the last band too, and you realized that you weren't that special. One girl from the Tri-Towns – Haileybury, Cobalt, and New Liskeard – was infamous. I saw her from the days of Harlequin right through to the days of Zon. I swear to God. She never changed. That was her thing. When you were on the road, you'd meet girls who were there for you when you came back to town. I remember falling in love with a couple of them. In Harlequin, every one of us had a girlfriend in Brantford, Ontario. Wherever we played, they'd come to see us, the four of them, all together.

RA MCGUIRE: We had the pleasure of meeting some amateur groupies in Portland, Oregon, when we were still an amateur band. They were practising being groupies on us in the bars, and when we went to play the Starwood Club in Los Angeles, they had graduated to being professional groupies. It was very impressive. We had this shiny, metallic cloth on our pants, fairly tight, and these women were insistent that we not go on stage in a non-erect state. So they rubbed each of us until there was more impressive activity.

ROB GUNN: All the groupies were remarkable. Max loved Quebec City. The band was trying to be good, so they kept sending girls into mine and John's [Erikson, the soundman] room. There would be knocks on the door in the middle of the night and girls would come in and start taking off their clothes. When we were on the road, we met Connie in Little Rock, the girl from the Grand Funk Railroad song: *"Sweet, sweet Connie was good at her act / She did the whole show and that's a fact."* Everything you heard was true. She was very proud of her art. We'd go to Memphis a week later and Dr. Nick would show up with his penicillin.

JIM MILLICAN: The Guess Who ran into Connie in Little Rock. She even had a bumper sticker with her name and phone number on it that she'd give out to bands.

DAVID HENMAN: In April Wine, we discovered the groupie scene in Toronto. During that period in the late '60s, it was their mission in life to look after travelling rock-and-rollers. One girl who was a waitress at Larry's Hideaway had an apartment right across the street. One night she took me back there and she gave me a tongue bath from head to toe.

RA MCGUIRE: In many cases, the groupies were your good friends. They vibrated at the same frequency, they understood what you were up to and shared in your life in the way their male counterparts in the audience couldn't. The guys were awestruck, but the women were more likely to just drop into the groove with you. They wanted to experience things with you, rather than watch it. They'd take you in their cars to the cool places, introduce you to their culture. That was important to us all.

RIK EMMETT: A stripper showed up at a gig and was very, very forward about the fact that she wanted me. I was going, "Thanks a lot, I'm flattered, but, you know . . ." When I went back to the hotel after the gig, she was there, too, and was not happy that I was giving her no as an answer. A couple of weeks later, we were playing a gig in St. Louis and AC/DC were on the bill with us. Bon Scott comes into the dressing room, completely pissed, wearing a plastic thong sandal with his big toe all taped up. He's bleeding. Apparently, he'd walked on broken glass. I went "Bon! Nice to see you, man," but he was, like, "Fuck you! I'm gonna pound your lights out, man!" I said, "Whaddya mean?" and he said, "My girlfriend told me that you said my band's shit!" I said, "No. I never said any such thing!" By this time, I was worried for my life because this guy, all drunken and angry and bleeding, wants a piece of me. I peeked by him and down the hall there's the peeler. She'd been putting thoughts in poor Bon's head. I said, "Oh, Bon. Look, buddy. Are you gonna take the word of some girl that you met backstage two weeks ago, or are you gonna take the word of a fellow musician who would like to buy you a beer?" He looks back at her and said, "Oh, all right, mate. Fuck. You know I fucking love you, baby . . ."

SKINNY TENN: Fludd's singer, Ed Pilling, was a beautiful guy, great personality, an English accent, real English, Birmingham. He was a drinker, a rocker. He was out to have a party, to be friends with every guy, to love everybody. Every chick in the country was after him. He really played it up. At the same time, Goddo was the horniest guy in the music business. If they had held a contest at the time, he would have won it. He'd corral the

chicks over at the side of the stage after the gig, pick out the prettiest one with the biggest tits, and then Ed would just amble
down and the babe — the one beautiful girl in town who'd been
using Goddo to get to the singer — would see Ed and then that
would be it. One night in Thunder Bay, Goddo was pissed off
because he'd had his eye on this one chick, and Ed had just come
in and scooped her. Later that night, Ed got on the bus, but
instead of rubbing it in, he said nothing. For two hours, he was
white. They had a ten-hour drive ahead of them and Goddo
finally got it out of him. Ed told him, "Man, I reached down and
it was a cock down there." Goddo was glad he'd lost that battle.

U. S. A.

"When I was young I had an old guitar
That I learned to sing and play
From a book I bought on how to be a star
Written in the U.S.A."
Stompin' Tom Connors, *"Ripped Off Winkle"*

Leaving Canada, Das Bus barrels doggedly south down the white highway, leaving thousands of miles of freakish landscape at our backs. For anyone who's ever done a west-east run of the country and ended up travelling through the U.S.A., you can't help but notice how the geography flattens and pales and greys once you pass south of the border. This isn't so much a reflection of the terrain to the south as it is the incomparable strangeness and diversity of the Canadian land. Before this tour, I promised myself that I wouldn't fall prey to writing endless paragraphs about the majesty of my native soil, but sitting here looking at the moonish, blue snow-fields pooling into the magenta sunrise, I have to express a word or two about how astonishing this country is to travel over.

Canada is a triptych of visual delights. To start, there's the Rockies, and they scare the shit out of you. There's nothing you can do to prepare yourself for the shocking size and pointedness of the young, towering range. Speaking while in their midst is to voice the feeble titterings of a mouse-person. Whenever I'm among them, I experience the same kind of sensations that I felt as a kid, back when anything that was larger than me seemed frighteningly monstrous. However absurd, there lurks a very real fear in the back of my mind that, like the Thing in the Fantastic Four, one of these glacial behemoths will wake up and grab our puny vehicle, sputtering gamely between its slopes, and crush it with a stony, oversized fist. Part of this fear, I think, stems from the fact that the first time we travelled through them, our car broke down, stranding us in Rogers Pass. It wasn't like being abandoned in a big city, with bars and movies and casinos, or in a prairie town, with farmhouses and diners and bingo parlours. It was way weirder; the falling purple light of the day, the silence of the empty highway, and the mountains looming above us, displeased and unimpressed. While we stood there with the hood open gazing at our troubled autoworks, Martin took off into the woods. When we found him hours later back at the motel up the road, he told us that he'd climbed the nearest mountain looking for fauna and wildlife and places from which to sketch the scenery. Sure he did. Had it been me, I would have peeled down to my underwear and pounded the craggy rockface, gladly accepting whatever fate was cast upon me by a force far greater than mine.

After the awesome Rockies, the prairies come like a vaudevillian gag. I can only imagine the conversation between migrant workers in British Columbia in the '20s: "You mean to tell me that on the other side of these mountains, there are thousands of miles of flat, unbouldered terrain?" "Yes, I've seen it! It's as smooth as a velvet snooker table!" What a laugh. It's as if some eggheaded geographers got together and smoked a joint for the first time. "What if we . . . (huff) . . . what if we . . . (huff) . . . made that space on the other side of the mountains really really really fla . . . (huff) . . . *Flathahahaha!*" It's a ridiculous and absurd piece of natural planning (way to go, superior entity). It takes a day to adjust. What this does to one's consciousness, I'm not sure; however, I wouldn't doubt that some sort of chemical activity is the cause of all those travellers running through yellow wheatfields, yelling "*Wula-wula-wula-woooo!*" Emerging from the Rockies is like getting spat out at the end of a roller-coaster ride; to drive across the prairies is to milk that off-ramp momentum before the road gets wavy again. We've crossed it many different ways: bus, van, car, train, even taxi. Once we broke down outside of Brandon and had to hire a cab to bring us to a show at the Walker Theatre in Winnipeg; 250 dollars later, we made it with ten minutes to spare.

The boundless prairie eventually narrows, and the Canadian Shield rises to smother you in a storm of rock and wood. It is both a difficult and beautiful part of the country, hard and rugged to travel over, but breathtaking to view. I'm fond of this part of Canada because it means that I'm nearer to home, and even though Northern Ontario looks like a different planet from Toronto and Georgian Bay, at least I'm in my own province, and this comforts me. But as much as I remember this chunk of Canada for its *Field and Stream* tableaus of glistening lakes, menacing rock outcrops, and murky forests, when I think of up-province, I think of Thunder Bay. I mostly associate Thunder Bay with Spencer Musselam, whom we met on our first visit in

1987. At our initial performance at Crocks and Rolls (a long-gone staple on the national rock circuit that everyone — really, everyone — passed through), I remember asking from the stage if anyone was interested in showing me the city limits the next day, and Spencer obliged. The next morning, I awoke to find him sitting on a couch across from the mattress in the living room of the house where I was sleeping. He'd let himself in. It was one o'clock in the afternoon and Spencer had been sitting there since early morning, waiting for me to rise. This loyalty and good nature led us to stay at his parents' house on subsequent visits, and I'll fondly remember the morning that he shook us awake and told us to look under our pillows, where we found four brand new Old Dutch Potato Chips shirts, which we wore all the way to Vancouver and back again.

But I think of escaping Thunder Bay as much as I do of arriving there. My memory is still vivid of missing our train home after our inaugural visit. We arrived late at the station to find the locomotive pulling away, so, having seen too many Steve McQueen films, we chased after it in our friend's Jeep, which was loaded down with drums, guitars, suitcases, and people hanging over the sides. We sounded our horn and screamed at the conductor to get it to stop. We ran parallel with it until we were diverted by the rising treeline of the forest. We gave up, but it was a beautiful place to be abandoned. We stopped right there at the crest of the forest under magnificent fat stars and watched the steel beast charge into the black horizon without us, just another great moving thing in the silent line of the night.

Cobo Hall, Detroit.

I'm strumming my battered black guitar and staring into the eye of the hall. The eye looks back; it always does. Dark shapes take their seats. The building is round, and even though the upper deck seems as distant as any, I can make out the expressions of those sitting farthest away, their faces glimmering in the shadows. I'm relieved that they aren't stoners, but kids, and instead of smoking chillums, they are eating ice-cream bars. They will not egg me nor assail me with their fists despite the fact that we are in the very cradle of power rock, the place where *Kiss Alive* and *Yessongs* were recorded. If they did want to hurt me, however, I would excuse them for behaving instinctively. The MC5. Grand Funk Railroad. The Iguanas. The Stooges. Alice Cooper. Ted Nugent. They all started here. Detroit Rock City. This is Mecca.

I expect little from tonight's show. It's the last performance before our three-day bivouac in Toronto and it's hard not to look beyond it, to home, to sleep, to Janet. Besides, our dressing room has an overflowing toilet and a kettle that sets itself on fire when you plug it in (which provides us with a pre-show charade: "Hey, Donny. You feel like making tea?") The rider in our contract has produced five green bananas. Down the hallway, two three-hundred-pound security guards are having an argument — "Aw, that's fuckin' bullshit, John! How was Pete supposed to know it wasn't his car? He was *drunk* for chrissakes!" — and, for the pre-show snack, the caterers have put out trays of pinkish roast beef, ham loaf, and baskets of Wonder bread.

But you can never read a gig until it's played. You can go out with all the expectations in the world and fail miserably, which I suppose is the folly of gods. By the same token, the most intractable conditions can also create inspired performances. In Limerick, Ireland, for instance, we performed at a Texas-themed pub called the Barn. It was depressing from the minute we arrived; in the land of Joyce and Yeats and Synge, we found posters of the Dallas Cowboy cheerleaders. We'd also hauled most of our equipment on a train from Dublin only to discover that the promoters had neglected to hire amplifiers for our guitars. Guitar and bass amps, we found out, are called "backline" in Europe, and not knowing that word, we hadn't requested it. So we played the show with our guitars plugged into a P.A. system, an "amp" as it were.

The band was on the verge of breaking up. Before the gig, Martin sat in a corner and wrote out his resignation. It was an awful time. It should have been the worst show ever, but at the beginning of the set, Dave Clark peeled off his shirt and wrapped himself in the Canadian flag, at which point our fortunes turned. He swung from a pipe that ran across the ceiling and the audience could not believe their eyes. It was like watching a professional wrestler in action. The show caught fire. One of the reasons we felt so high afterwards was because we'd expected it to be shitty and depressing. The rest of the trip was a similarly wild series of highs and lows. When we left our bed and breakfast the next morning, Martin realized that he'd forgotten his wallet. We convinced him to retrieve it, and when he did, the host family were waiting in their doorway, dressed in their Sunday best. He thought that it would be rude to count the money in front of them, so he waited till the train ride home. One hundred Irish pounds were missing. It was cheese sandwiches and half-pints and borrowed smokes for him the rest of the way, which, fortunately, was pretty much his diet anyway. But he had to ask for a cigarette every time he wanted one. Poor fellow.

So it's comforting to know that while I sit here remembering these heart-sinking times, the others have something different on their minds. On most nights, I can guess where Martin and Don are at, but it's difficult to read Tim, which is odd considering that I've studied him the longest. It's hard to tell what Tim is thinking even at the best of times. His contribution to the band's intellectual alchemy is to provide reason and foresight, and when paired with my pop-gun impulsiveness, this can lead to a strange mental dance. My arguments with him are often like flinging paint against a wall, so I'm surprised when his behaviour reminds me of myself. Tonight, with my body feeling as if it's already lying on my cool bed in Toronto, he commands the gig, and I'm reminded of why I play with him.

Before the show, Tim found himself in front of the Maritime Sailors' Museum. It's where the families of those missing on the *Edmund Fitzgerald* congregated on the evening the ship went down in 1975. It's also where Fred "Sonic" Smith of the MC5 was eulogized. This gave Tim the notion to sing Gordon Lightfoot's "The Wreck of the Edmund Fitzgerald," a song that we rarely perform live. There are many reasons why it's not a regular part of our repertoire. First, unless the song is rendered with passion and grit, it can sound disrespectful; we've had people come up to us whose grandparents were on that ship, and I'm glad they saw us on a night when we didn't miss the sixth, tenth, and fourteenth verses by mistake. Also, since the song is so long and dynamic, having to listen to a tepid interpretation of it is too much to ask of even the most forgiving audience. Sometimes we even find ourselves in the middle of a zipless version thinking, "Oh, geez, not another ten minutes of this . . ." The size of the song is daunting; it's hard enough for Tim to remember all the words, let alone infuse them with the kind of tension and drama they demand. We often have to coax him into performing it for these very reasons, but since he has suggested that we do the tune, I spend most of the gig anticipating it. It will be the last song of the first half of the Trouble at the Henhouse tour.

Perhaps I'm being cynical, but I doubt that any record-company executive would see much sense in devoting seventeen minutes of a forty-five-minute set in a premier American market to an epic folk dirge about death and water. "Play the hit!" they'd cry, their hands cupped around their mouths. But this song exists beyond the pale of commerce; it has more to do with the blood of our culture and the breath of our people than *Cashbox* magazine and *Pop-up Video*. That's why, when Tim sings it, his voice will ring through the hall like a depth sounder of sorrow, and Donny will smash his cymbals into ocean waves. The song will end and I'll lay my guitar at my feet like a wreath. I'll look into the crowd and notice the dark shapes rising out of their seats, standing. Martin will roll his languorous sea swells and seagull cries over the deep pooling silence and Gary Stokes, the lone figure at the sound board, will fade the last round note as if it were a half-dollar sinking into the abyss. To sleepy applause, the eye of the rink will close, and we will move, unbowed, from sea to home, if for a moment.

We were once a major-label band. Sire Records. I'm reminded of this every time we cross the border, because that's where it all went down, in New York City, mostly. Our first gig in New York was in 1991 and it was spectacular. We played at a place called Kenny's Castaways in the Village, a narrow, wood-panelled club with the front windows thrown open and American life pouring in. We shared the bill with four other Canadian groups as part of a northern showcase during the New Music Seminar, a yearly convergence of unsigned and up-and-coming alternative bands. Before our set, I was in a falafel place up the street and I remember looking down at my hands and noticing that they were shaking uncontrollably. Across the table, Martin bit into his pita and choked on it like he'd lost control of his functions. Outside, the streets were crowded with people there for the seminar and, being paranoid and naive, we believed that they were there for us, even though there were thousands of other gigs happening. We put tremendous pressure on ourselves thinking that if we didn't perform well, we'd be passed over in the rock-and-roll duck gallery. It felt like this was our one big chance, and even though we knew that our musical lives would be played out in Canada, we intended to win over the States. Our careers seemed boundless. World domination was not out of the question.

When we showed up at the club, the room was crawling with record-company moles. These people have the reputation for mining talent and spotting trends for their bosses, and they have an obvious look. With industry laminates looped around their necks, they appear too straight for rock-and-roll but too rock-and-roll to be straight, lacking credibility either way. Like young executives of other industries, they travel in packs, and you can spot them leaning together against the bar and nodding

approvingly, even if they think the band is shit. They're the
cyborgs of the music industry, totally bloodless and impassive
until they sniff potential, in which case they overdo their praise.
Craig Aaronson, Geffen's junior A&R scout, who once bid for
our services after *Whale Music* came out, described himself as
being like a "match on an oil slick, a spark at a brush fire," suggesting that he would make us famous, ostensibly at the cost of
environmental devastation.

So that night at Kenny's, we stood there pale and shaking, our
arseholes puckered, as the eyes of the industry set upon us, their
scorecards drawn. Our first few songs sounded breathless and flat
and my mouth was chalky and dry when I sang. But fear was our
engine, and we ended up playing the most inspired show of our
lives. The gig was like that classic film sequence where the guy
who's getting chased by the cops suddenly finds himself at a
track meet outrunning the competitors. The crowd is cheering,
absorbed by his performance but unaware that he's running for
his life. At Kenny's, the audience roared at us as we leaped across
the stage like acrobats. They didn't know that our performance
was nothing but a frantic attempt to keep the phantoms at bay.

The show ended with a medley of "Horses" and "Record
Body Count" that had all the suddenness of a fistfight. When
we finished our set, the crowd applauded wildly and slammed
their bottles against the tables in a terrifying din. I was panting
and bathed in sweat, and being admired across the room by a
young woman. On the tour bus a while later, I noticed that she
was looking at me through the window. I stepped out and asked
her why she'd been following me, and in difficult English (she
was Brazilian) she replied, "When I first saw you up there, I had

to know you." It was that kind of a night. I followed her on an odyssey through the streets of Manhattan on a quest for hashish. We snaked through traffic, cut across playgrounds and basketball courts, ran down alleyways and climbed over fences, until we came upon two men in their undershirts sitting on a curb in front of a New York deli. They exchanged a few words in Spanish, then one of them reached into his pocket and handed her the dope, at which point she lifted her skirt, flipped up the band of her panties, and slipped the stuff in her underwear.

Now, we are mostly a chaste band, so I did not have sex with this beautiful Brazilian fashion student because, well, I never thought it was possible (some would call us a dumb band). Besides, not only was I in love with Janet, but I'd also hooked up with my friend Joe, and it was enough just to be drinking and smoking with him in Manhattan. Joe had been in a terrible accident years earlier and we'd drifted apart. He'd suffered serious head injuries when he and his girlfriend stopped their car on the paved shoulder of a highway to look for a contact lens. They were slammed into by another motorist trying to pass a truck. Months after the accident, Joe's girlfriend sneezed and a two-inch sliver of glass shot out of her nose. They'd sued the offender, who had committed suicide after the accident, and Joe was awaiting settlement. That night we slipped back in time to before any of that happened. We drifted through the evening lost in a long silvery dream, the blue night dissolving into pink morning outside the Mayfair Hotel. We sat on a curb tipping back cans of beer, zealously toasting the Rheostatics' ascent to stardom. The sidewalks became crowded with men and women solemnly marching to work, to whom we raised our drinks and laughed. Two cops passed us in their police cruiser and just shook their heads. I'd made it through the night.

The following year, we played a showcase at Tramps in New York City, this time for Sire Records' president, Seymour Stein. Seymour was interested in signing us because Nigel Best — our manager and the rainmaker behind the Barenaked Ladies' early success in Canada — had a personal relationship with him. It's not unusual for record executives to sign groups on the advice of friends and confidants (it saves them the trouble of actually seeing the bands themselves, lazy bastards), so when Nigel asked Seymour if he was interested in buying the rights to two of our records for seventy-five thousand dollars, he probably figured that he could do a lot worse than sign the Rheostatics. He also offered deals to three other Toronto-based groups — Meryn Cadell, the Waltons, and Acid Test — and the rock press at home was once again atitter that one of America's most prescient talent scouts was interested in new Canadian artists.

A few months later, back in Toronto, we met Seymour face to face. Stein is a rock-and-roll legend, and I was acutely conscious of this at our meeting at the Four Seasons Hotel. I had read somewhere that when he went to ask for a job at *Billboard* magazine in the '50s, he spoke with such a thick Brooklyn accent he could not be understood. I also knew that Seymour and two other Warner Brothers executives, Mo Ostin and Lenny Waronker, liked to charter airplanes and just circle. He was also the man who had introduced punk and new wave to mainstream America, releasing time-defying albums by Blondie, Television, Talking Heads, the B-52's, Patti Smith, and the Ramones. Whether our deal was good or bad, the main reason I wanted to meet Seymour and sign with Sire was because it was the label that had put out records by the bands who had affected my life. There was an aura about that yellow label and its sinuous *S*, and Seymour, after all, had signed my favourite band, the Ramones.

Seymour is an eggman with silvery sideburns and a sunburned head. He looks perpetually tired. At our meeting at the Four Seasons, he never looked at me. Not once. I'm not sure he made eye contact with anyone in the band or if he even knew who we were. I could have thrown water in his face and he would have just kept staring over my shoulder, nonplussed and sleepy-eyed. Dave Clark asked him what kind of vision he had for the group, and all he could say was that he found our music "quirky," which is not what I expected from one of the world's greatest pop thinkers. Seymour sat at one end of the table and Nigel, who'd just dyed his hair blond and was looking stylish, sat at the other. It must have been a pretty weird scene: four guys in ski jackets and winter boots, bookended by two music-industry freaks. Later that night, Nigel got us invited to a Juno party, where we rubbed elbows with k.d. lang and Blue Rodeo, which I took as another sign that our time had arrived. At one point I saw Gordon Lightfoot standing alone in a corner of the room. He appeared as he does on the cover of *Endless Wire*, with those dark sunglasses and moustache. When he left the party, I followed him to the elevator, hoping to give him the copy of *Whale Music* that was in my pocket, but he was gone. On my way back into the party, Nigel grabbed my arm and said, "Dave, I really think you guys should take this deal."

The next week, we signed.

That was the last I saw of Seymour Stein. We opened for Blue

Rodeo at the Bottom Line and Seymour was supposed to come, but he didn't. I still have the card saying STEIN, which we'd used to reserve his table.

KEN TOBIAS: After I moved to Montreal from Halifax, my manager called me up and said, "Bill Medley from the Righteous Brothers is in town. I'm gonna try to get in touch with him and tell him about you. I want you to put on your coat and get your guitar ready." My manager called him and spoke with Michael Patterson, Bill's pianist and one of his partners in management. Patterson told him, "Well, if he can get here in fifteen minutes, we'll listen." Bill was staying just down the street at the Holiday Inn, so it was easy. The next thing I know, I'm pounding on the door of Patterson's hotel room. He greeted us wearing a tuxedo top and boxer shorts. He let us in and told me to start singing. I sat down on the bed and played four or five songs, and after I finished, he said, "You're good. I like these songs." He called Bill up to the room and I sang them again. Bill asked me if I wanted to be his guest at the club where they were playing, and, of course, I said that I did. That night I found myself sitting at a private table with my manager, watching the Righteous Brothers. It was incredible. About halfway through the show, Bill stopped the band. He went up to the microphone and announced, "Ladies and gentleman, I'd like to introduce to you an up-and-coming star of Canada. I'm sure you know who he is. Kenny Tobias. Stand up, Kenny!"

RICKY PATTERSON: Three's a Crowd were hired to play Expo 67 in Montreal. At the time, our lead singer, Donna, was going out with a guy who was an entrepreneurial drug dealer around

Toronto. He had a reputation for being involved in all kinds of bullshit. Cass Elliot and Denny Doherty of the Mamas and Papas were coming up to Canada to go to Expo and he was hired to be their I'll-get-you-whatever-you-want guy. They were staying at the Bonaventure Hotel and he made sure that they came to Expo just as we were playing. The Mamas and Papas were getting ready to break up, and Cass was thinking about becoming a producer. As soon as she saw us, she thought, This is it. This is a band that is like the Mamas and Papas. They're entertaining, can sing, and have great songs. She picked us as her first band to produce. So we left the Ontario Pavilion and drove straight to New York. We did three songs, sent them to L.A., and that was it. Within a month, we were signed to ABC–Dunhill. They told us to pack up our gear, go home, say goodbye to our parents, and get on the next plane. When we got off the plane, a limo was waiting for us and photographers were taking our picture as we came down the steps. I thought, "This is it. This is what you've been dreaming about all your life. If it stops tomorrow, it doesn't matter, because you've got here." Well, it didn't stop tomorrow, but it didn't last very long.

KEN TOBIAS: After the Righteous Brothers concert, Bill Medley loosened his tie and walked over to a little piano set up on the stage. There was no one in the club except for a few people sweeping up. He turned to me and said, "Come here, Kenny. I wrote this song and I'd like your opinion." Right then, I knew he was testing me. All I could do was say to myself, Now, whatever you do, Tobias, don't lie. Don't fuckin' lie. It was a good song, I enjoyed it. He finished it, looked at me for a response, and I said, "Well, I really liked the song, but there was one part in the middle that didn't really grab me." "You're right," said Bill. "That section's been bugging me too." Then he looked me straight in the eye, and said, "Kenny, how'd you like to come to California?"

GREG GODOVITZ: We had big dreams. We went to San Francisco for the first Fludd album. We were signed to Warners. We flew down to do the record; it was the first time I'd ever been on an airplane. I was nineteen years old. There were two limousines and a beautiful girl waiting for us. She said, "This is from the record company. Enjoy your evening," and she gave us five hundred dollars each. We all caught the clap.

We recorded with Freddie Kitaro, who did Santana. Adam Mitchell of the Paupers produced us. Later, we went to the Manor in England to record. Mike Oldfield was there making *Tubular Bells* and people like Graham Bond were stopping by. Richard Branson gave me a black top hat for my twentieth birthday. The people at the studio expected a bunch of lumberjacks to show up, but by then we'd already been to England a few times, so when we showed up, we were dandies, dedicated followers of fashion. The first night I was there, I banged two of the chambermaids by pretending I was afraid that the house was haunted. I'm told that they named a room in my honour – the Fludd Suite – because of the debauchery. When we weren't in the studio (which was more often than not), we were either in the pub or the wine cellar or at this beautiful bacchanalian feast every night. The fire would be going, we'd be dancing on the table and drinking. Who wanted to record? This was absolute paradise.

RICKY PATTERSON: Cass Elliot eventually bowed out of producing us because she really didn't know what she was doing in the

Three's a Crowd. Left to right: David Wiffen, Dennis Pendrith, Colleen Peterson, Bruce Cockburn, Rick Patterson

studio. Steve Berry ended up doing the album. It was still a thrilling time. Dunhill used to get free tickets for their artists to go to concerts, movies, and events so that they could be seen. We saw the premier of *Camelot* at the Cinerama on Santa Monica Boulevard. Dunhill sent a limo to pick us up. When we got there, there was a crowd, spotlights, the whole deal. When our limo pulled up and we stepped out, people looked at us, like, Who the fuck are they? We didn't care, we were stoned and having fun. After the movie we went to a deli to eat. Everybody was talking about Richard Harris; they'd all fallen in love with him.

A week or so later, we got a call from Steve. We had four more tracks to do on our album. He said that they'd just signed a song-writer who had some new songs and he wanted us to go over to the Dunhill studio and hear him play some of them. So we did. A guy wearing a leather jacket came in and sat down at the piano. It was Jimmy Webb. One of the first songs he played was a number called "MacArthur Park." It bowled everybody over. Steve said, "How would you guys feel about doing that one?" and we told him that it was a wonderful song but that it would use up half the album. Besides, we had great songs by Bruce Cockburn and David Wiffen written already. We left it. Steve said, "Okay then. I'm gonna get Richard Harris to sing it." We looked at each other and rolled our eyes.

GREG GODOVITZ: One night at the Manor, I went down to the living room and Mike Oldfield was there. I said, "It's a bit chilly in here. I think I'll start a fire." I went over and, honest to God, I grabbed a sheet of music from *Tubular Bells* and I lit it on fire. Mike started screaming. He jumped over tables to get to it, and he finally stomped it out. He wouldn't come near me for the next two weeks.

During our visit, Ed had leaped off the dining-room table and broken his foot. One evening, while he was sitting by the fire in his cast, we went out back and loaded our pockets with eggs. We asked Ed, "Comfy? Foot hurting a bit? Enjoying the drink, are we? The fire?" Then we pelted him. We just unloaded. This was in this amazing mansion with these beautiful tapestries. It started a fight that had people pouring buckets of ice water on each other. We destroyed tapestries worth tens of thousands of dollars. We went berserk. Finally, I went back to my suite. There was a fire going, the bedsheets had been turned down. It was so peaceful. I

Fludd at the Manor. Greg Godovitz, second from right.

crawled in; I just slid in and closed my eyes. Then I went, "Oh, fuck." I pulled back the sheets. They'd put shit in my bed.

SKINNY TENN: Fludd signed with Warner Brothers in Los Angeles. We should have all fuckin' moved there, man, and just played the local bars. But we didn't know better. We waited for things to happen. Warner said they were gonna do things for us, but they didn't.

BOB SEGARINI: After the Family Tree broke up, I sat in a room in a little house with an old AIWA reel-to-reel tape machine and an upright piano and I wrote a pop opera called *Mrs. Butters* that told the life of this person. It was very Harry Nilssonesque. I slaved over this record for a year. Of course, we weren't allowed to play on the record because, in those days, the studio guys did everything. For this session, they used Mike Melbourne and Larry Knechtal and Jim Gordon, crazy Jim. The first thing he ever said to me was, "You know the Red Chinese are gonna atomic bomb the rest of the world in 1969?" Years later of course, Jim chopped his mother up into tiny little pieces and then sent his grandmother a mother's day card. He's still in a rubber room.

Robert Moog himself set up a Moog synthesizer for us to use. It was as big as a swimming-pool wall; he was up there on a little platform operating it, and he looked just like Dilbert. So we did the album: George Tipton did the horn charts, Derek Taylor played it for the Beatles, and Dick James, their publisher, wanted the rights for England and Europe. So RCA sent a reel-to-reel tape over there. Bernie Taupin and Reg Dwight [Elton John] were working in his office at the time, and later Bernie told me that that record was what had inspired them to get good. We did one more single for RCA, and then they said, "Um, we're sorry. We don't think we want to continue." It was devastating. *Mrs. Butters* was in American libraries for thirty years. The Joffrey Ballet was going do a ballet on it. I couldn't understand why it didn't work. It was heartbreaking.

GREG GODOVITZ: Goddo had the same management team as Long John Baldry, Angela Bowie, and Cathy MacDonald. One night, we were playing at Uncle Sam's in Niagara Falls, and they tried to get Clive Davis, head of Arista Records, to come and see us. That night was the worst snowstorm of the year, but the place was still jam-packed; Goddo was in its heyday. All night, we kept looking out into the crowd, thinking, Where are they? Where are they? They picked up Clive in New York and flew him to Buffalo where the plane sat on the tarmac for three hours while Clive fought with his boyfriend. What the management should have done was take Clive and his boyfriend to the hotel and said, "Let's do this another night." But instead they insisted on driving them to our gig. When they got to the club, the boyfriend came in and the place was going ga-ga. We were in the middle of an encore, people were going nuts. Clive Davis refused to get out of the car. He wouldn't sign us on the principle that the band had ruined his evening.

RONNIE KING: In 1965, our manager, Mel Shaw, came to us and said, "There's this Calgary loyalist who wants to invest ten grand in a band who will name themselves after something that represents Calgary. We've come up with something. I want you to guess what it is." Kim Berly, our drummer, said, "Oh no, Mel. Not the Stampeders. For god's sake, not the Stampeders! There's the Stampeder football team, the Stampede hotel, Stampede outhouses, Stampede Motors . . ." To which Mel replied, "Yes. But they don't know that in the States or South America or Europe!" So we became the Stampeders. Mel Shaw thought the Stampeders were going to invade the East with something he called WestBeat.

SKINNY TENN: A lot of Canadian bands used to be pretty schmaltzy. But nobody was ever more schmaltzy and had worse promo shots and costumes than the Stampeders. God bless them, they had a top-five *Billboard* hit, but they were managed by Mel Shaw. I never talked to him because, frankly, I thought he was pretty square.

RONNIE KING: After two years of touring northern Ontario in obscurity, the Stampeders came to Toronto. The first place we went was the Bigland Booking Agency. We thought we were going to see a Capitol Records–sized building, but it was just a one- or two-storey place. We arrived in our Cadillac hauling a U-Haul, and Mel said, "Hats on!" We went, "What?" And he repeated, "Hats on!" We said, "You gotta be kidding." But he said, "Listen, we've got an image, okay? We've got a WestBeat image that we've gotta project." So we rummaged in the back of the U-Haul and found our cowboy boots and matching hats. We traipsed up there, around eight o'clock at night, only to find one guy – local musician Bobby Chris – doodling on the desk. "Where is everybody?" asked Mel. Chris looked up at him and said, "Nobody's here, man, but me."

STEVE SMITH: Jason was predominantly a cover band. We played at Cornell University and Deep Purple's manager came to see us. We had a great night, and I thought this was going to be our ticket. After the show, he said to me, "You did all those cover tunes. I know all these people whose songs you're doing. They do what they do better than you do what they do. What do *you* do?" When he said that, I knew he was right. My wife and I decided we had to do our own thing. It was really hard to talk the rest of the band into it because we'd become very comfortable with our show, so we left the group. We started Smith and Smith because we wanted to do something that was ours, whatever the consequences.

RIK EMMETT: When I was in Act Three, Gil Moore and Mike Levine made me an offer. They wanted to put together a three-piece hard-rock extravaganza. They needed a guitarist who could sing and write. They'd already auditioned Jerry Doucette and a few others, but they wanted me. These guys were sharp. Levine already had his own record label and had set up distribution. Gil Moore had been on the executive of the Toronto Musicians Association. Mike had managed Leigh Ashford, a Toronto band. Gil had had a band that did well, too. So here were these two guys sitting at a table in a bar with a cheque for fifteen hundred bucks from Attic Records going, "Look. Look. We have an advance and a real record deal." I didn't know what to think. At the time, I fancied myself a musician, so I had to find out what these guys played like before I did anything, even though that aspect didn't seem to matter much to them. They already had lots of contracts for gigs. Gil was his own booking agent; he had an agent's licence, his own little P.A. company that he was running out of his garage, a nice house in suburban Mississauga, a couple of Ford Thunderbirds in the driveway. He was very together business-wise. They had posters printed up with the devil's head and fire and brimstone. The band was going to be called Triumph, but they had all this devil imagery; there was something very Second City about it.

We sat down and played, and I won't put any Shinola on it: they were terrible. Levine had no technique and Gil was sloppy. I was thinking, Oh, my god, but then they sat down and talked more about business. I could tell that they could play, they just didn't really care about that end of it. Here I was, thinking, I can change them! I can mould them! They were more than happy to give me the answers that I wanted to hear. I asked them, "Would you guys dedicate yourself to the aspect of writing and rehearsing?" "Absolutely!" they said. So I went and stabbed my good friend Denton from Act Three in the back. That's how it started.

DENTON YOUNG: Rik and I started a band called Act Three. I made a mirrorball, we got costumes, I made a drum riser. Guys from Max Webster were coming up the street to see us play at Yonge Station. We were playing very progressive stuff. We were exciting; three white kids, all of whom sang and were proficient on their instruments. We were so progressive that the Canadian recording industry never would have signed us. They would have never thought we were saleable. Then Rik took the offer from Triumph, and that was that. There was no point going on with the bass player, because we never really got along anyway. Rik and I were the band. I was upset, but I couldn't blame him. He wanted to get married and have a future. It was presented to him. If he'd stayed with me, he might have regretted it anyway because our managers at the time were jerks. They just sent us out to bars and collected the commission. If the band got lucky and got a deal, management cashed in. But really, they just soaked you.

JERRY DOUCETTE: In '67, I played in Toronto with a band called Tribe. They were a good band but they were managed by this woman who musta weighed three hundred pounds. She was real domineering. She was lying, cheating. Our bass player was screwing her, so they were in cahoots. She owed me a lot of money. I went to Gil Moore at the musicians union and I told him about this. He called a meeting. I asked her lawyer what was in his briefcase, and he said, "Dynamite. We're gonna nail ya." My heart fell down to my crotch. The meeting started and I explained my part.

The next thing I know, a long-haired guy came through the door, a musician; then another and another. I'd never seen them before in my life. They'd heard what was going on – that I was taking her to court – and they all came to back me. They talked about their experiences with her. It shut the case right down. I got my money back.

KIM MITCHELL: My advice to young musicians: Get a good lawyer, a good accountant, a good manager, and bring along a large bottle of mouthwash.

HOLLY WOODS: My advice is to go as far as you can by yourself. Don't let anyone tell you how it's supposed to be done or how your records are going to be sold. Make it yours. Record companies and managers were trying to mould me all the time: how to dress, how to look, how to talk. Tighter, shinier, higher, longer, skinnier. All of those things. Make-up. A couple of times they tried to change the music based on directives straight from the head fat cat. I listened because I was under contract. But you had to stand up for yourself, even though when you do, you take flak. I was called a bitch and a moaner. You name it, I've been called it by people in the business. If I was a man, I probably would have been listened to.

DARBY MILLS: For a long time, I never blamed my problems on being a woman. I didn't want to admit it was a problem because I always felt like one of the guys. There wasn't any segregation. I had no better a vocabulary than most of the men I worked with. I did my best to fit in. But once I got into recording, I was by far

the youngest person around the Headpins. I was the most inexperienced. I was worlds away from where these people were, especially Ab [Bryant] and Bill [Henderson]. I was this little kid
they'd picked up. It became a problem; not always because I was a
woman, but because I was younger. I had to be tougher on the
tour bus after the show. I had to be one of the guys. If I'd acted
like a woman – or a lady, should I say? – and been completely
grossed by what I saw, then I'd have alienated myself even more
than I already was as a female on a tour bus with twelve guys. In
the hey, hey, heyday of the Headpins, I had a female companion
out there for a bit, but it didn't answer everything. It got to a
point after a while when I was like, "Check out the blonde, check
out the blonde." I still am. I look for women more than I do men,
by far, because I've lived with some crazy men. Crazy men. All of
them unmarried, of course.

SHARI ULRICH: In the days of the Pied Pumpkin, I was very
determined to be one of the guys. I knew how to schlep the gear
and set it up. Whenever some guy came along and tried to take
the speaker cabinet from me, I'd say, "I can do it." Of course now
I ask sweetly, and with great happiness, "Can you take this for
me?" Later on, in the Hometown Band, I never quite fit in; there
was pressure on me to be the rock chick. I didn't really represent
the guys in the band the way they liked. I'm sure each one of
them had a different idea, but the drummer, who was the rocki-
est of the bunch, felt that my appearance and my presence didn't
work for him. A friend told me once that, before we'd ever met,
she saw me set up my saxophone at the Hometown Band's A&M
showcase in L.A. and she thought, Gee, that's cool. They've got a
female roadie. I've never seen that before.

GALE GARNETT: I love music, but I *hate* the music business. I think that it's mobbed-up and bogus and filled with too many drugs, too many people acting badly, girls who lie down for people they don't like because they're in bands, people who expect you to provide them with girls, and roadies with packed noses. There was also a serious hygiene problem in the music business. Guys' underwear was as good as their girlfriends, and I was frequently on stage with a lot of people who smelled bad.

America. New York City. Sire Records.

Seymour Stein.

I signed because of the Ramones.

Along with Rush and Max Webster, the Ramones had a profound effect on my life. What really got me was their speed. To a fourteen-year-old kid supercharged on junk food and sports, they played at the ideal clip: fast. Compared to Kansas and Styx and Mountain and all of those other lazy rock bands who ruled FM radio in the '70s (these acts have been supplanted, I might add, by a younger, though no less indolent, rank), the Ramones' songs sounded as if the deejay had forgotten to return the format from 45 to 33 rpm. This probably explains why so few radio stations played them; they made a lot of deejays look like idiots, which isn't the best thing to do when you're trying to get your music aired.

I had no idea what the Ramones were about. I'd never seen a picture of them and I doubted that my neighbourhood record store, Music World at the Albion Mall, stocked any of their albums. But when I first heard "Rockaway Beach" and "Sheena

Is a Punk Rocker" coming out of the little radio propped up on
the curb outside my house – I was listening to Bob Macowitz's
Sunday afternoon show on Q107 at the time, throwing around a
Nerf football with my best friend, Johnny Wersta – it was one
of those few instances when I knew while it was happening that
I would always remember the moment. I never thought that
anything that positive would have such a strong effect on me.
That day, I asked myself two questions:

Who are the Ramones?

Is this what love feels like?

Then I saw them play. It was the summer of 1979, and like
thousands of other Etobicoke kids, I was into hard rock. Punk
was something you only saw on the news. I wore a jean jacket
with AC/DC, RUSH, AEROSMITH scrawled in red Magic Marker
across the back, which I'd illustrated at school with the jacket
spread on my knees under my desk so the teacher couldn't see. I
also carried around Rik Emmett's guitar pick, which I'd bought
at a Triumph show. Rik hadn't actually used it to play, but at least
it was signed. Not that he'd sat down and written on the thing,
mind you; it was only an imprint of his signature. They sold
them in three-packs outside their shows. Still, he'd endorsed it,
and I was convinced that it had magical powers.

The Ramones performed as part of the Canadian World
Music Festival at the CNE. It was billed like that, I think, because
Nazareth were from Scotland. Otherwise, the line-up reflected
the biggest hard-rock draws of the day – Ted Nugent, Aerosmith, Johnny Winter, Goddo, Nazareth, and, inexplicably, the
Ramones. My dad dropped my friend Rick and me off at the
show at around four in the morning. We lined up with the stoners
and heads, who were already into their dope-bong, air-guitar,

tongue-in-the-mouth, "Stairway to Heaven," sex-in-a-sleeping-bag, wine-jug, rock-and-roll-hootchie-koo party. They were like the people I'd seen on television at California Jam, only real. Hours later, the line-up dissolved into a mob around the front gates of Exhibition Stadium. Being small and unwieldy, Rick and I were helpless within the crush of long-haired yetis and their maidens moving towards the gates. We suffered an elbow or two to the head, but it was worth it when we found ourselves pressed against the bodies of teenage vixens who back in high school wouldn't even look at us. As the mob grew, police on horseback showed up, but the organizers rolled open the gates before things got out of hand. Rick and I spilled onto the turf, climbed to our legs and gambolled to the front of the stage.

We found a good spot about twenty feet back. The crowd went crazy when Goddo hit the stage. For their last song, bassist Greg Godovitz ripped apart his purple jumpsuit and threw it into the crowd; the fans fought over it like voracious sled-dogs. There was dope everywhere. The heads had taken off their shirts and were huffing joints and tugging on wineskins. Two enormous speaker towers framing the stage blasted "Jet Airliner" by Steve Miller while a hot-air balloon sailed over the stadium. Frisbees hovered above the crowd. The sun was blazingly hot, and a few young women stripped down to their bikinis. Rick had a camera and was taking pictures. He got most of the bands' performances and probably a bit of tit, too. Every now and then, we looked at each other and just nodded our heads. We couldn't believe that we were part of something so amazing.

Big old jet airliner
Don't carry me too far away, hey, hey

Big old jet airliner
'Cause it's here that I've got to stay.

GREG GODOVITZ: When we did those arena tours — playing with
Rush or Aerosmith — we never looked at ourselves as the opening
act. We went out and killed every night. There was not one gig in
an arena where we didn't get an encore. That day at the Ex, we
played and we were getting a good reaction for ten in the
morning, or eleven, or whenever it was. I remember, at the end,
trying to get the crowd involved in one of those requisite "Let
me hear you say *ya!*" things and they wouldn't do it. So I said,
"Fuck ya. You're gonna sleep? *I'm going to sleep!*" and I lay down on
the stage. Of course it's only a trio, so now the bass is gone, the
lead singer's gone, the front man's gone, it's just the guitar
pumping and the drums. All of a sudden, the crowd got on their
feet. I got back up and said, "*Are we awake now?*" Then I gave them
the line I'd tried before, and they did it. It was our last song, and
we walked off. I remember walking farther and farther from the
stage really feeling good. The crowd was going nuts. I could hear
this roar getting bigger and bigger and bigger. We went back out
there. I felt like a king.

Then the Ramones played. They were unlike anything I'd ever
seen. They had black leather jackets and jeans torn at the knees.
They had long hair that hung in their faces. They were loud.
They were ugly. And they were fast. Two things struck me: First,
while the other bands wanted to be perceived as fucked-up and
sleazy and lawless, most of them looked pretty, wore expensive

jewellery, and had fancy amps. The Ramones, on the other hand, looked like they didn't have two cents to scrape together and hadn't eaten in weeks. Second, they also sounded way better than any band I'd ever seen or heard. This impression is a little harder to figure. They were using cheap Mosrite guitars wired through Marshall stacks; basically crap equipment. They had an early position in the line-up, so they couldn't have had full use of the sound system either. But they sounded the best probably because they were communicating the clearest, at least to me. They knew who they wanted to be better than anyone else on that bill. As a result, the rest of the day has been effectively sluiced from my memory.

At first I was way too absorbed by the Ramones' set to realize that most of the crowd was not. I noticed something was awry when I looked up and saw a shoe flying end over end through the air. Then I saw a can of Coke go past. Then a belt, a saddlebag, a beer, some batteries, a baseball glove, an orange, some cookies, more beer, then a lighter. Then a seat cushion. The sky was filled with debris.

It was raining garbage.

I looked around. "Fucking faggots!" "Get off the fucking stage!" "Fucking queers!" "*You suck!*" The heads were screaming. They'd been lying around like sleepy cattle for hours, and this sudden explosion of hatred was the first bit of activity they'd shown all day. It was horrible. I watched as bassist Dee Dee Ramone got whacked in the forehead with an Insta-Matic camera, which exploded magnificently upon impact. A few years later, Joey Ramone told me that someone had thrown a bag of sandwiches at them which they ended up eating for lunch.

The Ramones fans howled back. There were about twenty of them, twenty against twenty thousand. Dee Dee and Johnny marched to the lip of the stage and gave the crowd the finger, pumping their arms up and down. They unplugged their instruments and stormed off the stage. By now the crowd had redirected their rage from the band to their fans, who were wading into the foam-mouthed throng. The stoners swarmed them and they were wrestled to the ground. The police finally jumped in as "Black Dog" thundered through the P.A., Bonzo's kick drum sounding like a prize-fighter working the heavy bag. The stoners eventually tired and went back to pawing their ladies, while the punks, ragged and bloodied, were escorted by the cops out of the park. The crowd booed. I was presented with a very important and fundamental teenage question – which rock-and-roll force would I align with?

If there hadn't been so many of them, would the heads have behaved the way they did? Probably not. The more I watched them – their bloodshot eyes and wild hair, stained teeth and sun-tanned chests – the more they gave me the creeps. They'd shown ten times the enthusiasm for driving the Ramones from the stage as they had in bringing Goddo back for an encore. I'd never be one of them. The punks, on the other hand, had put their skin on the line for their band. I might not ever be one of them either, but at least we shared a passion for music. I, too, would have bitterly defended my bands, it's just that I'd never had the chance to because, well, everybody liked Rush. However, no one liked the Ramones, except for those twenty fans in whom they had inspired fearless loyalty. My brain was wracked with uncertainty. Then Nazareth played. I couldn't even watch.

RIK EMMETT: One time we were playing River Bend, an outdoor festival in Cincinnati. We were going to the gig, it was the middle of the day. The limo driver usually does funerals, and he's very inexperienced. He seems to be going a weird way to the gig, not in the direction of where we think the backstage is. In fact, he seems to be going through the main gates of the park. We asked him, "Are you sure you know the way?" and he reassured us that he did. Now he's going down a roadway into the park. There's lots of people walking by going, "Who the fuck brought a limo in here? Who's in it?" He eventually gets down to the bottom, and now he's going really slowly because there's lots of pedestrian traffic. All of sudden, we encounter all of these people sitting down. We're pointing at the *front* of the stage. He tries backing up, but more and more people are arriving, blocking his way. He decides he'll just forge ahead and toot his horn and everybody will just clear out of his way. He starts doing this and people are turning around going, "Fuck off! We ain't moving!" They're planted on the grass; they won't so much as budge, especially for a limo. It goes from bad to worse. It's a nightmare being trapped in this little tiny box. By now, people are starting to kick the limo as it passes, hoofing the side panels as they roll out of its way. Some guy climbs up on top of us and starts doing a dance on the roof. You can hear the roof cracking and bending. Pretty soon, fruit starts hitting the car and splattering across the windows. Two guys get up and start rocking the car back and forth. By the time we get to the stage, the car is totalled. There's no hubcaps left, the antennas are broken off, there's smashed fruit all over it. Oh, I played a superb gig that day.

I got to know the Ramones. By their third or fourth visit to Toronto, Joey Ramone knew me well enough to call me by name. In 1983, I chatted with him at the Chelsea Hotel in Toronto, and after the interview, I thanked him for taking the time out of his schedule to talk to me. There was a pause.

"So what are you doing now?" he said.

"Not much," I replied.

"You wanna hang out or something?"

You wanna hang out or something?

It was beyond my most insane fantasies. He came down in the elevator wearing a striped pink shirt and jeans and running shoes. Joey stands about six-foot-five, so when he walked towards us across the lobby, everybody's head turned. He asked us if we'd take him to get his glasses fixed, so we climbed into the Delta 88 and drove around Toronto looking for a place. I remember checking my rear-view mirror before changing lanes and there he was, sitting in the back seat. It freaked me out. We ended up at the old Public Optical on Queen Street. A cherubic man in a lab coat looked the glasses over and said that he'd fix the nose piece free of charge. The fellow spoke mainly to us, as if he didn't think that Joey would understand. I finally said, "Talk to him, they're his glasses," but he didn't bother. I think he thought that Joey was from the mental home or that he was retarded because of his hard-to-understand nasal accent and because he looked so weird and sickly. We sat at the counter while the man fixed Joey's specs. After a few minutes, he came over and placed the glasses on our hero's face.

"There. Just like John Lennon," he noted.

He had no idea what he'd just said.

That night, the Ramones played at the Masonic Temple. After the show, Joey asked us if we wanted to go to their gig in Ottawa.

Joey Ramone, centre

Danny Clinch

We said that we did, and so four of my friends and I drove to see them at Barrymore's. Joey opened the show by saying "This one's for Dave and the boys from Toronto! *Take it, Dee Dee!*" One, two, three, four! Then they played "Blitzkrieg Bop."

My friend Gordie missed two exams because of the trip.

He failed grade thirteen as a result.

GEOFF DAVIS: Once, after a Max Webster rehearsal, Alex Lifeson of Rush drove me to high school. It was weird. He was asking, "So this is where you go to school, man?" I thanked him for the ride. Then he said, "No. Wait. What're you taking? Trig? Calculus?" He came in and walked around for a while and checked the place out. Then he left.

RONNIE KING: A lot of the instrumental bands were big in Calgary – the Ventures, Jimmy Gilmour and the Fireballs, the Shadows – and we tried to copy them. We all had echo units and did our kick steps. One time the Ventures played at the Gardens, which was the second floor of a community hall. I was thirteen years old and in a band called the Echoes and we had matching red vests, which we wore to the concert. The Ventures mentioned us on stage that night. They said, "The Echoes are here," and we almost put our hands up to show the crowd who we were. We got signed drumsticks from the drummer.

RICKY PATTERSON: I was very tiny as a child. When I was nine, I looked like I was six. I was a tap dancer and I used to compete in an amateur contest at a golf and country club in Hull. I won a lot, so eventually they said they'd pay me ten dollars to be a headliner on the show. So once a week my mother bundled me up, we'd go to the club, and I'd perform. One night, the bandleader, a fellow named Bob Simpson, said to my mother, "I want to take Richard somewhere to meet someone very special. It's sort of a secret and I can't tell you where we're going, but it'll be okay." So during one of the breaks, we jumped into a cab and went over to a nightclub called Standish Hall. We were taken through the side door down to a dressing room. We knocked on the door. I had a full set of tails on. We walked in, and there was Louis Armstrong. He was wearing a white shirt, white boxer shorts, black stockings with garters, and black patent-leather shoes. I was introduced to him as a great dancer, so he picked up his trumpet, started to play, and I danced for him.

BARRY ALLEN: We used to go down to Clovis, New Mexico, and record with Norman Petty, the fellow who discovered Buddy Holly. Norman had a band called the Fireballs who came up here and we shared the bill with them. We got to know them, so they said, "Why don't you come down to Clovis and record with Norman?" There were no studios in Edmonton; there were a few in Toronto, but for us it was easier to go to New Mexico than to drive all the way out east. We'd play a gig on Saturday night and then get in the car and start driving. We'd get to Clovis at about noon on Monday. When we first started recording, we cut straight to two-track, and then we went to four and then eight. It slowly evolved. The studio was where Buddy Holly recorded, too, and his parents used to come over to hang out and watch us record.

SKINNY TENN: The Witnesses did one tour with Roy Orbison. We did ten cities in fourteen days from Vancouver to Winnipeg, and on three or four of those days there were two shows. Orbison was on a bus and we were in a station wagon with a U-Haul, doing the same miles. We never missed a show. We played Saskatoon with him, feeling like the conquering heroes. Not that Roy Orbison said, "How about those Witnesses?" He said nothing. We never spoke to Roy. He never spoke to us. He didn't speak to anybody.

DANNY MARKS: Edward Bear opened for Led Zeppelin twice; once at the Rockpile, once at the O'Keefe Centre. I recently got this book of Led Zeppelin bootlegs, and in it there's a picture of Robert Plant plugging into my Fender amp. Being British, Plant had never used a Fender amp before, and he was going "Whoaa! I've never 'eard anything like this!" I thought, "This guy is gonna blow my amp up!" so I went over and flicked the toggle switch. One of the pick-ups on the guitar went silent. He looked at me and said, "Don't touch that, man, that's not your guitar!" I said, "Well, that's not your amp, is it?" People never bought that story because Robert Plant doesn't play guitar. But that picture proves two things: He does play guitar, and it was the first time he'd heard a Fender amp.

HOLLY WOODS: I saw Led Zeppelin each time they toured. One time, I somehow managed to wangle my way backstage. I kept screaming Robert Plant's name over and over. I was every bit of sixteen. Finally, during "Moby Dick," he came over to get a drink and he saw me standing there, screaming. I had no breath left, no voice. He folded his arms together across his chest and said, "Well, hello. I'm Robert." I can't believe I didn't pass out. After the show, I was driving home with my boyfriend and a limo behind us kept flashing its lights. We pulled over and it turned out to be them. They were lost, they couldn't find the Holiday Inn. Robert and Jimmy were in the back. We explained the way to the Holiday Inn, and as we were walking back to the car, Robert yelled, "I'd like to suck your tits!" I didn't have any. I was sixteen.

KELLY JAY: We worked a couple of gigs for Trudeau. It was really cool being paid by him. That was part of the agreement. I said, "We'll play if Pierre will cut the cheque." He did. And, you know, cats can talk to kings. He was such an interesting guy with remarkable people around him. Trudeau would talk about things that he wanted to talk about, and if you got him engaged in conversation, he'd stay there and give you eye contact. He was talking to you, he was with you. He'd listen to your ideas, give you his own, and scoff when you were out of line. I remember we did Lester Pearson's birthday at Maple Leaf Gardens. Before the show, we said to Pierre, "Look, man, come out and play tambourine with us or something. You can say some words in the middle of our set. You can talk to the kids." But he wouldn't. After our set, seven thousand kids cleared out, and I said to him, "See, you should have done it."

TERRY DAVID MULLIGAN: There was a coffeehouse in Regina called the Fourth Dimension. There was also one in Winnipeg, Saskatoon, and Calgary. That's where I first met Joni Mitchell, back when it was Chuck and Joni. I had a deal with the Fourth Dimension where I took care of the house where all the artists stayed. They would stay in one side, I'd stay in the other. Back then, artists didn't talk about going to the States to get famous. It was more a case of getting from gig to gig, of surviving. Joni and Chuck, for instance, were pretty poor. They couldn't have been happy either; a few years later, they broke up and went their separate ways. Joni gave me a sense of missing out. She'd talk about New York and Toronto and going on the road. I thought, "Here I am sitting around in Regina. I gotta get out of here."

Years later, a little older, a little less starstruck. I was walking down Grafton Street in Dublin when I noticed a poster on a wall:

RAMONES

THIS SATURDAY NIGHT

TV CLUB

I told all of my friends. They were over the moon at the pos-sibility of meeting their idols. On the day of the show, I hung around the club trying to convince the security guards that I knew the band. When they finally let me in, I found them in the middle of sound-check, which consisted of a roadie standing in front of Johnny's amp playing the same chord over and over again on his guitar at ear-splitting volume. I stood at the back of the hall and taped some of it. Afterwards, I found Joey back stage.

"Hey, Joey! How's it going?"

"All right. How're you?"

"Great. It's Dave. Remember? From Toronto?"

"Uh, no, man."

"Remember? We got your glasses fixed."

"Huh?"

"We came down to the gig in Ottawa. After the show we drove

to Hull and bought a pile of beer. Remember? The guy ripped us off?"

"Oh."

"Then we drank it in your hotel room. Remember? Dee Dee and Richie were hanging out too, and my friend asked if he could have your sock as a souvenir?"

"Oh ya. Ya, wait. Ya, ya. Howya doin'?"

"Great. It's great to see you."

"Ya. Okay. Now I feel right at home."

We talked about the tour and playing in Europe and the new record and about Canadian fans, whom Joey said were some of the best in the world. He told me that when they played Toronto in 1978, they were booked into a good hotel, for the first time ever. The promoters were the Two Garys, who'd also given us our first gig. I wished him luck with the concert, and he told me to come down the next day for their autograph session at Comet Records.

When I arrived, Joey was sitting at a table with a bunch of posters in front of him. His skin looked blue and he could barely keep his head up.

"You got something for me to autograph?" he asked, his eyes downcast, his speech groggy.

"Joey. It's me, Dave."

He looked up.

He had no idea who I was.

I left the store.

Outside, the rain felt like spiders.

TORONTO, PART I

"Above the din, we listen for other music."
B. W. Powe, *A Canada of Light*

When we first started playing around Toronto in the early 1980s, Canadian bands were not our heroes. We were taken with the new-wave groups from the United States and England. The few Canadian bands we admired – the Rent Boys, Inc. and the Dave Howard Singers – had fled to England to further their careers. The lesson seemed to be that if you were a cool and progressive-minded group, you had to leave town in order to achieve real success. Chances of maintaining a career playing interesting, original music in Canada seemed slim, so I was certain that I would leave. It was only a question of when and where I'd go.

At the time, the record business did little to promote Canada as a bountiful place to make music. The Canadian Association of Recorded Arts and Sciences (CARAS) made foreign stars such as Aerosmith and Rod Stewart the main attraction at the Juno-award shows; critics overstated the contribution of American residents such as Joni Mitchell and Neil Young to the national rock scene; and record companies offered up artists such as Honeymoon Suite as stellar examples of an indigenous pop machine. It was inevitable that we turned to the Ramones and other new-wave DIY bands for guidance. If we'd been aware of the existence of the Nihilist Spasm Band or DOA (who, while unknown to us, were in the process of transforming modern music), we might have thought differently. It didn't help that hundreds of other strange and exciting bands – Plasterscene Replicas, Woods Are Full of Cuckoos, Vital Sines, The CeeDees, Fifth Column, Jolly Tambourine Man, DV8 – were also being neglected by record companies and ignored by college kids, who still thought that alternative rock was fag music. Teenage Head, Goddo, Rough Trade, the Government, L'Étranger, Martha and the Muffins, and the Diodes were doing okay, but I still thought that if making it big in Canada meant that I had to dress and sound like Mike Reno, I would just as soon move away.

Then I heard Stompin' Tom.

The first time I held one of his records was in 1985 at the Vinyl Museum on Lakeshore Boulevard in Toronto, a sooty old record store that sold albums with encrusted goop on their covers for ninety-nine cents apiece. Besides its reputation as a goldmine of unwanted vinyl, the store's main attraction is its owner, Peter Dunn, who pastes Bible quotations on record sleeves. The cover of, say, *Yanni Live at the Acropolis* would proclaim "The god of this age has blinded the minds of unbelievers!" even though Yanni fans are among the least likely people to freak out and axe-murder their parents. Still, how Mr. Dunn ever reconciled selling W.A.S.P. and Megadeth albums to kids is beyond me. Whatever his reasoning, his pious record depot did deliver unto me *My Stompin' Grounds*, and for that I owe him no small debt.

The cover was chewed at the corners and the vinyl had embossed a half-smile at the bottom. At the top was the signature of its former owner – Sylvester Lefforts – a name best sounded with a wheatstraw stuck in one's teeth. The cover featured postcards of the Calgary Stampede and Niagara Falls floating around Tom as he walked down a railroad track holding a smoke. Tom looked visibly concerned – and not just because rodeo horses were charging at his goolies – but because he was staring into Canada's future and was clearly not at ease with what he saw. From his expression, I should have known that there was strong stuff on this record, but at the time, I thought that Canadian music was all René Simard and Percy Faith and the Laurie Bower Singers – laxative artists who wouldn't know a fuzzbox if it thunked them in the head.

I gave the record a few spins. Then it lay around for awhile. Every now and then, my friends and I would play the songs about snowmobiles, "Wop" May, and the Reversing Falls for their comedic value. I experienced no sense of cultural enlightenment while listening to it, nor did I feel anything close to the epiphany that would later hit me like a ham shot from a cannon. In fact, I found the sound of Tom grinding his boot heel into his wooden plank was sometimes too much to bear, and when I read on the back of the album that the percussion parts were actually credited to "Tom's foot," I almost split a gut. I put the record away and moved on to more sophisticated groups, like the Headboys, Fingerprintz, and Flock of Seagulls. You know, future music.

But the strong ones sneak up on you. It's taken me years to absorb records that I now count among my favourites – *Sailin'*

Stompin' Tom Connors

Shoes by Little Feat; *Doc at Radar Station* by Captain Beefheart and
His Magic Band; *Talking Heads 77* — and I had to get out of
Canada before I could enjoy the poignant heaviness of *My
Stompin' Grounds*. I spent the summer of 1985 in Dublin, Ireland, at
Trinity College, where I kept a small, sunny room overlooking a
croquet pitch first turned by Queen Elizabeth in 1592. That
summer, like any young thinking person, I spent countless hours
sitting on my window ledge rolling around ideas about my life
and where it was headed. At the time, I was caught in a crossfire
of muses. I'd been a junior new-wave musician in Toronto, but
the Rheostatics' skinny-tie pop experiment had seen little audience growth and even less promise for a hit-making career. We'd
added the Trans Canada Soul Patrol horn section, and our sound
soon became wearied by exhausting saxophone solos. At the
same time, I'd also written scads of articles for newspapers and
magazines, and was enjoying a double life as a hopeful music
journalist. Finally, after a few months wandering around Dublin
in a remarkable Guinness-and-whiskey fog, I felt my life's trajec-
tory change. I decided to cast off my aspirations to be a fourth-
generation CanRocker. I pitched the glitter. I would be a writer.

But in the end, Stompin' Tom had something to say about
that. He'd found his way across the ocean too, on a C90 tape
along with selections from Dylan and the Band's *Basement Tapes*. I
played Tom's music for my Irish friends and, to my surprise,
they liked it. *My Stompin' Grounds* became my way of communicating what Canada was like without having to stumble through
my own hazy ideas about home (Tom, after all, had a song
naming the provinces and their capitals, a handy geography
lesson in under three minutes). Soon I found myself listening
to the tape in private as I sat at my desk writing the first fifty

pages of a novel. Tom's voice drew me back across the ocean, and the songs about bobcats and Wilf Carter that I'd once been embarrassed to listen to anchored my identity in a culture where nationhood was everything. They taught me who I was and where I came from. To a twenty-two-year-old kid unsure of his character, Tom's voice – a hoser's cocktail of Hank Williams and Popeye – was a reminder that I wasn't born yesterday, and that I lived somewhere, too.

When I returned home later that fall, I decided to find Tom and tell him about this revelation. I seized on this quest partly because of the cultural free-fall most people experience after arriving home from a strange land. Toronto seemed drab and uptight compared to Dublin, but I was excited at the idea that Canada was waiting to be explored, a Canada that I hadn't known before going abroad. *My Stompin' Grounds* had conjured up a panoramic winterland of railways and folk music and taverns and hockey rinks that was as unlike suburban Etobicoke as Europe had been. I'd had to cross an ocean to find Ireland, but Stompin' Tom's Canada was just up the highway.

Of course, I had no idea what I was getting myself into. Tom, I discovered, had gone missing in action. He'd been in self-imposed exile since 1977, withdrawing from public life to protest the American bias of the Canadian music industry. In 1977, Stompin' Tom asked to play the Grandstand at the CNE, only to be offered the smaller Bandstand by organizers. When Tom visited the CNE offices to discuss the matter, he was told that the talent-bookers were in Las Vegas scouting American acts. Tom called a press conference, gave back his Juno awards, and cancelled all public appearances for one year to prove that he'd taken his stand in the interests of Canadian musicians, not, as some

had suggested, to attract publicity. When I heard this story, it
endeared him to me further, as did the news that no one in
Canada — not even Peter Gzowski, who'd put out a nationwide
call — had seen him for almost a decade.

I took up the search. I found the old footprints: newspaper
clippings, concert films, tour programs, magazine stories, songbooks, and gold records — the basic kit box of an aging Canadian
pop legend. These documents showed that, in the mid-'70s,
Stompin' Tom was Canada's most famous musician: twenty-eight
consecutive sold-out nights at the Horseshoe, an audience with
the Queen, his own show on CBC television, and an introduction
by Toronto mayor David Crombie before the first of two sold-
out shows at Massey Hall. He'd also moved huge numbers of
records nationwide, which explained why he continued to elicit
requests for public appearances; it was as if his audience was in
denial about their hero's exile. But nine years down the road, it
was obvious to many that Tom wasn't coming back. I assumed
that his story would end like those of so many other Canadian
entertainers — as a footnote in the Great Canadian Rock-and-
Roll Encyclopedia that would never be written.

But in the winter of 1986, I found fresh spoor. I put in a lot of
time at Boot Records, Tom's record label in Mississauga, where
everyone knew of my quest. I got on well with the receptionist,
who prepared files for me whenever she saw me pull into the
parking lot. Sometimes she'd say, "You know, you just missed
Tom. He was here not five minutes ago," but I was never sure
whether she was being straight with me or was just keeping alive
my dream that one day I'd walk in and find him waiting in the
lobby to talk to me.

Then she gave me a gift.

I asked her whether the record business slowed down in the winter. She shook her head and said that, on the contrary, she was worn out by all of the work. When I asked her why, she looked over both shoulders to make sure no one was watching, then held up a letter addressed to New Brunswick premier Richard Hatfield. It was an invitation to Tom's fiftieth birthday party on February 10. In the top corner was the address, date, and time, and the name of the town where Tom lived. I gave her a hug, then ran to my car where I scribbled it all down.

On the day of Tom's birthday, snow emptied from the sky. We headed out of the city towards Halton Hills, and one hour later, we turned off the highway and disappeared into the country, the roads white and empty. I carried a petition in my back pocket with seventy names written on it under the plea "TOM, WE WANT YOU BACK." I also took a Rheostatics tape with me. I wanted Tom to know that I was a musician too, not just an interloper, but I later discovered, much to my chagrin, that I'd given him the wrong cassette. It had only one Rheostatics song on it. The others were Patti Smith doing "Hey Joe" and "Piss Factory."

As we climbed the wooden steps of Tom's local community hall, we could hear laughter and fiddle music coming from inside. A young woman came to the door and asked if we knew Tom. We told her that we'd come to give him something for his birthday. She told us to wait a minute while she got him. It was the longest minute of my life.

Then he appeared.

Dressed entirely in black, standing about six-foot-two and wearing a black cowboy hat, he stepped towards us.

"Well, hello there," he said, exhaling smoke.

"Happy birthday," we said.

"Thanks. What's this?" he asked, pointing to my petition.

I handed it and the tape to him. My memory flutters at this point. I believe, however, that I quoted from a manifesto I'd penned the night before, which included stuff like "the youth of Canada need you to come back. Our country's in trouble, save it. The Tory scourge. My band loves Canada, hockey, the National Dream, besides, we think you're really, really great . . ."

He laughed.

He looked us over.

"Where're you from, then?" he asked.

"We're from Toronto," we replied.

"You came all the way from Toronto?" He sounded pleased. "Geez, you come all the way from Toronto, you might as well come in and have a few drinks!"

It was like a dream. The hall was dark and wooden, and felt as if it had been built overnight by great men in beards. There was a head table on a little stage at the front, with a lectern and a microphone stand to the side. The guests sat at long tables with foil tins for ashtrays and benches for chairs. We sat beside the local OPP officer and his wife, dining on a pot-luck dinner and drinking many bottles of 50, which Tom had recently taken to drinking after decades as a Golden man.

After the meal, the lights dimmed, and Tom's daughter rolled out a monstrous cake, which she'd made in the shape of Canada. It looked exquisite. People cheered and howled and stomped their feet. Tom was all choked up and he gave a little speech. He acknowledged Bud Roberts and Stevedore Steve, two mythic characters from Tom's songs, who were parading the room telling road stories. He played four songs with his band — "Green, Green Grass of Home," "Sudbury Saturday

Night," "Gumboot Clogeroo," and "Bud the Spud." I couldn't believe that I was hearing his voice live. Having spent years trying to fuse it to my own voice and writing songs that sounded like his, it was a benediction to watch Tom perform. He strummed and growled and legendary bassist Gary Empry pasted his trademark hoofbeat to the floor. We tapped our feet and smiled and everyone sang along.

After the ceremonies, Tom came over and talked to us. My throat closed up when I told him about my epiphany in Ireland and the words didn't come out right. But Tom listened intently. He chain-smoked Rothmans from a long gold and black cigarette holder, which he said was supposed to cut down on the nicotine. After I finished my long-winded, fumbling dissertation, Tom sat with us and expounded the virtues of Canadian music and the importance of travelling the country. He talked about meeting a couple of schoolteachers while he was riding the rails in the '60s, who asked him why, if American musicians wrote songs about the United States, in Canada there weren't any Canadian songs. Tom told us, "so that's how come I started writin' them." By the end of his soliloquy, he's ripped the filter from his cigarette and thrown it to the floor, cursing free trade and the record business, waving his beer around his head. We listened to him like hypnotized rabbits.

The next year, we toured Canada for the first time.

Suddenly, there we were, on the road . . .

JEANINE HOLLINGSHEAD: In 1966, I was with Neil Young and Bruce Palmer when they left for Los Angeles in the hearse. I was the only person who got to drive that hearse other than Neil. He was very picky about it because he'd already burned one up with the Squires. It was a standard, an old three-speed, a monster. We were six young, Beatle-haired, guitar-totin', shirt-flappin' hippies. Besides Neil and Bruce, there was Mike Gallagher (who was invited because he had gas money), Tannis Neiman (because like Neil, she was going to California with the idea of getting into the music scene), Judy Mack (who was in love with Neil and was just along for the ride), and me (the only other one who could drive standard). The hearse broke down in Albuquerque and had to be fixed. The fellow who ran the garage thought that Neil and Tannis were Sonny and Cher. Neil went a little bananas. It was the beginning of his epilepsy. We had to hospitalize him. He was suffering from exhaustion, basically. While he was in the hospital, I wound up in the hospital, too. I had suffered two serious injuries. One was blowing up my face in a gas oven in a motel room. I went to light the oven and it took my eyebrows and hair and skin off. Then about a week into that, while walking around with this bandaged, mummy face, I developed kidney stones. When Neil was ready to move on, I wasn't. Tannis wasn't about to leave me alone and Mikey wasn't any more interested in going to L.A. than anywhere else, so he stayed with us.

After I got better, we hitched all the way to L.A. together. The first person we ran into was Neil. We went over to Ben Frank's Drive-In and the first thing we saw was the Pontiac hearse with Canadian plates. Tannis had managed to get herself pregnant in Albuquerque, so she wasn't in a great mood. She was six to eight weeks' pregnant and starting to show. She really needed to get back to Canada. She didn't leave me in Albuquerque, so I didn't leave her out west. The only thing I'd ever really wanted to do was go to Vancouver, so she and I hitchhiked and bused up the coast and we finally got to Vancouver. We made it back to Toronto under separate cover. We hiked back with two guys from Vancouver who wanted to see Yorkville. Instead of the four of us travelling together, we split up into couples because it was easier to get rides that way. It was also safer, for everybody. We'd been away for six months. When we got back to Toronto in July or August, Yorkville was really starting to happen.

RANDY BACHMAN: After the song "Hey Girl" became a hit in the U.K., the Guess Who flew to London with all our equipment to record an album for King Records. I was so excited at the possibility of buying rare Cliff Richard and Beatles singles; I was just as much a fan as I was a musician in those days. We showed up at the record company's office, where they laid out a contract on the table. It promised us 160 dollars per week for the next five years. We asked about royalties and they said, "Right. Well, you'll get 160 dollars per week for the next five years." We said, "Yeah. But what about the percentages?" and they just repeated themselves. They didn't realize that we were already making that kind of money playing high-school dances in Winnipeg. They were trying to trick us into letting them own the Guess Who, but at that point, we didn't want to be owned by anybody. We told them no thanks, and walked away. We were 20,000 dollars in debt to Air Canada and had only 420 dollars to spend between seven guys. That's when we really became a band.

TERRY DAVID MULLIGAN: When the Guess Who first went to England, no homework had been done. Management let them down. They were supposed to be there to record and tour, but they got no support when they arrived. The ball had been dropped, big-time. I was with them in the Marquee Club on the

Courtesy of John Einarson

The Guess Who. Left to right: Gary Peterson, Randy Bachman, Jim Kale,
Burton Cummings

day that the Who released "Happy Jack." The Who did a set and
it was just wild. They destroyed everything; Pete Townshend left
his guitar sticking through the acoustic tile in the ceiling. The
next day, I went to see Pete and he was lovingly restoring the
guitar that he'd smashed up. He was sanding it down and putting
the neck back on.

RANDY BACHMAN: We went to talk to the Who. Not a lot was
said, really. We asked them to change their name because we were
getting requests for "My Generation" and they asked us to change
ours because they were being confused with the band that did
"Shakin' All Over." Neither of us budged, of course. I saw them
perform at a club later that night. They were so loud that the film
crew who were shooting them complained that the volume of
John Entwistle's bass was vibrating the film inside their cameras.

JIM MILLICAN: KY58 was a huge top-forty station in Manitoba for years. My favourite deejay was a fellow named Darryl Berlingham. Darryl was the guy who recorded Burton Cummings for the first time in the KY58 studios when he was in the Devrons. I sort of followed in his footsteps. I was a fan, and then I became a top-forty deejay in Winnipeg. When the Guess Who had that run of singles from "These Eyes" on, there was a lot of pride among the fans, the clubs, the deejays, everyone, about what they'd accomplished. I'd be on the air, taking calls from Jim Kale or Burton Cummings from Birmingham, Alabama, or San Francisco, California, and talking to them a little about what they were up to and what was going on. I felt connected to them.

TERRY DAVID MULLIGAN: The first time the Guess Who were ever interviewed on a television show in England, they asked everybody's name, and when Randy said his, they laughed like crazy because, in England, "randy" means "horny."

JIM KALE: I was in awe of England. We were just little kids. I'd get up in the morning just to watch women go to work in their miniskirts. One night we went to the Who concert at the Marquee and they blew up the P.A. The BBC were there filming and they weren't too happy about it, because the band ruined their sound system.

JIM MILLICAN: Randy Bachman was off the road for a long time because of gallstones. So they got another guitarist to fill in for him. Without Randy around, the other guys got an idea of what it was like to conduct business without him. It gave them the confidence to think that they might be able to go on without him. Randy was tight with the purse-strings and he believed that they could get on with a very small road crew. In those days, their manager did their road managing and they only had one full-time roadie. Sometimes they picked a guy up on the road to do some work for free. This was right up until the time when "American Woman" was the number-one record on the planet. They were playing huge places. After the split, they decided to expand. So they hired me as tour manager.

RANDY BACHMAN: One night the Guess Who were playing in Kitchener with Junior Walker and His All-Stars. We were doing our last song of the night when I broke a guitar string. After the set, I restrung it and went back out and started jamming on this riff, you know, nothing special. The band joined in and we had something going, so I looked around for Burton. He was outside the back door of the club, talking to friends. I guess he thought the music he was hearing was some tape over the P.A. system, 'cause when I yelled, "We're jamming! We're jamming!" he didn't even move. Finally he realized what was going on, so he hopped up on stage and sat down at the piano. I yelled, "Sing something!" And he started screaming: *"American woman! Stay away from meeheee!"*

JIM MILLICAN: It was unusual back then to be a Canadian act on the road in the United States. We developed a shtick with a beaver logo superimposed on the Canadian flag. We made stickers and T-shirts; people loved them. We also had a Canadian flag backdrop that we'd raise from the floor during the long solo in "American Woman." It used to get an unbelievable response from American audiences. Canadians loved it too, of course, but the

Americans were just crazy about that part of the show; they really ate it up.

RANDY BACHMAN: I remember going to Kresge's in Winnipeg, picking up *Billboard*, and reading that "Shakin' All Over" was number 22 on the charts. The lady behind the desk didn't believe me when I told her that this was our group, the Guess Who. She didn't believe that a band on the charts could be from Winnipeg. A few days later, we got an invitation to appear on the *Ed Sullivan Show*. We cut school and arrived in New York expecting all these people to be waiting for us. Instead, we spent most of the day knocking on the door of the TV station, trying to convince an elderly security guard that we were booked for the big show. As it turned out, Ed knew nothing about the invitation, so we ended up at our record company's office, where they introduced us to Burt Bacharach and Hal David. The rest of the time I spent sitting quietly in a corner of the recording studio, watching Dionne Warwick make her new album.

RICHARD FLOHIL: Ian and Sylvia were the first Canadian act to play Carnegie Hall and sell it out. They brought Lightfoot down to Albert Grossman, Dylan's manager. From '65 on, folk music here was becoming very nationalistic, due in part to Expo 67, which proved for the first time that we could do something bigger and better than the Americans. We'd spent all this time sponging up American music, and now it was time to move on. Earlier, there had been no record labels, no recording studios, no managers, no industry infrastructure. The idea of the Canadian Content regulations, which came out of this period of musical growth, was to build the whole infrastructure. That simple regulation got radio people to do something instead of slavishly playing whatever came from America. Of course, it was awful at first. Everybody formed bands, record companies, built bad studios, and went crazy, and the quality was very low. But once over the hump, the greatness emerged.

BARRY ALLEN: Can Con impacted dramatically on us. When we first put records out, there weren't any Can Con laws. You got played because you knew the deejays; when it clicked, it was because it was a good tune. We were lucky because our single "Love Drops" was on Capitol (we were signed by Paul White), so we had promo men in there saying, "Hey, this record is getting good reaction across the country, get on it." But Can Con made the regional acts happen. It was critical in making radio stations expand their base. Otherwise, it would be worse than it is now in terms of playing the American stuff. When you think of all the incredible bands and music being made by Canadian artists, it's disgusting that the infrastructure here doesn't support it in a big way.

TERRY DAVID MULLIGAN: After the Can Con rules were brought in, in 1970, Anne Murray, the Guess Who, and Gordon Light-foot held a press conference and said, "Canadian Content is killing us." At the time, there was only a handful of acts, and since radio had to fulfil 33 per cent Canadian content, they'd played the shit out of those bands and there was a backlash. These artists wanted them to knock it off, to play other bands. That's when the deejays started to loosen it up, and we found out that people like Gene Cornish from the Young Rascals had been born in Ottawa and Zal Yanofsky was from Toronto. Their Canadian connections qualified them under the code.

RICHARD FLOHIL: Gordon Lightfoot and Bryan Adams bitch about the Canadian Content rules for three reasons: One, Canadian talent's good enough, it doesn't need it. Two, it breeds a huge amount of mediocrity. And three, it hurts those who are successful because Americans think they can't be good because they're being propped up by the system. But the people who're complaining have all made it, so what're they worried about? Talk to the guys who ran agencies in the late '60s. Back then, Canadian bands could not tour outside their own local area because no one outside knew who they were, not until a system was in place where radio stations would play their records. I was managing Downchild in the late '60s and home-recorded our first album in the basement of Rochdale for five hundred dollars. RCA picked it up and paid two thousand dollars for it. We couldn't believe the money. The first gig we played in Winnipeg was triumphant. These days bands tour all the time, but in those days, it was unheard-of. The agents would be lucky if there were four or five bands on their roster who could tour across the country.

SKINNY TENN: Why do we need regulations? Well, when some song about living in the ghetto is getting airplay over a great Canadian song, what does that say about our industry? That's why I've always thought that the Can Con rules were totally necessary. Always. Anybody who's ever suggested that they're not is wrong. The sad thing is that radio could do a lot more to support Canadian acts and, in fact, get bigger ratings than they already do.

SHARI ULRICH: If we didn't have Can Con, Canadian music just wouldn't get the support that it now gets. For the longest time, the unfortunate reality was that Canadians didn't support their own until they were successful in the States. I think that's less true now, but that's because Canadian music had a shot on the airwaves. It got a chance to grow to the point where success in Canada could actually be considered real success.

PETER GODDARD: The whole nationalistic music movement that came out of Can Con was very false, very forced. It was all promotion. Canadian music was developing naturally all around North America, and the push that this movement gave it tended to capitalize on what was already happening. For instance, I went to Gordon Lightfoot's opening in Las Vegas. I was put at a table near the front next to this woman from Sacramento who was Lightfoot's biggest fan. She just loved him, this American woman. I told her that I was from Toronto and we talked a little about the city. But when I told her that I occasionally went to Georgian Bay, her eyes lit up. It was like the magic kingdom to her. So the music was already resonant. An identity was being established and we didn't need the government to define what it was.

RA MCGUIRE: The whole issue of Can Con is bullshit. Either you're a good band or you're not a good band. If you're marginal, the rule helps and that's really cool. Those who created it had their hearts in the right place, and I think it's important that somebody's watching out for Canadian artists in that way. But, as for whether it hurts people's careers, that's a separate issue.

DENTON YOUNG: Back in early days, record companies came to see you in bars, but not until the mid-'70s were they even looking to sign Canadian bands. There was only the Guess Who, Gordon Lightfoot, and Anne Murray. Canadians didn't look at Canadian music until it got noticed in the States, which is not uncommon now, even though we have a lot more respect for our abilities. Now, you can get a group of guys together with some good recording equipment and if you put together a decent enough product you can take it to a record company and sign a deal without having toured anywhere. But bands back then didn't make albums. We didn't imagine in a million years that we'd really do an album.

GREG GODOVITZ: We played a simulcast gig at the Bathurst Street Theatre. It was a big-time TV production. I played piano live for the first time; that was terrifying because I'd never played piano on stage, with horns behind me, lit beautifully. The next morning, I took the subway to my mom's place at the end of the line, and there was a little old lady sitting across from me. She looked at me and she said, "I liked your TV show last night." I thought it was funny. In Canada, you can't equate fame with the amount of money you have in the bank. Being famous in Canada means you can have a fantastic gig at the Gardens, but you go home on the subway.

QUEBEC

"All the musicians in the town, it seems, are a backsliding lot,
who want strange new hymns that nobody knows at an ungodly
pace that nobody can keep up with."

Sinclair Ross, *As For Me and My House*

"Béliveau played here."

I say those words and they float there. Next to Tardif's,
Lafleur's and Tremblay's, Béliveau's silken banner points
down from the ceiling rafters of Le Colisée, where riggers
outfitted with great metallic belts are draping cables and
hanging rope like spiders slinging thread. They're raising
steel poles and pulleying iron skeletons up the walls of the iceless
rink, rippling Béliveau's flag, reminding me that I am walking
where he once walked, and that not even Canada's grandest rock-
and-roll circus can outshine the aura cast by this heroic man.

"Béliveau played here."

Daniel Larocque, Cargo Records' francophone promo rep, is
the first to say it. I have an immediate kinship with Daniel; like
me, he is obsessed with hockey, or rather, with its demise. In one
breath, he talks of Le Colisée being built because of the explosion of Quebec hockey in the '40s and '50s, and in the next he

breaks the news that the legendary Quebec Remparts have been sold, and that next year the city's junior-A team will move to the hockey hotbed of Lewiston, Maine.

"It's not that far, eh, so if people wanted to go, they could still visit them. But in Quebec, things haven't been the same since Les Nordiques left," he says.

Neither, it seems, has the building. It is a dump. The blackened floors look like they've been wiped down with a greasy rag, and because it was built long before the sizzle of electronic billboards and pixelated scoreclocks, the rink feels dark and close. Unlike the spit-clean, brilliantly lit Corel Centre in Ottawa (where we played two twenty-thousand-plus shows before crossing the provincial border), Le Colisée has the damp feel of an old garage. Two days earlier in the nation's capital, we dined in a candlelit suite, where handsome chefs spooned out victuals from sparkling silver trays. Here, the catering area resembles the engine room of an old steamship, and the food is prepared by two sweating women standing over cast-iron pots that sit on ancient stoves, the kind my grandmother has in her kitchen. Their beef stew is thick and glutinous, and you can smell it all the way to the ticket window.

I like it.

I tell Daniel that I want to buy a hockey jersey. Actually, I ask if I can *have* a hockey jersey. In every arena we've played on this tour, the Hip have been given uniforms of the home team. They've collected Oilers and Flames and Senators sweaters, often with their names printed on the back. While I do not begrudge the Hip their popularity and related financial rewards, this aspect of their success makes me wobbly with envy. But Daniel says that I won't be given a jersey. "Who do you think you are? Eddie Van Halen?" he says, laughing. He promises, however, that he'll track down the woman who runs the arena's boutique to see if he can get the one I want at cost. The only souvenir I want to bring home from the tour is the jersey of an obscure Canadian hockey team, and the local International Hockey League franchise fits that description. They're called the Rafales, and their name means tenacious cold front or marauding wind or really, really strong breeze. I'm particularly drawn to their emblem, which features a cloud that looks like Santa Claus riding across the sky on a hockey stick. It is coloured silver and purple and green and gold stripes fly along its sides, as if the team couldn't decide what their colours should be and so used them all. It is very garish. It is very French.

The arena is draped with a mammoth black curtain that hides about a quarter of the seats. It lends the place a look of style, an intimacy rarely found in sports bowls. Le Colisée starts to feel more like a theatre. (In Ottawa, by contrast, the upper reaches of the arena seemed harrowingly infinite.) This relatively small size is a treat for everyone except the promoters; the show hasn't sold well. I find this odd considering that no fewer than three Hip cover bands are playing in town – Road Apples, Nautical Disaster, and New Orleans – and you can usually measure the popularity of a band by the number of local musicians willing to torpedo their own muse by mimicking a band who followed theirs. From a musician's or fan's point of view, the downsized venue proves to be a good place to rock.

We come out and play our first song and immediately people start laughing. One of the reasons we are wearing crooner's jackets on this tour is so that we will look nothing like how we sound. Too often, we're called "difficult" and compared to eggheaded bands we've never heard of, so we set out to corrupt that image as best we could, not to mention look dapper at the same time. The Québécois are the first crowd to clue into the irony of our stagewear; then again, their mirth may have something to do with Tim's modest resemblance to a young Jerry Lewis. Sitting in front of me are three teenage girls with milky complexions and twinkling teeth, gazing up at the stage and paddling their hands together after each song. They are so beautiful to look at that I spend most of the night watching them, feeling loved. My guitar more or less plays itself. I swipe at its strings with my pick, and every note sounds rich and clear. When I climb the neck in search of a difficult, poignant note, I close my eyes and hit it, even though I have no idea what those notes at the top of the neck mean anyway. In this area of the instrument, I'm usually chucking darts. I'm sure the fellows will be happy to read this.

Some nights, it all lines up, and that's tonight. We are each our own player, which makes for a stronger brew. Martin has two main guitars, and they're polar opposites. One of them is an Ibanez doubleneck, on which he's painted a twig of maple leaves, after A. Y. Jackson's proposal for Canada's flag. When Martin plays it, the weight of the guitar makes him appear stiff and rigid, and because it's so big and square, he looks like a man trapped inside a picture frame. His other guitar is a Steinberger (which isn't even technically a guitar; it's a "Steinberger System"). Its defining features are a body the size of a shoebox and a neck that lacks closure. Most people think it's ugly. Because Martin is so fond of it, I'll go on record as saying that it's ideal for his style of playing. Once, Neil Peart (Rush's drummer) asked Dave Clark and me, "Is Martin a genius?" Dave Clark said, "Yeah!" but I'd

never thought of him that way before. I'd been too amazed by his
playing and singing to put a word to it. But I suppose that he is.
In performance, his musicianship can be humbling and inspiring
at the same time. He possesses Malmsteenian powers on the
guitar and an otherworldly singing voice, but his role in the band
is as much accompanist as leader. I could say the same about any
of us, but Martin has the ability to take it farther out there,
which makes his turn on lead guitar or harmony vocal all the
more dramatic. Sometimes when we do "Rich, Beautiful, Mine"
or "A Mid-Winter Night's Dream," I like to focus on someone in
the audience who doesn't know what he's in for, and watch his
reaction as Martin's singing climbs higher and higher. It's a magic
act that can still take me by surprise, which makes playing with
Martin terribly distracting, for all the right reasons.

When Tim has a great night, the show hums. Tim is having
a great night. His voice seems perfectly suited for arenas —
especially Le Colisée — because his timbre, newly fostered, encom-
passes an upper range that soars and a lower range that rumbles,
resulting in a breathy sound with weight. His singing in "Claire"
resonates like a pipe organ, evoking a voice like Neil Diamond's,
who I believe is Tim's least-favourite artist. Tim gets to play three
instruments on stage, sometimes four: bass, electric guitar,
acoustic guitar, and piano. Tonight, we do a version of Tim's
"Bad Time to Be Poor," a political song written by the least political member of the band. On this song, Tim plays his Telecaster
through an old Fender amp. He uses a yellow fuzzbox to effect
a raucous, ear-battering tone, but his right hand is so heavy that
the effect is double-*grnnnged*, and while this sometimes causes
much eyebrow-raising, tonight the song moves broodingly like
a griffin. You'd never pick Tim out as a snarling, politicized,

Martin Tielli

Graham Kennedy Photo

high priest of hard rock, but he is tonight, and has been most of the tour.

Neil Peart told me, "Oh, I prefer playing the smaller rooms. You can hear your drums a lot better in hockey rinks." Knowing this, Don Kerr must feel like the Jolly Green Giant of rock. Standing in the wings of an arena listening to a rock band – even running from the parking lot on your way to the bandstand – you're hit first by the drums. Don doesn't look like he's hitting the drums that hard because he's thin and wiry-armed, but in the arena, his kit sounds like a Brobdingnagian heartbeat. It gets the stoners' heads swivelling back and forth even in the cheap seats, and the more forthright he is, the better we come across. Dave Clark was a stylist, and he'd change tempos in mid-song. While this was often the source of musical frustration, it was also the impetus for a lot of innovative ideas. It's taken Don a while to play into this (and a while for us to let him), but tonight, during "Four Little Songs," he executes Beatlesesque, punk, pop, swing, ska, metal, prog, and new-wave drum patterns all in the span of five minutes. Frankly, I can't believe we're doing this song in a stadium. It requires quick-headed tempo changes – it has four distinct songlets separated by a chorus, stacked with vocal flurries. Don has to play in four different tempos while remembering how to get back to the head, not to mention taking the breaks and pregnant pauses and drum licks that define where the songlets begin and end. Tonight, Don does it perfectly, and with a few bonus surprises. When he joined the band, I started to see ourselves through his eyes, and one of the things I realized is that being a Rheostatic is sometimes like being a math nerd. Even more reason to dress like Bobby Vinton.

Cathy Bidini

Don Kerr

Because of the black drape and the smaller crowd, we come across better. Here, the audience can pick up our nuances and subtleties (and egregious mistakes) that get swallowed up in the larger joints. The arena's shortened length also means that when people shout at us from a distance, we can actually hear what they're saying. Because a lot of it is in French, none of it sounds like "You fuckin' English faggots suck!" even though they may be saying this. But I doubt it. Don speaks French to the crowd and there is a smattering of applause, and more laughs. This sets off a round of between-song patter from the rest of us, in English, defeating the purpose of Don's magnanimous linguistic gesture.

Because the crowd is so affable and well-behaved, when we ask them to be quiet so we can hear what a particularly robust group of fans is yelling, they fall silent.

"We came to see you guys!"

We feel wanted.

Our last number is "Dope Fiends and Boozehounds," and the audience consents to every musical arc. Martin is so relaxed by the crowd's good nature that once he's warbled the song's final, dramatic line, he shapes his hands into tiny devil horns behind his head, and makes like he's gargling. I can't believe he's doing this in front of ten thousand people, especially since, in the early days of the band, he'd be so uptight, he'd write out things to say between songs. Underneath the gargling, Donny cues us on his hi-hat for the song's outro and, on the three-count, we lower the hammer. Martin and I hurtle airborne across the stage, Donny slashes at his drums, and Tim wallops his bass with the flat of his hand. After four cycles of this, we collapse into the hushed coda of our children's melody, "You Are Very Star," while lying flat on our backs, staring up at Béliveau's silk. We pretend to fall asleep, and as the stage darkens, we creep down the ramp through the ugly hallways, past the office where the pot-bellied arena manager is asleep at his desk, and into our damp and dimly lit dressing room, where a tray of Charlebois beer is given our full and immediate attention. The beer is La Fin du Monde. It's our best show of the tour.

KEN TOBIAS: We played Baie-Comeau, Quebec, when they were building that big hydro-electric dam up there. We got isolation pay. It was winter, about forty below zero. No one wanted to go up there, it was such a long drive north of Quebec City. There were white-outs, there were wolves. We drove there with our heaters on full and we're going, *Oh boy, don't let us break down.* The cold was creeping in even with the heaters blowing. After two weeks up there, we heard there was a snowstorm coming, so we said, "Let's leave tonight, let's not wait till morning." We didn't want to have to stay there any longer than we had to. Now, of course, in *habitant* country at night at forty-below, nothing is happening. There's nothing but 'long roads, maybe an occasional village. We had two cars: Donny was driving a Buick his father had given him, and Charlie, the guitar player, and I were in the other. We hadn't been paid, and Donny, who always had money, didn't give me any when we took off. Charlie and I only had a few dollars between us. At around four-thirty in the morning, it got cold. It got so frigging cold that the snow stopped. Everything froze. Then I blew a tire. I pulled off the road and honked the horn. The other car stopped, and we rolled into an old, overgrown service station. We were sheltered there, but even so, it took us an hour just to get the frigging lug-nuts off. It was so cold that we had to take turns. We finally got it done, and Donny jumped into his car and, instead of waiting for us, he took off. I started the car but as soon as I put it into gear it went *blppluuu . . .* With a little condensation, it had frozen that fast. We tried again and again: nothing but *blppluuu . . .* We were so beat, so tired.

The heat immediately left the car. It just disappeared. We sat there talking, and Charlie was starting to sound very tired, exhausted. The cold was going into our brains so fast. Within an hour, we were defeated. The car was still going *nnnnnnrrr* and we couldn't think what to do. Charlie was going, "I don't know what to do, man, I'm so tired, I just want to sleep." I said, "Don't sleep. Don't sleep, Charlie. You don't want to go to sleep." I was saying,

"Maybe we should light the back seat on fire, but what about the plastic?" "What about up the road, do you remember seeing anything up the road?" And our voices were getting quieter, we were slower and slower. Then I said, "Charlie? We might die, you know." "No big deal," he said. Then all of a sudden, I hear . . . whistling. I've got good musician's ears, thank god. "Did you hear something, Charlie?" I asked. I looked up through the steering wheel and there was this guy, this woodsman. He's got on these big boots, all laced up, really cool woodsman's boots. He's wearing a short vest, very thick, and he's got a double-bladed axe over his shoulder, and he's wearing a tuque. He's walking down the road, past the entranceway to the shelter. I leaned my head on the horn; it was the only part of my body that wasn't drained of energy. The horn went *eeeouuuuu*, a pathetic, weak honk. He kept on walking, so I did it again. The horn was even weaker. I couldn't honk the horn again. Then he stopped. He walked back. He came to my door and I looked out at him and in my dull eyes he noticed extreme terror. He shouted, "Mon dieu!" and he grabbed the door, opened it, grabbed me, hauled me out and banged me against the car – slammed me against it – then walked me around real fast. He said something in French – "Stand there!" – and then he hauled Charlie out and did the same thing to him. It shocked us out of it.

My legs could hardly move, so he put his arms around both of us and he walked us. No more than fifty or a hundred yards down around the corner was this small farmhouse where he and his mother lived. Inside there were two roaring fires, two stoves just belching heat, and as soon as we hit the heat, we fell to the floor. I never felt anything like it in my life. I've had cold fingers, a cold nose, but I've never been cold in the middle of my back or in the

Ken Tobias

muscles of my arms or in the flat of my ear or in my knees. Charlie is a guy who never, ever cries, never shows his emotion, but he was sobbing. The pain was unbearable. The woman grabbed the son and said, more or less, "Come, leave them alone; they have to go through this. Give them their dignity." That's what I got from her. She closed the door and we just lay there. We went through it. They saved my life. We stayed there all night. In the morning a mechanic came up, charged me twenty-five dollars to take a blowtorch and melt away a little piece of ice. That left us with ten bucks.

We drove. I'm saying to myself, "When I get ahold of Donny, I'm gonna kill him." We had to pay all the autoroutes and when we got to the last one, we had no money left. We drove up to it and stopped. I said, "Look. It's a long story. We've been through hell and back. We almost died. We have no money. What do we do?" The attendant could see it in my eyes. He said, "Okay, drive through and go park over there." It took an hour and a half before they let us go. Finally, we pulled into the yard at Donny's place in Montreal to drop the equipment off. His car was there, they'd already eaten. They were inside having a good time. We walked through the door and told them the whole story. Years later, I finally decked him.

The woman who runs the boutique at Le Colisée drives in from the country to open her store. She sells me a Rafales jersey at cost, and says something about Eddie Van Halen. I ask Daniel what the deal is, and he tells me the story. The last time Van Halen played Le Colisée, Eddie asked this woman for a Rafales jersey. He wore it that night to play a solo and got a standing ovation for flying the local colours. This apparently upset bassist Michael Anthony, who felt it unfair that Eddie had received applause for posturing. The next evening, in Montreal, a fan threw a Canadiens jersey on the stage, but before Eddie had a chance to pick it up, Anthony raced over and put it on. The response from this crowd was twice as loud as it had been the night before. But they weren't cheering. The Habs were mired in their first losing season in twenty-five years, but no one had told poor Michael Anthony that the people of Montreal were pissed off. They kept booing until he took the damned jersey off.

THE EAST

"Danny was doing his thing, his hands twisted in the air,
his head shyly buried into his chest. The kids started doing
this too, it became quite the rage, you know, this dance
of awkwardness and crippled emotions."
Paul Quarrington, *Whale Music*

As we glide over the low, rolling New Brunswick terrain,
under a light, spitting drizzle, past the dull grey trees,
Tim Mech is reading to us:

There's always some mail waiting for me, too, mostly
from women who tell me they are in love with me, or
that they want to do me. I take it up to my suite, where I
relax with some prime hash and a couple of beers. After
I call room service to send up some food, I'll skim through
the letters, and look over the snapshots. I get lots of shots
from open-legged women who hope to turn me on – and
they do.

Tim Mech calls himself our stage technician so that, one day,
people will stop calling him a roadie. It's Tim's job to maintain
our gear, stock the stage with beer and water and towels for the

show, drive the van, haul amps and guitars from truck to gig to van to hotel, and repair Martin's effects unit. He performs these tasks with such efficacy and aplomb that performers from Bruce Cockburn and Spirit of the West to the Pursuit of Happiness have enlisted his expertise. He carries with him a hefty, metal-enforced road case, which includes a strobe tuner, a carpeted work bench, and a glass jar of guitar picks that smells of garlic and pepper. Tacked to the lid of this multi-purpose suitcase are photographs of Tim's martial-arts instructor, Master Pan, scowling at the camera, of his girlfriend, Rebecca, in an alluring pose under a boudoir canopy, of his guitar hero, the late Danny Gatton, of his grandfather, of Tim on a motorcycle, of Tim with Bob Mould, and a pink Power Rangers sticker.

Tim's current band is called Peep Show. It's a rock-and-roll–blues revue featuring slide-guitar-based songs set to narratives of lust, love, temptation, and dirty sex. Tim takes Peep Show quite seriously. While shopping in Calgary between shows this tour (making sure we visited Recordland, the best used-record store in Canada), Tim asked if we could stop at Half-Price Adult Video. A friend who was with us at the time turned to me and whispered, "What? Is this guy into pornography?"

"Oh no," I said. "He's just looking for song titles."

In Vancouver, I had glanced over Tim's shoulder while he was writing in his tour journal expecting to find personal ruminations about life on the road, and noticed a list of words that I could not immediately identify. I soon realized that they were adult-film titles. *Sleeping Booty. Hot House Bush League. Edward Penishands. Battlestar Orgasmica. Terms of Endowment.* In Half-Price Adult Video, I watched him stroll bookishly down the aisles of dildos and lubricants while holding a pencil and pad of paper,

Cathy Bidini

Tim Mech

scribbling down the names of blue films and scanning video boxes for variations on the word love-hole.

Gary is driving and Tim is riding shotgun. We have traded in our tour bus for a van. We don't need sleepers because there are no overnight drives on the East Coast. The cosiness of the van provides for a little more interaction and chatter. In the van, even though we may not want to, we can actually hear the lurid details when Tim quotes from his bound collection of *Penthouse Letters.*

Over the years we've learned to get along in small spaces, so long drives like this one from Quebec City to Halifax aren't a problem. Just as on the tour bus, it's all a matter of defining your space and establishing a routine. Tim Vesely usually occupies his time reading long, demanding books – Josef Skvorecky, V. S. Naipaul, Dostoyevsky – something that will effectively gobble up the hours and leave more for the next drive. It's either that or he's trying to look smart. Martin is the closest anyone in our band comes to Duke Ellington, who wrote arrangements on the bus for his orchestra to play that evening. Martin is the most likely one to whistle through a melody-in-progress or write down tablature for a song he's trying to complete. Then again, he's also the kind of guy who'll take hours to eat lunch, but never quite finish it, so that, two days later, you'll wake up with a flattened French fry stuck to your ear. Don is probably the busiest of the six of us. He likes doing difficult tasks with little room, like repairing his talking drum, which is made from shoelaces and the rim of a tire. This is all very well unless you have to sit beside him. Gary, on the other hand, is a stay-put magazine reader, though he cannot hold a candle to our old soundman, Roger Psutka, who would bring with him a stack of *Details, GQ, Esquire,*

OUT, Rolling Stone, and *Spin* magazines, providing endless hours of lightweight reading.

But sometimes, living in close confines results in aggression. When we toured Ireland in 1988, we roomed together in a tiny hostel with two sets of bunks; you could barely get up to pee without planting your foot on the other fellow's forehead. In Cork, we were billeted with two young girls who gave us a closet-sized room in which to sleep. I woke up in the middle of the night to find myself chewing on one of Martin's kneecaps, which were splayed apart in the middle of the room as he clawed an awful case of athlete's foot. I have no doubt that living in such tiny spaces contributed to our first break-up. Martin and Tim were already at loggerheads; neither of them was speaking. As an Italian, I found it very difficult to watch. Then Martin's tension was redirected at me and Dave Clark. It all came to a head one afternoon at University College in Dublin, where we were waiting for word from a student organizer about where to set up for our lunchtime performance. The word never came; we were ousted in favour of a student debate on abortion (possibly more fun than a free rock show; more lively, anyway) and as we sat on our amps feeling glum, for some inexplicable reason we started fighting about Neil Young.

Actually, it wasn't much of a fight. Dave Clark and Martin exchanged words and I joined in, yet another example of not keeping my yap shut when I should have. One of us called Neil a "wanker" (yes, a wanker), and before I knew it, Tielli had wrapped his hands around my throat. I was taken aback, not to mention a little frightened. In the two years that I'd known him, Martin had been quiet, docile (albeit slightly edgy), and I was dumbstruck by his actions. I tried to break his grip, but he held on tight. Just as I started to panic, Martin let go and broke down in tears. Collectively, individually, we were a mess. It was only after we broke free of each other and did our own thing that we enjoyed our time abroad. Tim hopped on a bus and headed north to visit his mother's ancestral home; Martin took up with a flame-haired flautist and escaped to her flat; and Dave and I held court in Mulligan's, the best pub in the entire world.

It was there that Dave Clark and I bonded. We'd been close before, but this cinched it. We had about twenty Irish pounds between us and we spent it all drinking and meeting people and enjoying each other's company. When we weren't doing that, we hung around our friend's office at Trinity College, writing many of the songs that would end up on *Melville*. In those few weeks, Dave and I developed a musical intuitiveness and sixth sense that allowed us to trick-ball rhythms and ideas and melodies back and forth, switching gears in concert in the bat of an eye, the tweak of a note. This rapport became a blueprint for our live performances. While Martin is the probably the wildest, most expressive musician I've played with, Tim the most unfailing, and Donny the most ambitious, playing with Dave Clark was like playing with my other half. Ours was a rare chemistry that allowed me to evolve from novice to hack to musician. It's still hard for me to come to terms with what happened to make Dave leave the group. But there is a story in there, and I suppose that I must tell it.

All of those years sharing vans, hotel rooms, beds, couches, pullouts, and floor space damaged us. Over the last few tours with Dave, it was part of our sport to argue with each other. Sometimes

it was a show. Other times, we tried to wear each other out with
our wit and intellect and humour, though that makes it sound
more clever than it was. It was often just an Olympics of Idiocy, an
attempt, by both of us, to diffuse the tension and paranoia which
had surfaced on our early tours. Occasionally, however, it was nasty
and visceral. These bouts reflected a brewing unhappiness; I was
angry because I felt my friend slipping away, and he was upset
because he could feel my allegiance softening. The change in our
dynamic was almost imperceptible. I don't know why it happened,
all I know is that it did. Tim and Martin were the first to get pissed
off at him, perhaps because they noticed things that I could not.
When they'd come to me and complain about his unpredictable
and explosive behaviour, I'd defend him indignantly, as if they were
criticizing the both of us. If I had loved and respected him less, I
might have seen what they saw.

   In Edinburgh, we almost fell apart. One night during an
abysmal week of shows at the Fringe Festival, Dave left his kit
and he and I led the band into the audience. We'd done this a
hundred times before. Our philosophy was, if the show's sucking, change it. Sometimes it worked, sometimes it didn't. This
time, Tim and Martin took it as a personal affront. They'd had
enough of Dave's improvisations and spontaneous song follies,
activities I fully and completely supported. We had a meeting
after the show where Tim and Martin told Dave and me to stop
wreaking havoc on the music in an attempt to amuse ourselves. I
expected a war, but instead, Dave submitted. He was tired and
disgusted, and he left me to battle Tim and Martin alone. Our
artistic alliance – we'd effectively represented one hemisphere of
the Rheostatics' brain – collapsed. The next two gigs were the
saddest I have ever played. Dave rendered his parts exactly as they

were put down on record. He wouldn't even look at us. I left the stage after the last song of the last night and told Roger Psutka that I was quitting the band. He talked me out of it. After sulking for a few hours, I spent the rest of the evening with Tim and Martin, wandering around the old city, boozing and making up. Dave went back to our flat and slept on his misery. Things were never the same.

Back in Canada, we had a terrible fight. Telling the story now, it sounds stupid and juvenile, but at the end of a tour, I chucked a box of chocolate milk at Dave. Hit him right in the face, too. The box bounced off him and exploded against a white kitchen wall. Before this happened, I had parked the van behind the house. I'd backed up as Dave tried to get out, trapping his leg in the door of the van. I did this on purpose. Once inside, he said something about my trying to hurt him (which, disingenuously, I denied), and then I threw the milk. If it had been a rock or a brick or a knife, I would have thrown that. I would have. I wanted to hurt him. I threw the box as hard and violently as I could. My best friend. I both loved and hated myself for doing it.

Rock-and-roll bands are horribly political. We can be sick, awful people, particularly in the way we treat each other. You wouldn't know it by looking at us driving through the sleepy countryside, dozing off into vapid dreams with our heads tilted against the cool windows; but playing in this band means behaving monstrously, at least some of the time. Any relationship does, really. Over the years, we've resorted to all manner of in-fighting and head games and mind-fucks to assert ourselves and to take the music where we wanted it to go. In Saskatoon, once, I asked Martin why he continued to play in the band, to which he replied, "Because I want to beat you." In our time, we've stolen

girlfriends and manipulated loved ones and told the most horrible lies about each other. We've gone through long stretches of
deceit and cowardice to protect ourselves, to guard our egos. But
for sixteen years, the most extraordinary thing we've done has
been to sacrifice our own identities and impulses to create something that each one of us alone could not. We've given ourselves
over to the music, to the art, which is more than some people give
to the man or woman with whom they spend their lives. Dave
Clark left the band that he joined when he was fifteen because,
for him, the sacrifice was no longer worth it. The collective
reward was not worth the individual suffering. He hated who he'd
turned into. I hated who he'd turned into. He hated seeing his
best friend try to break him, and he hated having to absorb the
blows and count the scars. He hated fighting back. He hated
having alternatives taken away from him, of the life being
knocked out of his hands. He no longer believed that the
Rheostatics were worth it. I think he wanted to be in a rock-and-
roll band rather than in a painting of his life. By 1994, Tim and
Martin had had enough of him, and I found myself defending
my friend for the last time. Then Martin, speaking for the rest of
us, told Dave Clark, "I don't hate you, Dave, I hate *you*." That was
it. Not a day passes that I wish it weren't true.

DAVE HENMAN: When we finished recording *Electric Jewels*,
the members of April Wine went our separate ways. Myles
Goodwyn was just way too headstrong, too ambitious, too driven
to be in a democratic band. It was driving him crazy. He kept the
deal and the management and asked me to sign over the name
"April Wine" to the organization. I didn't have any business
acumen, so I didn't know that I could ask for anything in return,

like merchandising. I was twenty-three years old and I still had my idealism.

RICHIE HENMAN: Dave and I left April Wine together. I left because of the way the band had started performing. We were playing in the wrong places too often and, as a result, the band was often performing poorly. I never saw any other bands have as many bad nights as we did. We were having them 50 per cent of the time, and it was becoming more and more important to me to play in a band where I didn't feel nervous about how we were going to do every time we walked on stage.

We had an ace crew who trucked our stuff across the country, and when I went out on stage with the lights down and sat behind my drums, everything was within a millimetre of where it had been the night before. We had good sound, good lights, good crowds, and yet it still wasn't enough to get the band up as a whole night after night. When we played at the Capitol Theatre in Halifax on the first night of our cross-country tour, we were deadly; a week later in Corner Brook, Newfoundland, we just sucked. It was night and day. The whole tour was like that. In Winnipeg, the gig was sold out, and the CBC were filming it for a special. It was us and Downchild. They opened, and they rocked the house. I thought that their set would get us up, but we had one of the worst nights of the tour. Halfway through the show, less than half the audience were applauding, and about 10 per cent of them were gone. By the end of the show, 25 per cent had left. There was no encore. I walked off stage, and as I went down the stairs to the dressing room, I said, "That's it. This is not what I want to do."

JERRY DOUCETTE: The arguments that bands have are ridiculous; often they're about the most ridiculous things. Petty, petty things. The Seeds of Time used to go at it all the time. But that's the way it was. When you're young, you've got a point to prove. Everybody has their own ideas, and when you've got five, six ideas going at once, the next thing you know, one guy doesn't like the latest idea, and you spend the next half-hour trying to convince him that it might work if only he'd try it. But he's stubborn and he cleans his keyboards while you're trying to get the idea across. You just go on, weeks go by, and it gets hotter and hotter until, "See ya!"

RIK EMMETT: For eight years I tried to extricate myself from Triumph. I tried to reach a financial settlement. A contract is just an agreement, a basis for two parties to get along with each other. If things go bad, then it doesn't matter if that contract is 150 pages of "notwithstanding the generality of the foregoings" or a one-page letter that says, "You and I are going to do business together, okay?" It's going to be open to interpretation. You can find a lawyer who will interpret it to your benefit, and vice versa. The more that's there, the more you'll fight about. That's why there's always going to be horror stories in show business.

KEN TOBIAS: Gene MacLellan and I were good friends. He played "Snowbird" for me before he played it for Anne. I liked the song a lot, but I only did my own stuff. That's the way it goes. It's history now. Gene also wrote "Biding My Time" and "The Call." The guy was brilliant. Years later I saw him in Toronto. He was married, and we used to go to his house and sing in the kitchen. We'd get wasted and play guitar — they were some of the best times I've ever had. Then all of a sudden, Gene got rich, very rich. Even Elvis recorded "Snowbird." So with all of this money around, Gene's wife divorced him. She took virtually everything. He was devastated, absolutely devastated. After a while, he got her back. They remarried, but then she divorced him, and she did it to him again. She took everything. Twice. Now, I know you might say, what's wrong with this guy? But Gene had a child in him. He needed a lot of special love, and he should have got it. Instead, he was burned by it. He hanged himself.

DARBY MILLS: I was working with a seven-piece band from New York called Business Before Pleasure. Seven black guys and me. We did Donna Summer, Anita Baker. Their manager was a young Fred Sanford. They held an open audition and I joined. They'd moved from New York to Edmonton because the manager's girlfriend was there. They were real characters. There was a seven-foot-three guitar player who wore a size fourteen shoe; another guitar player who was an albino with white hair and blue eyes; and a five-foot-two conga player who was the leader of the band and who sewed all of their uniforms, which came from Vegas. You can't imagine how they dressed. They wore one-piece bell-bottom jumpsuits with silver and gold lightning bolts. We had choreographed steps and dances that we did. The night I decided to quit them, not only did we have our money ripped off from the dressing room, but their drummer left with the van that carried the gear. This was in Lethbridge. It was awful. When the drummer took off, they went to the local schools in Lethbridge and auditioned kid drummers to see if anybody could fit the bill.

DENNIS ABBOTT: We played Regina with Witness and the Dave Clark Five. After the gig, the mayor of Regina held a reception for us, but both our band and the Dave Clark Five wanted to get away from all the backslapping. So we split with the beer and the Kentucky Fried Chicken, which was what they were feeding us at the reception. We took off and sat in the back of the bus. We carried on for several hours and had a great time.

We had a bass player named Dave who, the more important it was to not be a fool, the more likely it was that he would. He came in and sneezed into his fist, but what he was doing was blowing sneezing powder all over the place. Sneezing powder and itching powder. He put it in our sleeping bags, which pissed me right off because you can't get it out of a sleeping bag. He got pretty drunk and went to sleep.

We all crashed for a while, but got up as we were driving, and noticed that Dave was still crashed. We emptied all the ashtrays into his sleeping bag, but he didn't move. We dumped them over his head, and it was like he was dead. We took some beer and started trickling it into his sleeping bag, but still, no movement. We poured beer into his hair, on his head. Then one of our equipment guys smeared shoe polish all over Dave's face, made a horrible mess of him. Dave still didn't wake up. We shoved a chicken bone up his nose and put one in his ear. Nothing.

Then we got stopped by the RCMP. They were looking for some guys who've escaped from jail. They asked if we minded if they looked in the bus and we said no. When they flipped open Dave's bunk, the cop looked at us and said, "This place is a pigpen." Of course after that, Dave became known as Pigpen. People called him Pigpen for years and years. I ran across one of our old roadies a few years back and he said that he'd seen

Pigpen. Apparently, he was a heroin addict living in Vancouver, totally fried, in a room with nothing but a hot plate.

The East Coast leg of the tour started in St. John's, Newfoundland, at the Memorial Arena, home of the Toronto Maple Leafs' farm team. Before we walked on stage, kids were climbing on each other's shoulders and waving their arms. They even screamed at Tim Mech as he laid down towels in front of our microphones. They were the most boisterous crowd of the tour, and what made them doubly charming was the fact that three-quarters of them had absolutely no idea who we were. We've played St. John's, Newfoundland, three times now, and I can say without reservation that it is impossible to have a bad show here.

The morning after the gig, I took a cab from the hotel to the CBC. When I got in, the taxi driver asked me how I felt about last night's show. "Oh, it's always great to play in St. John's," I said. "Well, you've been terrific every time," he replied. "In fact, I was there when you played the university." I realized then that he was confusing me with someone in the Hip. I didn't have the heart to set him straight because he was quite excited to have a rock star in his taxi. A few times, he even honked at people he knew on the street, drawing attention to the fact that he was escorting a celebrity. He reminded me of that famous night at Memorial, when the crowd almost got out of hand. "Oh, yes, that really was something," I said, trying to figure out which member of the Hip he'd confused me with. I could have been Gord Sinclair on the most frightening morning of his life. Maybe. Maybe not. When he dropped me off, he said that he regretted that he didn't have his camera to capture the moment. I walked into a coffee shop. The woman at the counter poured me a cup and said, "Hey, by the way, great show last night." "What?" I blurted. "Yeah, and the Hip were excellent, too," she said.

GARY PIG GOLD: I had quit York University to live with a friend of mine in Hamilton. Our band was called the Specs. We were a progressive bar band for 1976 because we did Abba and Beatles songs as well as Aerosmith, Steve Miller, and Peter Frampton. We hooked up with a really crooked agent in Oakville, and because we were really young and stupid, we accepted her offer to send us to Newfoundland. We didn't know any better. The place looked really close on the map. We had a two-week engagement in a town called Holyrood, which was literally atop some rocks near the ocean. We drove all the way, staying in campsites because we had no money. She didn't fix us any gigs on the way out, and none on the way back.

We finally got there and found two big, white houses; one of them was the band house, the other was the club. They were next door to each other and at the back there was a big dog pound with *Hogan's Heroes*-type fencing. We noticed this, but didn't think anything about it. The guy who ran the club said that we wouldn't get paid until the end of the first week of the two-week engagement. I'd been elected to be the manager-slash-guitar guy, so I had to go into his office at the end of the first week to get the money. The first thing I noticed was the cut-off warnings from Hydro. Sure enough, we didn't get any money.

My dad was a musician, and he'd taught me that one's only bargaining power in a case like this was to refuse to play. We thought it would work because there were no other bands on this rock, so we didn't show up for our second Monday night. Tuesday morning, we decided to leave because it didn't look like we were going to get paid at all. We were starving; we had no money or any food. The union was no help. We phoned the 1-800 number and said that we had no money. They asked how much they owed us, and when we told them it was eight hundred dollars, they seemed to think that it wasn't worth worrying about such a little amount. We realized that we had to go back to Hamilton if we wanted to eat.

When we were ready to leave we noticed that the big fenced-off area was filled with gigantic dogs the size of horses. It didn't look good, but at least they were behind a fence. But then we saw the club owner opening the gate to the fence. The dogs leaped out and rushed the house. We were all at this window looking out and the dogs were jumping up, trying to tear out the window so they could eat us.

Our van was parked away from the house, so we knew that, in order to escape, we'd have to pull it right up to the door of the house. But this required that somebody get the van. So we got a sleeping bag, stuffed it full of pillows, and threw it out the upper window to distract the dogs. It worked. We ran to the van and called the police when we got away. They knew exactly what was going on because this was something that regularly happened. They had a big laugh over it. That was my first experience on the road. We drove from Newfoundland to Hamilton without anything to eat. The punchline is that when we got back to Hamilton, we found the house that we were staying in had been condemned and boarded up.

RIK EMMETT: One time, Triumph was booked to play Puerto Rico, South Padre Island, Anchorage, and Honolulu, all in the space of six or seven days. A couple of days before we got to Puerto Rico, the promoter was shot while he was picking up box-office receipts from ticket outlets. Then, as we were going through customs, Gil [Moore], who was carrying a briefcase that had five thousand U.S. dollars cash in it for per-diems, left it on the counter at customs. He got sidetracked, and when he went to get it, it was gone. There was nobody else in customs except the customs agents, who, of course, denied they'd ever seen the thing. Thirty-six hours later, they called to say they found the briefcase, minus the cash.

We went to Anchorage, found the hotel and checked in. At that time of the year there was twenty-four-hour daylight, which was strange to begin with. Then at 5:30 in the morning, I woke up. The room was shaking. Plaster was cracking down the walls, and my heart was beating like a jackrabbit's. I jumped out of bed, and then it stopped. Four-point-six on the Richter scale. We played the gig, and went to the airport. One of our key production guys was dead drunk. We had to walk him through the airport, pretending that we were chatting him up. We got him into the plane and flew to Honolulu. I got to my hotel, I got into my room, I closed the door, I went to the television, turned it on, and the whole room went black. I went onto the balcony, I looked out, there were no lights, nothing. There was a power shortage: no elevators, no phones, no food, no kitchens. Things were getting weirder and weirder. At the gig that night, some guy chucked a beer and it got on Levine. Levine stopped the show, stopped the band, and yelled, "I want that fuckin' guy! I want you to give him to me! No music until I get that guy!" The crowd was going, "It was him! It was him!" pointing to this guy who was saying, "It wasn't me! It wasn't me!" Then the crowd started passing this guy over their shoulders, offering him up to us. He was pleading, "It wasn't me!" so Levine said, "Well, if no one's going to 'fess up, then fuck it!" and walked off the stage. Refused to go back on. That was it. Show over.

We flew to Nova Scotia only to have the gig postponed because the waters were too rough for the ferry carrying the concert trucks to make the crossing. This caused much consternation among the promoters and tour managers, but it was all right with us; a free day in Halifax was a reprieve. Being the opening band was getting to us. Night after night, it felt like the audience was cheering (or not cheering) out of anticipation for the headliners rather than in appreciation of our music. We were disheartened and needed positive reinforcement (besides the kind offered nightly by the Hip themselves) to offset the fact that we were starting to be mean to each other.

On the road, I get cranky. My health slips and I can't sleep. I get upset because the rest of the guys are cavorting and having fun. I get annoyed at the crowd for not being sympathetic enough and jealous when my band-mates perform with athleticism and energy. My misery reaches the state where I mail in my performance, at which point someone else – usually Martin or Don – has a worse night, and then I feel better. Donny hits a similar wall whenever he's sick. Because he is thin and requires a diet that needs to be finessed, some illnesses tear right through him, resulting in hellacious fits of pique during which he throws stuff around. It's a scary thing to witness, but only until you realize that it's not your head that he's kicking, it's the wall. Then you stop worrying about yourself and start feeling sorry for inanimate objects.

Tim and Martin are closely related in their dolour. Because they are the only two smokers in the band, they are roommates, and their cohabitation has a shelf life. After performances, Martin will return to his hotel room with leftover booze and drink and chain-smoke Marlboros until he's too tired to watch any more bad television. Tim, protecting his wits, will try to salvage at least a few hours' sleep from the evening. This febrile environment works for a while, but soon wears thin. Once, I walked into their room to find Tim buried under the covers while Martin sat up drinking warm Carlsberg, watching surgery. "All Tim does is sleep; he won't even talk to me," Martin tells me in private. "Martin stays up until four or five in the morning drinking and smoking cigarettes; I can't get any rest," Tim tells Donny. Their battle is waged with nary a word passed between them until Tim eventually says something curt to Martin. By then, the tour is almost over. Looked at in a positive light, our behaviour does have one benefit: When one of us feels depressed or sick or angry, the rest of us are glad we're not him. This makes us feel better about ourselves. We're nasty, awful people.

When we landed in Halifax, we were in the final period of this cycle. Anxiety and tension and neurosis and ill-health were peaking, and to make matters worse, we encountered a spot of real trouble. The seeds had been planted weeks ago. Before the tour, Martin was interviewed by a Halifax newspaper about one of our CDs — *Music Inspired by the Group of Seven* — which we released in 1995 after being commissioned by the National Gallery to write music for the Group's seventy-fifth anniversary. The article was published in the Friday, December 6, edition of the *Halifax Daily News*. Here is his exact quote:

> We got started because bands in Toronto are singing with American accents about New Orleans. Well, I've never been to New Orleans and I actually don't care about the United States. I've got nothing against it but it's not my home, it's not in my heart.

No matter whether he intended to call out the Hip for writing "New Orleans Is Sinking," Martin still spent the aftermath racked with guilt. We drove around Dartmouth and talked about it. Martin sat hunched over in the passenger seat, his face pond-green. Earlier, Gord had told Tim that he couldn't really understand what Martin had meant or why he'd done it. Martin was aghast at himself for even opening his mouth. It was killing him. It's not that what he said was unfounded; it's true that our identity was born out of a rock scene where kids from North York affected Birmingham accents to be cool, who spoke of achieving glory in the U.S.A. without ever seeing Saskatchewan. In the early days, we probably heard the Hip on the radio and thought it was more Americanized crap. Part of our reaction came from our defensiveness and insecurity about who we were, and part stemmed from our belief that anything that wasn't like Stompin' Tom or Max Webster was antithetical to our vision. But over the last few years, both the Hip and ourselves have edged closer to one another in style and sensibility. There's actually very little to choose from when it comes down to which band writes more about Canada. Besides, the Hip have always been supportive and gracious towards us; that's what made Martin's remark unfathomable.

MIKE TILKA: A bad thing happened between us and Rush. We were scheduled to open Rush's three-day stint at Massey Hall, and in the meantime we were playing at a bar in Hamilton. I was sitting with a bunch of guys who were rabid Max fans. We were talking about Rush, and I told them that, in the States, Rush didn't deserve to make it based on their radio airplay. Back then, there were hit singles, but Rush didn't have any; you had to be a hit band to get airplay, but Rush were a genuine fan-band. That's what I meant. It wasn't a matter of whether they *deserved* to be big or not. It was just how their success related to radio airplay, or lack thereof. As it turned out, the woman two seats over from me was Neil Peart's new girlfriend. She didn't hear it that way. The next day, we got kicked off the tour. Now we were friends with the other guys in Rush. I knew them before we even formed Max. They were cool guys. So Ray Danniels, whom we shared as a manager, set up a meeting. They said, "Tilka can't come; he's got a rap." Now I'm a talky guy, and I do have a rap. Kim Mitchell told me I had to apologize. I said that I would, it's just that I didn't know what I'd said. Kim went to the meeting and told them that we'd never say anything like that about Rush, and they forgave us. We stayed touring with them, but it was never the same.

GREG GODOVITZ: We recorded the third Goddo album, *An Act of Goddo*, at B.J. studio in Orlando and we safety-mastered it at Criteria in Miami. I drove in a van with the masters to Criteria and when I got there, there was a sign that said, "Home of the

Bee Gees' *Saturday Night Fever*." I had written a classical piece called "ANACANAPANA" which incorporated themes from all the songs of the album. Maurice Gibb was in working that day. He listened to the piece and asked, "That's part of your album?" I told him it was, and he fetched Albhy Galuten and the other guy who did *Saturday Night Fever* and told them, "Listen to this guy's stuff!" Then he said to me, "You must stay at my mansion tonight. I want to introduce you to Robert Stigwood [of RSO Records]. You should be a big star!" He started going on about re-recording the song with a sixty- or ninety-piece orchestra, at which point Albhy Galuten and the other guy went, "Maurice, it doesn't need anything. It's fine the way it is." They split, and then all of a sudden, there was a flutter on the tape. The engineer rolled it back and, sure enough, there was this horrible flutter — on the master tape. I'd driven these tapes down in the van myself and now there was a flutter? I said, "What the fuck is this?!" Then Maurice said, "Well, this is brilliant! We can do it again! We can re-record it properly!" I turned to him and said, "You've got six months to make an album. I've got two *weeks*. Your fuckin' machinery is eating my master, now get the fuck out of here so I can get back to work!" Out he went. As it turned out, the engineer hadn't spliced the tape properly, and when the song started up again, it was fine. I went out and found Maurice to explain. He just looked at me and said, "Fuck off! I don't want to talk to you!" Needless to say, I never met Robert Stigwood.

GALE GARNETT: The 1965 Grammys took place in a big hotel in Beverly Hills or Bel Air. I went with one of Jerry Purcell's apparatchiks, one of his sub-managers, because I didn't know who else to go with. I rented a pale bolero mink stole. It was like a little jacket, a slouchy little jacket, with pockets. I rented it from a place called Somper Furs and, when I won the Grammy, I bought the fucker. At the Grammys, I said this very ungrateful thing that I didn't mean to sound ungrateful. Jonathan Winters was the presenter. He gave me the Grammy that I never expected to win. You know that line, "It's a great honour to be nominated with these people"? Well, it was. I was an actor who made up songs. The musicians who were up for the award were the likes of Peter, Paul, and Mary, Joan Baez, and Bob Dylan. When I got up on stage, I said the first thing that came into my head: "I always thought it would be the Oscar."

It's teeming rain outside the Harbour Centre. The gig this afternoon in Saint John went a long way towards cleaning the chalkboard. The Hip were upset at what Martin had said, but they weren't mad. Gord seemed more bewildered by it than anything. By the next day most of us had forgotten that it had ever happened (except maybe Martin). After our set, there were lots of other things to think about. We'd been pelted by the crowd. Sort of. At the beginning of our show, a projectile flew out of the audience and glanced off Tim's shoulder, who swore when it hit him. When we looked down to see what it was, we discovered that it was a T-shirt with YOU ARE VERY STAR, RHEOSTATICS written on it in sparkly blue paint. It was a gift. Before we started the tour, people had suggested that the Hip's crowd would eat us alive, but they were wrong. "Tell us, mister, was the audience evil and cruel?" some kid will ask me one day. "Oh, terribly," I'll say. "They pelted us with gifts."

We've only been hit while performing once before; twice if you count liquids. At the old Channel One club in Regina, some sausage tossed a cup of beer at us from the balcony while Dave Clark was removing his clothes during one of his poems. Dave confronted the human sprinkler in his Jockey underwear and we played the rest of the gig without incident. At the Kanata Speedway just outside of Ottawa on the Another Roadside Attraction tour, I was clonked on the shoulder with a large shoe dripping with mud. It splattered magnificently across my white shirt and I held up my thumb and said, "Great shot!" to the fellow who'd chucked it. Being a little bit of a sandlot hurler myself, I knew that this kid had excellent aim and I felt it only fitting that I point this out to the crowd. It never crossed my mind that he'd tried for my head and missed.

DARBY MILLS: The worst night was in Weismuller's Country Club in the Valley, outside of Los Angeles. We were bombarded with everything from wooden matches to shoes. We had beer cans, cups, playing cards thrown at us. A running shoe hit the guitar player in the head. It was scary. We only did a five-song set that night. The record company flew people in from New York to see us. There were about fifteen or twenty people in the audience who could get the band more money to continue on in the tour — agents, publishing people, record-company types. We were opening for the Romantics, I think. I don't know how the Headpins ever got booked with them. It was our first show of a twenty-date tour. There were minors in there, young people, two hundred on the dance floor and three hundred people in the seats. We came on with a song that was written by Brian MacLeod and Bill Henderson for Long John Baldry called

"Welcome to the Midnight Show," which was kind of a rocka-
billy tune. The kids up front weren't sure what to make of us. We
were wearing rock clothes at the time. Then we broke into
"Don't It Make You Feel Like Dancing?" and it was over. We
were ducking and dodging things. At one point, I came so close
to kicking a girl in the head. She threw something that hit me in
the face and I saw red. We did five songs with our manager backstage going, "Oh, my god!" I finally pulled it.

ALAN KELLOGG: One of the worst nights of my life was playing
the Rockpile in Toronto with the Ohio Express. Because I had
Canadian roots, I was proud to play there, although we probably
weren't the right sort of band for the place. As usual, we stunk
the joint out, but this time, instead of kids throwing us jelly-
beans, they were throwing Beef-A-Roni cans and all manner of
garbage they'd found in the dumpsters. It was humiliating and, in
retrospect, quite funny. Years later, I interviewed Nash the Slash
and he told me that he'd been there, throwing garbage.

DENTON YOUNG: One night a kid threw up a piece of one-by-six
with ZON cut out of it. It bounced across the stage and hit me
right in the nuts. It nearly killed me.

STEVE SMITH: I've had underwear thrown at me. Unfortunately, it
was men's underwear.

RA MCGUIRE: I once saw Robbie Bachman get knocked off his
drum stool by an alcohol bottle. Hit him right in the head. We
never had anything serious fly at us, just lots of bras, panties,
flowers, notes. The things that get to me are the really sad ones,

Darby Mills

people who are in their last days of cancer and who want to meet you. One show, a woman came up to the front of the stage with an envelope and a bag. I was in the middle of introducing a song and she was standing right in front of me, so I had to react to her. I made fun of her. Later I talked to her backstage. Her daughter had recently died in a car accident. The woman had brought with her a bound collection of the songs her daughter had written. She thought that by presenting Trooper with it, in some way her dead daughter would achieve the dream of stardom.

GEOFF DAVIS: One night we played at the Century Gardens in Brampton with Max Webster, Goddo, and Wireless. The crowd really got into the first two bands. They were a normal crowd, a chanting, fist-pumping crowd. But the guy who was doing front-of-house freaked out. He turned on the lights and said, "If you don't settle down, we're not bringing on the main act!" Everyone erupted. They tore the brand new urinals right off the wall in the men's washroom and ripped out the toilets. People were using metal bits from the washroom on each other. I'd never seen anything like that before in my life. Max fans were usually just stoners who liked to have a good time.

Harbour Centre, Saint John, New Brunswick.

For the first time all tour, kids danced to our music. The Saint John crowd hollered requests and danced: "RECORD BODY COUNT!" "HORSES!" "SHAVED HEAD!" "ALIENS!" I felt like we were a sports team playing an away game with fans who'd travelled to cheer us on. Every now and then, security staff told the kids to sit down. They complied for a few songs, only to rise up again and dance. This cat-and-mouse game went on until the show ended. As you can imagine, playing to a responsive crowd made the world of difference to our performance. When there's no one to play to, it's like throwing a rubber ball at a snowbank.

Graham Kennedy Photo

Dave Bidini

You go out there thinking, *Okay. Martin will start the concert by playing an extended intro to "Song of Flight" and then we'll segue into "California Dreamline," which will blend into "Claire" which will give way to a clipped, economy version of "Fan Letter to Michael Jackson." We'll have the crowd drooling on their shoes by the fifth song!* and then you walk out on stage and there are more people lined up at the concession stands than sitting in the first forty rows. By the third or fourth time this happens, there's a jousting match going on in your head. One voice is saying, "Just play your eight songs, it doesn't matter what they are," and another is reminding you what Joe DiMaggio said when asked why he still hustled after years in the big leagues: "Because there's the chance that someone out there might not have seen me play."

The kids didn't stop dancing until the last note of our last song faded. Martin and I looked at each other and we knew what to do. I once had to wrestle a fan from the clutches of a burly security guard at Ontario Place after he leaped over the fence to pogo during "Horses." This incident set a precedent. We scampered down into the audience and made a beeline towards our caperers. There were seven or eight of them, sun-faced girls and boys in long-sleeved shirts with nervous haircuts. We grouped them together and told them to move. We marched them all the way backstage. Before disappearing behind the curtain, a few of them turned and waved and made faces at the disbelieving crowd. They were rubbing it in a little. I looked back and waved with them.

TORONTO, PART II

"I had this dream where I relished the fray."
The Tragically Hip, *"Nautical Disaster"*

Home. Some musicians have trouble gearing down from months of chaotic travel, but it's never been a problem for me. While I enjoy the carousel of hotels, big bathtubs, room service, cable television, and the passing affluence that accompanies life on the road, I am a suck for my home. I'm ever fearful that my life will one day mirror that nightmarish *Flintstones* episode, where Fred dreams he is a wayward old man who returns home to find his house gone and his children grown up and moved away. After a road trip, some musicians find themselves sitting on their front porches, longingly waiting for the van – any van – to whisk them to the next city. I, however, am more than happy to lie in bed and not move for days. Once I'm home, I'm comforted by the growl of traffic outside my window, the patina of sunlight as it slathers my bedroom wall, the warmth of another body next to mine; these are the things that make me think about never touring again, and each time we go out, I probably come a little closer to pulling myself off the road forever.

Most tours, you arrive home leaving all of your gigs behind you. Not this one. The best was yet to come. *The Gardens*. I repeated these two words to myself, aware that my job for the next two days would be to play music at the most famous hockey rink in Canada. I was also aware that this would probably never happen again in my lifetime. I'm not being fatalistic; the Gardens is set to lose its most famous tenant – the Toronto Maple Leafs – in the winter of 1999. The months between now and then may well be the last chance for *anyone* to rock the old cashbox. Knowing this, every activity of the day – putting on clean socks and showering thoroughly for the first time in three weeks, riding my bicycle up and down neighbourhood streets in search of a newspaper, fielding telephone calls from relatives and friends – is a tiny step down the path that will lead me to my place on stage in *The Gardens*. The name has a mythic tint. When our tour was announced, I was asked by friends where it would play in Toronto, and when I told them, they looked at me as if they'd lost their breath. It's the dream of every Ontarian who ever sounded a note to play there, to walk through its gold hallways with a purpose other than to watch a game. It also carries substantial weight in social circles. A co-worker might ask Martin's father, "So, where's your oldest son performing these days, Enzo?" and instead of having to reply, "I'm afraid it's still the Bovine Sex Club, Jim," he can say, if only once, "*The Gardens*."

These gigs are no less an achievement for our parents. It was my dad who drove us down to the Edge for our first gig, and the same selflessness that he and my mother showed me was true of the Clarks, Veselys, and Tiellis (Don's parents were fortunate enough to have escaped our tumult, though I'm sure they had their share; after all, their son is a drummer). Each of them opened their basements so that their kids could find out for themselves whether to pursue life as an impoverished, societal pariah. I'm certain that Dave Clark's mom suffered hearing damage from our countless versions of "Soul Glue," which featured a three-piece novice horn section and a rookie guitar player, whose riffing was as mellow as the sound of raking gravel. Tonight, while I'm up there singing and strumming the guitars my parents paid for, I'll be thinking about them.

RIK EMMETT: This is how we ended up at the Gardens: Gil Moore went to Peter Goddard and said, "They won't let us play Massey Hall because of the fire regulations, so we're gonna play the Gardens, but we need some help." Gil wanted Goddard to write "TRIUMPH TOO HOT FOR MASSEY HALL" to make us look incendiary and amazing. It happened. We announced that we were playing the Concert Bowl at the Gardens. We'd played every high school in the Metropolitan Toronto area, we'd played every bar, the ground work was there. We played to seven thousand kids that night. I'd sprinted at the Gardens at track meets when I was in high school, so it was really something to go back there as an adult and walk out on stage in the dark and see everyone waving their lit matches and lighters. It's a spine-tingling moment.

GEOFF DAVIS: The first time Max played the Gardens, it was a huge deal. These were hometown boys, New Year's Eve, they had all the momentum in the world. CHUM-FM loved them. It was packed, sold-out. The guys from Rush were there. I went down there at ten-thirty in the morning and the old pensioners took twenty minutes to clear my credentials. But when I finally walked in there, man, I was in awe. The place is so historic. At the second Max Webster show at the Gardens, Kim wore the yellow satin one-piece costume from the *Universal Juveniles* cover. In the second song, he ripped the crotch right out of it. Everything was hanging out behind his guitar and so he said, "Break into a vamp till I get back, maestro," and then headed offstage to change.

RICHIE HENMAN: Playing the Gardens was scary. I don't think any of us had even been in it before. We'd seen it on TV, watching hockey games since we were four years old. We opened for Joe Cocker. Playing in a big, big hall like Maple Leaf Gardens in front of seventeen thousand was the E-ticket. It was the number-one drug. Especially when we started to play the song that they really came to see us play. That reaction was the best drug yet. If we had any doubts before that we were really hooked on this life, it was cemented right there.

Were the club still there, it would take you a matter of minutes to walk from the Edge to Maple Leaf Gardens. Before a concert at the exalted rink, you could stand on a table in the patio of the club, throw a dirt bomb, and hit one of the cars dropping off a back-seat supply of kids too young to know about Pere Ubu or Drastic Measures or any of the other misfit bands who played at the bar with the postage-stamp stage. They'd be kids who,

instead, were just right for Thin Lizzy or Status Quo or Slade —
hit FM bands who played riff rock to soda-sucking crowds sky
high on strobe lights and weak pot. These two venues were the
rock-and-roll opposites where I explored music, and their sur-
rounding neighbourhood — from Carlton to Dundas, Yonge to
Church — was where I first ventured beyond Etobicoke's sleepy
pastures. The area between the Edge and the Gardens was like
New York City: The Pin-Ball Spot. The Imperial Six. Le Strip.
Cinema 2000. Sam the Record Man. Records on Wheels. The
Eaton Centre. The Terrace Roller Rink. The St. Charles Tavern.
The House of Lords. Flash Jack's Head Shop. Doug Laurie
Sports. A&A Records and Tapes. I could travel the globe to
mysterious cities fraught with danger and beauty, yet nothing
would match the intensity of those first impressions of the city.

Downtown. Streets packed with strange faces, rooms filled with curious voices. Dirt. Poverty. Action. Drugs. Music. Sex. You get out of the way and you watch.

When we first played the Edge back in 1980, the only time we'd been downtown before was to rent equipment at Long and McQuade, attend a concert at the Gardens, buy records at Sam's or the Record Peddler, play pinball on Yonge Street, or get our hair cut at the House of Lords. Of all of those activities, the haircut was the most explicitly urban experience. Only a downtown culture could produce the kind of women who worked at the House of Lords: saucy, ditzy, gum-snapping girls in T-shirts with the sleeves ripped off, blasted on coke or weed while snipping your bangs to "TVC15" or the soundtrack to the *Rocky Horror Picture Show*. They were unlike the girls I'd come across at the Albion Mall. They wore tight spandex pants and no bras. They leaned over a lot. A haircut cost twenty-five dollars, and if you were lucky, you saw one of the guys from Teenage Head or the Diodes or Hellfield hanging around. Rock stars. Whenever they were in town, Tim Curry, Alice Cooper, Jayne County, and Iggy Pop dropped by to hang out with the owner. One afternoon, David Bowie held a signing session at the House of Lords, and it made the national news. The line-up stretched all the way to the Gardens. They blasted music over speakers hanging at the front and back of the store, and you could hear it all the way down Yonge Street. Nina Hagen. T Rex. The Normal. "Jet Boy Jet Girl." Once you sat down in a chair, you felt like you were part of something wicked and dangerous, even though the only bad thing you were getting was the haircut.

It was on Yonge Street — at the New Yorker Theatre — where I first found out that we'd be playing at the Edge. I was covering

The Great Rock and Roll Swindle and *Let There Be Rock* for the *Sunshine News* (they were both screened as part of the Festival of Festivals, for which I'd been given the kind of all-access press accreditation that I appreciated only years later, when modern cinema meant more to me than *Caddyshack* or *The Blues Brothers*). A month earlier, we'd recorded a four-song demo tape at a place called Evolution Sound 2000 in Brampton, and we'd sent it to a few small record companies and club owners in town. In 1980, our group comprised Tim on bass, Rod Westlake on drums, Dave Crosby on keyboards, and me on guitar (for the record, Dave Clark replaced Rod, who had been replaced briefly by noted jazz trappist Graham Kirkland). We knew each other from high school. We rehearsed three times a week in the Westlakes' air-conditioned basement, next to the washer and dryer in a room decorated with brown and gold macramé wall hangings and Pink Floyd album posters. Rod's brother had built a drum riser for us to simulate a "concert setting" in the basement. Rod was a small, hyperactive kid who even when standing still often appeared to be vibrating. His mad energy lent itself to speedy drumming, which was perfect for a young band who couldn't learn how to rock fast enough. Crosby, who played an analog Korg synthesizer with a patch bay and knobs emblazoned with sine waves, was Rod's opposite: a stiff-legged string-bean with feet the size of canoe paddles. He had a long, rubbery face and one eyebrow that caterpillared across his brow and his hair sat high on his head and cleaved into two perfect half-moons. Together, we wrote such songs as "The People Who Live on Plastic Lake" and "Sometimes I Feel Like an Elevator," paeans to new-wave rock that featured plucky bass lines carved out with a pick and whooping synthesizer patterns, heavy on the pitch wheel. I'd still stand by most of those early numbers if it weren't for a ditty called "Letter to the President," an embarrassment in seven–eight time, which included a bizarre political tract read by yours truly in a British accent.

Our demo tape included four songs – "On TV," "Suburb Shuffle," "Radio 80 Fantasy," and, yup, "Letter to the President." One of the people I sent the tape to was Gary Topp, who, along with Gary Cormier, was the top new-wave concert promoter and talent booker for the Edge. There was no immediate response from anyone. All we'd hoped for was to land one gig from the tape, and it looked hopeless until that afternoon at the New Yorker. Gary Topp had called me at home to tell me that he liked the demo and that he could give us an opening spot on a week-night. My mom answered and told him that I'd gone downtown to see a film at the New Yorker. He said that he was headed there himself and so she described me to him. When he walked into the theatre's café, I recognized him immediately; along with CFNY program director David Marsden, he was the most influential new-music maven in all of Canada. He sat down and I tried not to stare at him. I thought about telling him about our band's tape, but was way too intimidated. When I looked up again, he was staring at me. Embarrassed, I looked away, but as I did, he said, "Excuse me, are you Dave?" Then he told me. I couldn't believe it. I phoned my mom, and then I phoned Tim, who called the rest of the band. We had a gig. A gig downtown.

KELLY JAY: I started playing in the Zanzibar on Yonge Street in the 1950s while I was still going to art college. I soon realized that I could make more money backing strippers than I could as an artist. Back then Yonge Street was alive. There was the Towne

Casino, the Brown Derby, the Le Coq d'Or, the Edison Hotel. The crowd at the Zanzibar was made up of gangsters, boxers, jockeys — guys who'd be out at the track during the day, then come down to the big, glamorous night clubs in the evening, guys in silk shirts with monograms, smoking cigars. You'd also have the rock-and-rollers there like Ronnie Hawkins and Conway Twitty. Ronnie Hawkins was a combination of Lenny Bruce and Elvis Presley. He was hilarious on stage. My favourite Ronnie Hawkins story is the time Morton Shulman and his wife came down. Morty Shulman was the city's coroner. His wife was wearing this beautiful red velvet strapless gown, and we were all like hound dogs in the background, watching her. Ronnie introduced all these people — the big muck-a-mucks in the crowd — and he kissed Mrs. Shulman, and then he looked at Morty Shulman and said, "I suppose a fuck's outta the question?"

RONNIE HAWKINS: They put all the liquor licences in one area, Yonge Street. It kept everybody downtown. You couldn't get booze anywhere else. All the people getting out of work from Eaton's and Simpson's would stop by for a drink and sometimes stay over. Live music was new to bars and they would line up around the block because it was so new. Everything stopped at eleven-thirty on Saturdays, and the Lord's Day Act meant it was closed on Sundays. They had ladies and escorts — properly dressed — on one side. Business was super good for ten years. We had everybody from the rounders to the wise guys to all the élite, the Bronfmans, the Molsons, the Carlings, the Bassetts, the Eatons, the people who owned the Gardens. They all came in for the girls.

PETER GODDARD: In the 1960s the whole Beatles pop scene grad-
ually took over the city, but the centre part of the scene was
still a '50s thing. The Beatles were considered wimpy by a large
part of the scene, which was blues-based. Black-based. The look
was stovepipe pants and purple shirts. Heavy duty. It was a very
macho scene, and the women and the guys were both into it. The
Concord Tavern on Bloor was the toughest place. I've been in
pipe-fights in alleyways behind places like that over the kind of
money that was floating around, lots of it. Bad money, drug
money. Scams. You could get hurt badly if you fell in with the
wrong people. The managers and the roadies for the early bands
were scary guys. This was the scene at every level of music.

RONNIE HAWKINS: At first, we thought that the Beatles and the
Stones were just doing bad versions of the songs we loved. We
didn't buy them for a second, because we knew the real thing
too well.

KELLY JAY: Ronnie Hawkins did a lot for the music scene. He let
everybody know that the clock was running and that nobody
would get any better unless they practised. He made sure we
knew that we wouldn't get anywhere by sitting around drinking
and smoking pot. Heavy Andrews was one of Ronnie's cohorts.
Heavy used to say to us all the time, "Baby blue, Ronnie and I
saw a guitar player last night, and he had your job written all over
him." They were tough guys. You ask anybody who went through
it. Nobody had a rockin'er set of bands than Ronnie. When
these guys got cooking and found the groove, nobody had to
come along and tell them that it was rock-and-roll.

GREG GODOVITZ: Because of my marks in school, the principal made me the ticket-getter for when the Beatles played the Gardens. They gave me a few hundred dollars — tickets were three dollars and fifty cents — and I took all the orders. I went down by myself and slept overnight for tickets. It was great; we were in sleeping bags, and everyone was hyped. When I got up to the ticket wicket, they said, "Just two per customer." I said, "But I'm here for my school!" And they said, "Well, you'll just have to line up a few hundred times." The line-up stretched all the way down Carlton and up Yonge; there was no way I could go to the end of the line and get more. So I went back to school and gave the money back to the principal. I had the only two tickets in the school for the Beatles at the Gardens.

Now, at this point in my life, my nickname at school was Pimplehead. It caused me much grief. I'd ask girls to dance and they'd say, "Not with you, Pimplehead!" Then all of a sudden, old Pimplehead's got the only two Beatles tickets in the school. I became a very popular guy. They all came up to me — Earline Devonald, Jackie Hotten — I remember their names because they were so cool. I could have taken any one of them to the concert. But instead, I asked the fattest girl in the school, "Dorothy, do you wanna go see the Beatles with me?" She said, "Are you kidding?" and I said, "No. The ticket's yours." I took her to see the Beatles.

RONNIE KING: Yonge Street to us was Las Vegas. Seeing Sam the Record Man and all those neon lights, we thought it was the big time for sure. Then to go to Yorkville and see the club where we were going to play — the El Patio — it was unbelievable. Neil Young was plinking around the Riverboat; Gord Lightfoot was

there, too. Then along came David Clayton-Thomas. He came
to see us at the El Patio. Really, we were in no shape to be invad-
ing the East with our cover versions of "Da Doo Ron Ron,"
doing our little kick-steps and jump-ups together in our little
matching cowboy outfits. Clayton-Thomas saw us and said, "Are
you guys serious? How'd you get here?" We said, "We drove," and
he said, "Go down to the Le Coq d'Or, check out Hawkins, and
catch the first plane back to Calgary."

DAVID HENMAN: We played at the Mynah Byrd with April Wine.
I remember that because they had a nude chef.

BOB SEGARINI: First time I was ever east of the Rockies, we were
opening for Bobby Sherman at the brand new O'Keefe Centre.
When we left L.A., I was wearing shoes, no socks, jeans, and a
white Roxy PRETEND YOU'RE RIGHT AND GO AHEAD T-shirt. It
was March 13, 1968 or '69. I get off the plane here, and it was
twenty below and snowing. Wow, buildings and snow! I'd only
ever seen snow in the mountains. We were doing a tour of the
United States with Jefferson Airplane, and we spent a week in
Toronto waiting for the tour to start. I ended up in Yorkville at
a place called the Penny Farthing. This is what I remember: I
paid a dollar for a bowl of chili and a girl took me downstairs
into the sauna and blew me. The buck paid for the chili.

SKINNY TENN: When we were getting ready to go to Toronto for
the first time in the '60s, there was nobody to look to, nobody in
Saskatchewan to even ask for advice. We got a big house together
in Cookstown. There were three bedrooms and three beds for six

guys, so you'd sleep with another guy. Even when we got hotel rooms, we'd double up. We did it even when we were a semi-successful band. Whenever we came down into Yorkville from Cookstown to perform, we'd get into our station wagon and end up driving along Bloor Street. One night, we picked a couple of girls up after a gig and they followed us back in their car. Because we took Bloor, the trip took about an hour and a half. When we got there, they went, "You idiots. Why don't you take the freeway? It's just over there." We could actually hear the traffic on it, but it just never occurred to us to go that way.

JIM KALE: When we came to Toronto to play, we were the guys from the West. We were the farmers who were supposed to wear overalls and have shit on our boots. There's southern Ontario and there's the rest of the country, and it's still that way.

GREG GODOVITZ: When I was thirteen years old, we got a gig a few doors south of the Friar's on Yonge at this place called the Rocket A Go Go, where my mom was a coat-check girl. It was an after-hours bar, and I was in grade nine. My mom said, "Let him do it; see what he does." We played from midnight till three in the morning. The hookers would come in from Yonge Street and they'd let us put their tips between their breasts. We were cute, and they liked us. There were dopos and druggos and drunks there too; "rounders" was what they called them back then. We didn't even notice them, though. It was so innocent then.

Later on, I was in a band called the Back Door Blues Band. A couple of slick, entrepreneurial guys, agency guys, took us and put us in wild-looking black suits with coloured stripes. My mom remembers us showing up at the Friar's one afternoon and saying, "Hi, we're the Back Door, and we play Chicago blues." We were kids, fifteen, sixteen years old.

Our managers took us up one night to play with Ike and Tina Turner at the Masonic Temple. I couldn't see a bloody thing because of my poor eyesight, so my manager sent me upstairs to watch the proceedings and to run errands for him. Ike was up there, too, in the dressing room with the Ikettes, who were in their underwear. Now, I swear to God, I can't see my own hand in front of my face if I take my glasses off, so I had no idea what was really going on. Finally, Tina Turner chased me up the stairs and said, "Whatsa matter, white boy? Are you some kinda pervert or something?" I was crushed, because I thought she was a star. But as soon as I explained, she tore a strip off the guy who'd sent me up there.

When we played the Edge, I had no idea what I was supposed to do. Let me correct that. I had too many ideas. I'd imagined myself a thousand different ways, visualizing moves, cues, lyrics, guitar parts, stage clothes, between-song banter, the set list, everything. For weeks, I'd dreamed the performance over and over in my head, but once on stage, I ended up being myself. And it was okay. I think we played ten songs. Our friends came in packs and sat in the front; our parents came together and sat at the back. There were many thrilling firsts. Being in a dressing room. Setting up our equipment. Watching the other band arrive (I remember one of them arrived in a cab, which struck me as wildly eccentric). Getting a free Coke at the bar. Taking a piss in the stall with stickers and graffiti everywhere. Seeing our name on the flyer alongside XTC and Split Enz and the Demics. Talking to the waitresses. Looking into the upstairs office and seeing the promoter's desk stacked with papers. Sitting at a table under a window in the falling evening light, writing out our set list as the soundman unwrapped microphone cables and organized the stage. Cigarette burns and gum on the carpet. The stink of grease. The reek of beer. The way the traffic slowed outside and the streets emptied until suddenly a handful of people walked around the corner talking to each other, then climbed the few steps of the club, passed through the big wooden doors, and paid the tired-looking woman who sat at the table near the entrance. These were people we didn't know. Adults. Were they here to see us?

Sixteen years later, these people have become the carnival of voices and faces marching towards the Gardens in the snowy winter twilight. At the corner of Yonge and Carlton, ticket-scalpers bark across at the winter-jacketed, baseball-capped kids slushing along the sidewalks holding their tickets in their hands stuffed deep in their pockets. Candy-apple and peanut vendors push chestnuts and cashews around warm metal trays with shopworn spoons, their trolleys loaded down with balloons and whirligigs and blown-up plastic Curious Georges that pierced teenagers wouldn't be caught dead buying. Singles wait for friends under the white light of the Gardens' radiant marquee, turning over their wrists to read watches. Taxis *shwwwwwsh* through the streets, letting off concert-goers coming from dinner. Streetcars expel dancing-eyed kids who have just come from getting high. The pulse of the avenue quickens and the city heaves its chest and the streetlights cast a cloudy glow through the thickening December snowfall, and I realize that these strangers are the people with whom I will share one of the most important moments of my life.

In the afternoon, I learned the Gardens. I sat in every section of the rink and explored every room. Whenever I was met by security, I flashed my laminate, and their barricades moved. I sat in the Leafs' dressing room; the visitors' too. Martin and his friends climbed the catwalk to the toppermost of the building and looked down while I sat in the pressbox and wrote in my journal. I ran my hands all the way around the perimeter of the boards, then stood between the nets, which were stored near the loading bays. I sat in the penalty box. I used the scorekeeper's phone. I stood behind the Leafs' bench and imagined that I was Red Kelly pacing up and down the floorboards hollering instructions to my players. I climbed on the Zamboni and stood under the scoreclock and I ran around the mezzanines in my purple jacket and black hat and silk tie and white shirt and dress shoes. I talked to Vicki Gabereau on her national radio show from the lobby. I arrived in the morning and left in the morning.

This was the third time I'd been to the Gardens not as a patron but as a musician. Twice now, we've been lucky enough to sing the anthem before a hockey game. The first time was on November 26, 1993 (Quebec 6, Toronto 5, OT), which happened to be the eve of Janet's and my wedding. (It was also the day after Grant Fuhr was traded to Buffalo for Dave Andreychuk.) Since the band had already rented tuxedos for my nuptials, we wore them for our performance. Standing there in the middle of the hushed, sold-out rink that night, we looked like a million bucks. I'm not sure that our performance matched our appearance, however. We'd rearranged our nation's timeless anthem into a countryesque foot-stomper with guitar accompaniment and four-part harmony. It probably sounded sweet and funny to some, but terribly irreverent to others. I still have a tape of the radio broadcast. As the anthem ends and our last note flies above the cheering, the Leafs' colour commentator, Gord Stellick, says, "They're from Etobicoke, Joe, and they'd like to say hello to all of their families and friends back home." The organ romps, the crowd settles, and Joe Bowen, the Leafs' play-by-play voice, says dramatically, "*Felix Potvin is to my left.*"

The second time we performed at the Gardens, the Leafs were playing the Mighty Ducks of Anaheim (Ducks 1, Leafs 0). This gave us the chance to add "The Star-Spangled Banner" to our repertoire. We arrived late in the afternoon for sound-check, which involved playing the songs into two foam-capped micro-phones while standing five feet from the boards on a spongy blue carpet emblazoned with the Leafs' logo. We left the rink, had dinner at the Golden Griddle across the street, and came back about an hour before gametime. We sat in the old referees' change room, getting more and more nervous, *puke nervous*. I'd felt nervous before playing the PNE, and a few times before our shows at the Bathurst Street Theatre in Toronto, but this was worse, much worse. I was wrenchingly nervous, and there was little I could do about it.

I decided to shave. Christie Fletcher, the Gardens' PR assistant, said that I could use the executive washroom as there were no mirrors in the public ones. She showed me the way and left me to get on with it. The washroom was just a few feet beyond the kingly oak-panelled quarters of the Leafs' GM, Cliff Fletcher, Christie's dad. Very nice.

As soon as I started to shave, I heard voices outside the door.

"Hey, who's in the can?"

"Do you know who's in there?"

"Sylvia. Someone's in the can."

It was Cliff. I scraped away as fast as I could. Assistant GM Bill Watters and Joe Bowen joined Cliff outside the door. I chopped at my face with the blade, and blood spurted everywhere. Soon the sink began to look like a prop for a slasher film. The Leafs' braintrust kept pulling on the handle of the door, trying to open it. I finished up and wiped the blood from the mirrors and floor. I put my shirt and jacket on, opened the door, and was met by Watters, Bowen, Fletcher, and Hall of Famer Darryl Sittler. The Sitt. Number 27. I slunk past them, pressing a Kleenex to my bloody chin and muttering, "Uh, singing the, uh, anthem."

We were called to the rink while the players were finishing their warm-ups and the crowd was finding its seats. The gate opened, and we walked out onto the carpet and waited to be announced.

The first thing I noticed was how brilliant the light was, how it shot down from the giant TV lamps that hang above the rink and bounces off the ice. I became so consumed by the extraordinary aesthetic of the place that I forgot that the gladiators of winter were standing on either side of us: the Clarks, the Gilmours, the Potvins. When I looked up into the crowd, I could actually see people, see their faces. I could read their lips and follow their eyes. It was unlike any rock-and-roll experience I've ever had.

Then Paul Morris said, "Ladies and gentlemen, won't you please rise and join the Rheostatics in the singing of the national anthems?" It was the introduction I wish I could have every night: "Ladies and gentlemen, won't you please rise and join the Rheostatics in the singing of their obscure, cultish art rock?"

Three minutes later, the cheering swelled as we hit the last chorus of "O Canada." The song pulls up dramatically, and we drew out the last "*foooor theeee!*" There was an eruption of cheers and whistles, followed by the scuffling of shoes and the rustling of pants and coats as men and women and children settled back into their seats. The skaters broke from formation along the blueline and dashed and circled around the ice before heading to the bench. I exhaled. Our friends and families greeted us, tears in their eyes.

For this concert, our families and friends were there, too. They crowded the small dressing room, fathers slapping our backs and clasping hands, young children pawing the old blue walls, mothers and sisters gnawing fingernails, friends sipping Cokes and ales. They wished us luck and filed out of the dressing room minutes before we took the stage. Our manager, Paul Davies, and publicist, Tyson Parker, stood with us as we slipped on our sparkling purple jackets for the last time. Our hearts were still as we marched along the back wall of the ancient building and climbed up there on the great stage of our youth. For the next forty-five minutes we felt as if we were being pulled through a strange and beautiful dream. I can remember just a few details.

We were introduced by my friend Dave Bookman, who stood at the centre microphone commanding the stage with all the magnetism of a Talmudic prophet. His voice was so full of rage and passion and love that I went out there and I jumped higher than I ever have. I remember playing "Claire" and following Tim's eyes as they travelled around the rink, swallowing the moment; he looked beautiful as the lights glinted and danced

across his face. I remember that Donny got to play a drum solo.
A drum solo in Maple Leaf Gardens. That's something that
only a handful of citizens have ever done. I imagined him as a
child sitting behind his beginner's kit in his Mississauga basement, headphones clamped to his ears, playing "Moby Dick"
while the other kids ran around outside, lighting firecrackers,
and learning to swear. I saw myself become small, too.

I remember going over and walking to the edge of the stage
and pointing my guitar neck into the crowd. I remember seeing myself standing over my chair wearing my brand-new
Farewell to Kings tour T-shirt, gesturing to Alex Lifeson and
Kim Mitchell, howling at them for a guitar pick. I remember
what happened during "Feed Yourself." I remember looking
into the crowd and noticing a blue light glowing above the sound
board. It appeared to be pointing towards me. I watched it as it
hung there, unwavering, and I let myself be drawn to it. I
watched as it reached out like a long finger. The rink grew dark
and still and I was coaxed towards the light. I closed my eyes and
started singing, and I felt like I was being pulled through my own
consciousness. I felt completely lost. When I opened my eyes,
the light was gone. I searched, but there were no colours above
the sound board. I strained to see it, but all I saw was Gary
Stokes, his finger woodpecking his effects unit. We ended the
song. I remember flubbing the only line that I'd wanted to use
during the concert: "It takes only twenty-five minutes on the
subway to get from Kipling station to Dundas, but it took us
sixteen years to get to the Gardens!" I could barely speak. At the
end of our set, I was flabbergasted. I put my guitar down and
walked away with my chin drawn against my chest, my arms
limp at my sides. I looked back at the stage. There was Donny,

Rheostatics at Maple Leaf Gardens

standing on his drum riser, smiling and waving his arms above his head, his hands like semaphores, flapping over the crowd.

BOB SEGARINI: I'll tell you the exact moment it happened. The only place to play in my home town for long-haired groups was a place on the wrong side of town called the Minotaur. Everyone more or less called it the Beatnik Place. It was a coffeehouse. Gale Garnett, early Dylan on the jukebox. It was like a coalmine in that place, very dark. They had the Chianti bottles with the candles. They served food, so young people could go there, which we did. One day, this big guy came up to me and said, "You guys in a band?" I said, "Uh-huh." He said, "Well, we're not doing anything in here on Sunday, you wanna bring your crap in here?" So we started playing there. I remember standing on the little stage right in front of the fire door. The place was so full that girls were sitting on the stage just looking at us. You know the kind of crowd, the heat, where the walls sweat? That's what it was like. Real hot, people, young people, crushed in together, making contact.

That week I had just gotten a British version of the *Rubber Soul* album, and on the British version there was a song called "Drive My Car" that wasn't released in the U.S. We learned it and played it, and people in my home town to this day think I wrote that song. The audience that night went nuts. Goofy. They didn't know it was a Beatles song. The girls were touching my leg. They were just sitting there on the stage, looking up at me and stroking my leg. After the tune ended, there was a combination of applause and *oooos* from the crowd that made my ears go funny. That was The Moment. That was the heroin.

DAVE HENMAN: I've always loved really pretty guitar playing – the Shadows, the Ventures – playing that sometimes brings me close to tears. So I would try to play like that: pretty and melodic. I remember one time we were playing at a beach resort and people came up to me afterwards, telling me that girls in the crowd were sitting at their tables crying because of my guitar playing.

HOLLY WOODS: In Greenville, North Carolina, Toronto played at a place called the Attic, which was the exact same place I played in a house band when I was nineteen years old. It was jam-packed with old friends and relatives. Unbelievably, my father, who hates my music, was there. It was nerve-wracking because he's a baritone for a church choir, so he was right on my stuff. But that night he had a tear.

DENTON YOUNG: We played six days a week, plus a matinee, for almost two years without a break. Then Harlequin played a concert in western Ontario; I think it was Tillsonburg, somewhere near London. It was our first time on a big stage and where people were sitting down to watch us. A little while later, we did a show at the Institute for the Deaf in Milton, Ontario. During the encore, kids came up on stage and put their hands on my drums to feel the vibrations. It was an incredible moment, the feeling from these kids. That really stands out in my mind.

GALE GARNETT: All of my favourite musical moments and buzzes have to do with the same thing: the internationalism of it. That's the large heading. There's three of them. One: Standing waiting for a light to change in London and hearing somebody hum a melody I wrote, who does not know that I am standing next to them or that I am me or that it matters. Something that came out of my head is being hummed by a stranger? In another country? Hello? Two: When "We'll Sing in the Sunshine" was recorded in Japanese. Three: Being asked to go to Paris, Rome, and Berlin to record my songs in French, Italian, and German. Winning the Grammy was a buzz, but the real buzzes are the universal things.

KEN TOBIAS: One live moment stands out from the early days. We were at this place called St. Joseph's University in New Brunswick. The theatre was designed for music; the stage was round and you could go up on it with an acoustic instrument and spellbind anybody 'cause the sound was so beautiful. The tune I was doing was called "Alberta." *"Alberta, let your hair hang down . . ."* Almost like a pop swing. I remember that I didn't have to play my guitar; we had an acoustic bass player, a banjo, and another guitar player. I remember sitting in a chair and I remember the floor being dusty, and I remember singing the tune and hearing, literally, a pin drop. I looked down and I could see my tears dropping from my eyes, on to the floor, and watching the dust go *puhhhh puhhhhh* and when I finished the song, it was like . . . thunder. I cried because I was so there. I was so into the tune and I was in my sweetest voice and the people were getting it and it was a communication at *that moment*. I connected. And I connected by not trying to connect. The tune was everything; it was no longer a song. It was like life; it was alive. It was a birth. That gave me something that ego didn't give me. You know what I'm saying? It was something else. It hit me in my soul. To that day, that was probably one of the key moments of my life. I think if you have several moments in your life like that, you're lucky. I consciously seek that place, not for anybody else either, but for me. I wanna get my sorrow out; I wanna reach those points so I can spill it. When those moments come, they let you go, they really do heal you. They allow you to be free. It also means people around you are not dangerous. When you're that vulnerable, they're also vulnerable, and so no one harms anybody. That's what I like about *pax cultura*, "peace through culture."

RA MCGUIRE: Our defining show was at the Pacific Coliseum in Vancouver. It was sold-out. Mom and Dad and the neighbours and cousins were in the VIP box. As we were walking on stage, Sam Feldman, our manager, stopped me and said, "Look, you've earned this. You should try to enjoy it." That was an awesome piece of advice. He made me realize that this was something important. I should enjoy it rather than just give, give, give. I

decided I'd take a little bit. It started something that I've done
ever since. I used to walk out to the middle of the stage and start
shouting the lyrics to "Summertime Blues," but this time, I
walked up to my mike and just stood there. I held my arms out,
as if to say, "Give it to me." There was the spill of the stage
lights, the lighters in the crowd. I soaked all the love in.

We stood backstage in our underwear. We almost chickened out.
I wore an H across my chest; Donny had an I, Martin a P, and
Tim Mech had on red long underwear with a ! painted across the
top. We huddled behind the stage and gave each other the opportunity to back out. We lost one. Tim Vesely decided to end the
tour with his wife and newborn baby rather than in his shorts in
front of sixteen thousand hometown yowlers. Wise fellow.
Donny pushed Martin towards the stage and Martin pushed me.
Then Tim Mech shouted over the music, "*If we're gonna do it, let's
do it now!*" He pulled back the curtains and pointed to the ladder.

They were playing "Fifty Mission Cap." The Hip have written
a handful of great Canadian anthems, but this song is their most-
loved. It's a tune that every fan entering the rink secretly hopes
they'll play. This night, by the time the group reached the song's
first, climactic chorus, Bill Barilko's memorial jersey was fluttering like a ghost sheet above the fray. Gord's hand gestured north
and the kids waved their arms like lampreys. It was a profound,
dreamy moment. Then, as the band returned to the song's
choppy signature riff, the person controlling the lights tripped a
switch – one that I imagine being locked in a box accessible only

to a wizard with a magic key – and the arena suddenly became as bright as day, sunshine splashing across faces and bodies and burning the darkness of the rink.

This lasted for only a second, long enough for us to look at each other and think, "Oh, holy shit." Knowing that this epic moment would be repeated later in the song, we almost didn't make it up there. Part of my brain told me not to desecrate such an already wonderful thing. Before the show, when I told Dave Bookman what we were planning to do, he said, "Great. Little Jimmy drives down ten hours to hear his favourite song, and there you are, prancing around in your underwear." But there was no turning back, not with the entire backstage crew standing there laughing at us.

We took each other's hands and climbed the ladder. We shimmied across the stage in a grade-school angel chain. Gord spotted us first and stopped singing, like we needed more attention drawn to us. The heat from the crowd hit me like a chinook, bathing me in warmth. We paraded right to left across the stage, exposing our scrawny, pinkish bodies before the rock-and-roll denizens of our city. I'd felt naked and vulnerable at that first gig at the Edge, too, but I'd spent years trying to build up a resistance to whatever embarrassment had been there at the beginning of my rock-and-roll life. Over the years, I'd shouted down hecklers, screamed at my band-mates, frozen out friends, and battled parents to protect what was tender to me as a musician, and now here I was, so bloody happy and confident and comfortable in this environment that I could take off most of my clothes, shuffle along like a clown in front of a packed hockey rink, and still feel like I was where I was supposed to be.

Cathy Bidini

We walked to the very centre of the enormous stage, and I stood there purging the sweat and tension of every gig and rehearsal, every terrible mile of the endless road. I felt like I'd finally cashed in my rock-and-roll credit, and this was what spat out. It wasn't bad at all. We raised our arms. The floor vibrated under our feet. *I had this really strange dream last night that we were half-naked up there in front of sixteen thousand screaming people at Maple Leaf Gardens.* We slid a few feet to the right, then disappeared in a circus of colour and light. That was no dream at all.

That was us.

I was up there.

ACKNOWLEDGEMENTS

On a Cold Road owes its existence to a family of Canadian music books, each having proven itself indispensable to my research: *Heart of Gold*, by Martin Melhuish; *Axes, Chops and Hot Licks*, by Ritchie Yorke; *Canadian Records (from 1955 to 1975)*, by Andre Gibeault; *Neil and Me*, by Scott Young; *Rock Is My Life, This Is My Song: The Story of BTO*, by Martin Melhuish; and *The CHUM Chart Book*, by Ron Hall. The idea for the structure of my book came from Peter Golenblock's *Bums: An Oral History of the Brooklyn Dodgers*, and I must also tip my hat to Paul Quarrington's *Whale Music*, to my mind the best rock-and-roll book ever written.

This being my first long-player, I feel the urge to thank everyone who's ever helped me become a writer. Please allow me this indulgence. I'd like to acknowledge my favourite high-school English teacher, Mr. Clark, and my first editor, Sheila Wawanash. Cheers to Alan Maki, who sent me his personal copy of *The Elements of Style* after responding to a letter I wrote to him as a kid while he was sports editor at the *Etobicoke Gazette*. Kudos as well to Shakey Hunt, Trent Frayne, and the late Jim Vipond, each of whom wrote me back when I asked what it would take to grow up to be like him.

It was Mitch Potter of the *Toronto Star* who first published a version of these tour diaries in December 1996. I offer profound thanks to him – and to the eminent Peter Goddard – for helping to plant the seeds of this book. I would also like to acknowledge Dave Bluestein and Bernie Aubin for the many phone numbers they provided, Geoff Davis and Danny Marks for lending me their books, and Clemens Rikken and Graham Kennedy for the use of their photographs. Cheers as well to Martin Levin, Jeff Z. Klein, Steven Heighton, and Reed Books Canada, who, over the years, gave me a break when I needed one. Thank you to my editor, Dinah Forbes, and to Rudy Mezzetta, Peter Buck, and Sari Ginsberg of McClelland & Stewart, not forgetting my agent, Dave Johnston, who made wrestling this alligator memorable and fun.

On the band side, the Rheostatics wouldn't have existed were it not for Dave Crosby, Rod Westlake, James Gray, Dave Rodenberg, Ray Podhornik, Charlie Huntley, Gary Topp, Jimmy Scopes, Artistic Endeavours, Ron Gaskin, Dave MacMillan, "Brave New Waves," Richard Chapman, Jay Scott, Mark Smith, Intrepid Records, Michael Phillip Wojewoda, David Wisdom, Richard Burgman, Roger Psutka, Andrew Rourke, Nigel Best, Paul Davies, Tyson Parker, Dave Teichrobe, Lewis Melville, Dave Bookman, and all of those excellent folks who wrote about us, played our songs on the radio, came to our gigs, and, most importantly, shared the stage with us over these last eighteen years. Thanks as well to the Tragically Hip and their fine organization: the most upstanding of citizens. My deepest love and affection goes to Cathy Bidini for her photographs and to my beautiful bandmates, past and present. Most of all, I owe the creation of this book to Janet Morassutti, who, in my mind, is all that rock-and-roll stands for, not to mention the apple of my eye and a damned fine editor in her own right.

Dave Bidini
Toronto
June 1998

Please write:
P.O. Box 616
Station C
Toronto, Ontario
M6J 3R9